## Praise for *Adaptive Listening™*

"Great communication is not just about how you present and how you speak. It's about how you *listen*. *Adaptive Listening* teaches the skill you will wish you had learned sooner."

**—Dharmesh Shah, co-founder/CTO, HubSpot**

"The most productive conversations demand strong listening, yet so many of us don't understand how we listen. *Adaptive Listening* will help you in both your professional AND personal life. Invest the time to read and apply it. It's worth it."

**—Ryan Hawk, host of *The Learning Leader Show* and author of *Welcome to Management* and *The Pursuit of Excellence***

"Many leaders ask what they can *say* to persuade their teams, without asking *how* they can listen. This easy-to-apply *Adaptive Listening* model can challenge everyone, at every level, to shift their perspective."

**—Scott Miller, *Wall Street Journal* bestselling author and host of the world's largest weekly leadership podcast**

"I really like [Adaptive Listening] as I learned how to improve my listening/ conversations. It was easy to pick up and use immediately, and I had a sense of accomplishment and knowledge I could share with others. I also found that adapting through listening was easier than adapting through personality (Myers Briggs) or colors (Insights), which fell flat pretty quickly."

**—Workshop participant from Microsoft**

"I was able to understand how I listen, but also learn how I can adapt [my listening style] to match the needs of the speaker, be a better communicator, and build trust."

**—Workshop participant from Kaiser**

"*Adaptive Listening* inspires a major paradigm shift. It will help you realize that your listening skills are just as important as your speaking skills. This is wisdom that will help improve communication across your organization and create a much healthier culture."

**—Scott Harrison, founder, CEO at charity:water, *New York Times* bestselling author of *Thirst***

"Feedback starts with soliciting ideas from others and listening to what they say, with the intent to understand their goals before you reply, in a way that rewards the candor. That's easier said than done. *Adaptive Listening* will teach you how!"

**—Kim Scott, author of *Radical Candor* and *Radical Respect***

# Adaptive Listening

# Adaptive Listening

## How to Cultivate Trust and Traction at Work

Nicole Lowenbraun and Maegan Stephens

Coral Gables, FL

Published by Mango Publishing, a division of Mango Publishing Group, Inc.

Cover Design: Oscar Chacon, Ash Oat
Cover Illustration: Oscar Chacon
Author photos: Alexis Macias



For permission requests, please contact the publisher at:

Mango Publishing Group
2850 S Douglas Road, 2nd Floor
Coral Gables, FL 33134 USA
info@mango.bz

For special orders, quantity sales, course adoptions and corporate sales, please email the publisher at sales@mango.bz. For trade and wholesale sales, please contact Ingram Publisher Services at customer.service@ingramcontent.com or +1.800.509.4887.

Adaptive Listening: How to Cultivate Trust and Traction at Work

Library of Congress Cataloging-in-Publication number: 2023945356
ISBNs: (pb) 978-1-68481-259-2 (e) 978-1-68481-260-8
BISAC: BUS097000, BUSINESS & ECONOMICS / Workplace Culture

Printed in the United States of America

# Table of Contents

## Foreword

# A Note from Nancy Duarte

## How Adaptive Listening Changed My Life

Some people are natural at listening, and others work hard to develop their listening skills. I've historically *not* fallen into either category. Granted, if I were interested in what you were saying, I'd give you my rapt attention, but if not, I'd try to turn the conversation into something that could yield some sort of productive result. Classic listening literature tells me that the way I naturally enjoy listening is a no-no.

I was good at listening socially. I'd nod, smile, and remain curious so others felt heard. But at work, nodding courteously was more challenging because we have goals to reach and decisions to make, so I had a bent toward listening to accomplish something. Is it productive to spend time listening so someone else simply feels listened to? Yes. But not always.

This book is not about ***active*** listening because active listening should be everyone's baseline, and it only gets you part way. Yes, while listening, you should be sending cues you're listening attentively—like making eye contact, nodding, showing interest, and affirming you understand—but that's not enough. Behaving as if you're listening isn't necessarily always what is needed in a work exchange. Let's say a team member wants your input on managing a difficult vendor. If you solely pay attention, affirm your understanding of the problem, and suspend judgment, they'll walk away frustrated. At that moment, they need a leader who can listen—and respond—*adaptively*.

Combining ***active*** listening with ***adaptive*** listening creates a powerful skill that boosts your empathy, helps in the exchange of ideas, and ultimately, gets better results—for a person and an organization.

With listening, one size doesn't fit all. Before I learned about Adaptive Listening, I noticed that some folks enjoyed how I listened and came to me often, yet others left frustrated or didn't feel heard. It was difficult for me to parse why some pursued me to listen, and others didn't. Identifying and breaking my behavior patterns eluded me, and there wasn't a simple tool to help me develop a path to improve.

Maegan and Nicole's groundbreaking work anchored me; it allowed me to keep a clear mental model in my head so I could catch myself and then modify my behavior on the fly, which is the best way for me to learn. Because it's rooted in empathy, their model quickly connected from my mind to my heart—listening and empathy are among the most essential human skills driving day-to-day organizational performance.

Empathic listening focuses on the goals of the one speaking—which, of course, will vary from meeting to meeting or situation to situation. At Duarte, we define empathic communication as knowing the approach you default to, understanding others' needs, and *then* adapting yourself to their needs. Maegan and Nicole have studied listening for years, and their model applied to our company, Duarte, took deep root quickly. It's also been tested by hundreds of learners who've attended the courses.

**Table 0.1. Adaptive Listening Is Empathic Listening**

| Empathy | Empathy + Listening |
|---|---|
| Know yourself. | Know how you prefer to listen. |
| Understand others. | Identify how others need you to listen. |
| Adapt to others. | Listen in a way that will help you meet the other's goals. |

© Duarte, Inc.

## Know Your Listening Style

Identifying your listening style is a required first step to adapting. You can't adapt unless you know what you're adapting away from.

After Maegan and Nicole carefully studied employee and client communication patterns, they identified four listening styles that people rely on at work: the S.A.I.D. Listening Styles. Once you recognize your listening style, the real magic begins; you listen in a way that can be tailored to others.

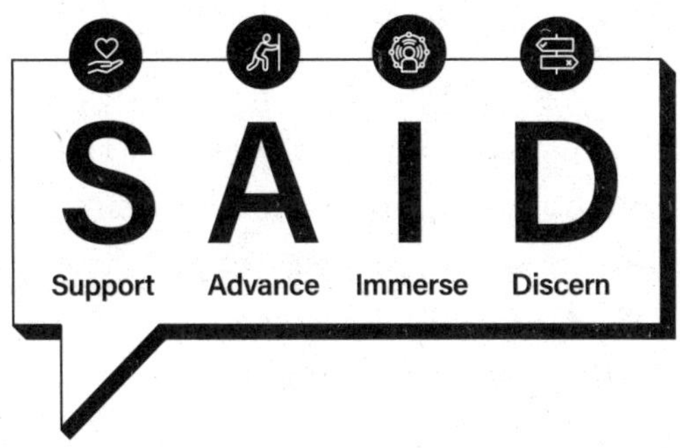

**Table 0.2. S.A.I.D. Listening Styles and Goals**

| S.A.I.D. Listening Styles | The Way You Prefer to Listen | S.A.I.D. Listening Goals | What the Speaker Needs from You |
|---|---|---|---|
| **Support Listeners™** | Prioritize the speaker's emotions | **Listen to Support™** | Meet their emotional need |
| **Advance Listeners™** | Prioritize forward momentum | **Listen to Advance™** | Move people, projects, or processes forward |
| **Immerse Listeners™** | Prioritize the content | **Listen to Immerse™** | Understand and remember the content |
| **Discern Listeners™** | Prioritize evaluation | **Listen to Discern™** | Evaluate the information |

Find your listening style at Duarte.com/adaptivelistening

Active listening mainly covers immersing or supporting the speaker, whereas Adaptive Listening draws on all four styles, depending on what's called for in each situation.

The tricky thing is that we all have one or two listening styles we default to, so going with what feels natural in the moment isn't necessarily the best move.

Like many executives I've talked to, my listening style is often to *advance*—I listen with a heavy bias toward solving problems and making progress. *Discern* is a close second. When others speak, I'm asking myself, "*Is this the best approach to reach our goal?*" or "*Is this efficient?*" or "*Is the risk worth the reward?*" Combine both my advance and discern styles, and you can see why, left to my own devices, I tend to jump in with unsolicited advice, asserting, "*I think you should...*" or offering, "*I can connect you with someone who...*" or directing, "*Let me break that down for you...*"

In the past, my mindset was: Why would people speak with me if they didn't want *my* decision? But now that Maegan and Nicole's work has created an easily applicable model for me; before any meeting, I pause to think through what else the speaker might need, so I won't just default to *discern* or *advance* mode.

The cool thing is that the S.A.I.D. Listening Styles are the same four ways one may need you to listen. Thinking through how the speaker wants you to listen *before* the conversation is key so you can get ahead of your strongest impulses—in my case, the urge to intervene.

> "Most of us think of ourselves as good listeners, but do we always react or respond appropriately to meet the needs of the speaker? This course provides strong background, theory, and practice for applying new communication methods for self-awareness, working with others, and becoming a strong partner to others. Excellent course, excellent facilitation, and delivery of content."
>
> ***—Workshop participant from Apple***

## Adapt Your Style to Meet the Speaker's Goals

Once you've sorted out what the other person needs from you, you're to meet their need to the best of your ability. For example, when my HR executive briefs me on employee concerns, I now listen to *immerse* so I can really understand people's issues. She has it all in hand; she needs me to feel and think deeply about the employees. When my sales leader does all the right things but has a week of low numbers, I don't listen to *advance*; I listen to *support*. When a CEO reaches out to me because they are stuck, I listen to *advance*. And, when someone proposes an idea for approval, I listen to *discern* the return on investment.

Well, I try to do these things. Sometimes I regress. Each of our listening styles is a strong, persistent habit. You have to remind yourself to choose how you listen and choose your response deliberately. Still, I already see the benefits of adaptive listening in my organization—smarter decisions at the top and better alignment throughout so that we will keep at it. Trust me. It's worth having the discipline to know yourself and adapt.

## My Listening Transformation

My listening style of "advance" transcends just listening for me. I feel most alive when I'm being a way-maker for others. A good portion of people want me to listen so things move forward, but not always. Especially not my kids.

My son is a whip-smart, deeply thoughtful, introverted entrepreneur. He carefully crafts what he says or it goes unsaid. When I took the Adaptive Listening course and identified my listening style as Advance, I also easily recognized the style my son defaults to: he listens to immerse. I knew instantly that my way of listening was why we had long patches where we'd only text. Because he's also an entrepreneur, I almost 100 percent listened to *advance* him and his company. I would say, "I can introduce you to someone who can help with that," or "I can take a look at that contract," or "You need to find an accountant to help with that." Nope, that's not why he was sharing things with me about his business. He needed to build his business his way and wanted me to immerse deeply with him to understand his thoughts. He wasn't coming to me to help him or his business. He just wanted me to listen and understand how deeply he thinks and why he's making his decisions.

As I adapted into an immersive listener, I realized if I counted to seven and let there be long moments of silence, he formed the next insight and volunteered more about himself. I wouldn't contribute or coach or advise. As I worked through my listening transformation and fully understood his needs, we began to understand each other more deeply. So much so that for Christmas, he gave me an hour-long conversation each week. That hour would turn into almost two hours many times. That never would have happened if Maegan and Nicole hadn't written this body of work and if I hadn't adapted to him.

Now, my entire dynamic with my son has changed. The conversations are a rich blend of immersing, and now that he understands my style more, he pulls on me to discern and advance—sometimes. The great news is that he gave me that gift of listening again the last three Christmases. We both understand each other's listening goals and have a thriving relationship because of that.

> "The framework is super valuable to help surface self-awareness as well as pre-consider how to bring the best and elicit the best from a call/meeting/interaction."
>
> — ***Workshop participant from Salesforce***

## The Company Benefits Too

Now that Duarte employees know their listening styles, it creates an honest and more productive environment. Both the speaker and the listener can have their needs met in service of helping the organization meet its goals also. You'll hear people in meetings catch themselves and say, "Gosh, I'm so sorry. I was listening to *Advance*, and now I realize that's not what you need from me." Or they feel safe saying to me, "I'd like you to suspend your desire to *Discern* and would like you to listen to *Support* instead." Having a common language creates a safe and productive culture.

I've said often that strong communication could solve the world's most pressing problems. So, imagine a world where every conversation has an ear bent toward empathy. Where leaders and individuals know the listening style they default to and adapt their own so others flourish.

I have read many books and reviewed many models. But this book and course might be the start of an empathy revolution. There's a beautiful balance between speaking and listening empathetically in a way that helps an organization meet its goals. So, next time you find yourself in a conversation, remember: the one speaking has a goal. Lend them more than an ear and adapt to what they need, too.

Nancy Duarte
CEO, Duarte, Inc.

## Chapter 1

# There's a Better Way to Listen at Work

You probably don't need to be convinced that listening at work matters. In your last job interview or promotion review, it's unlikely you said, "I try hard to avoid listening to the people I work with...so...can I have the job/promotion now?" You haven't asked anyone to endorse you on LinkedIn for your poor listening skills. If you've ever zoned out in a meeting, you likely apologized as you asked your colleagues to repeat themselves. You didn't say with pride and glee, "I'm more important than you, so I wasn't listening to a single thing you said (insert maniacal laugh)! Take that!"

You wouldn't do any of those things. Not only because it's rude but because those behaviors lead to bad outcomes. You've felt the strain when projects went sideways because your colleague, leader, direct report, customer, or supplier wasn't listening. You've felt frustrated when avoidable conflicts arose because someone wasn't listening. You've felt annoyed and even angry when you've had to repeat yourself because someone wasn't listening.

But you've also felt the power when someone *does* listen to you at work. You've felt excitement when your team worked together to reach their goals. You've felt energized when a colleague was in sync with you. You've felt relief when a supplier or vendor understood and could solve your problem. None of that would have been possible if they weren't listening to you.

The benefits of listening in the workplace are clear and numerous: Listening can increase your influence with coworkers.[1] Managers with better listening skills foster trust and create more psychological safety.[2] Executive recruiters are on the hunt for leaders with strong listening skills.[3] Listening is rated a top skill for successful salespeople, as enhanced listening skills improve customer attitudes and foster long-lasting relationships.[4] At the organizational level, listening leads to better business outcomes like increased engagement levels[5] and higher retention.[6] It's also been linked to a company's financial success.[7] Listening can improve workplace relationships and the bottom line regardless of your role, title, or industry.

If listening is crucial to hitting goals and building solid connections, why do so many people struggle with it? Sure, people are busy. And yes, attention spans are short. And it's true, technology has not only made it easier to multitask ("I'll just check my email quickly while this person is talking to me..."), but it has also granted a free pass to avoid listening altogether ("You'll send out the recording of this meeting, right?"). All these realities certainly make it harder to listen.

But with their over thirty years of combined experience as communication professionals, the authors of this book found two other reasons why people have trouble listening in the workplace. First, the way many people define good listening neglects how important, powerful, and nuanced it can be. Second, there's a lack of actionable, memorable listening techniques that fit within the flow of a hectic, fast-paced workday.

After three years of research, interviews, focus groups, and testing in US-based business contexts, the authors developed a new way of listening: Adaptive Listening.

Put simply, Adaptive Listening™ is a model for processing and responding in a way that meets the speaker's goals. That doesn't mean you'll say yes to every request they make, but you'll think less about yourself and more about them. This chapter lays the groundwork for a better way to listen at work by challenging common misconceptions and introducing Adaptive Listening as the solution you didn't know you needed.

## Paying Attention Isn't Enough

The authors met while working at Duarte, Inc., the longest-running, woman-owned communication agency and training firm in the San Francisco Bay Area. Most days, the authors help leaders at Fortune 100 companies align on their message strategy, craft compelling speeches and presentations, and elevate their delivery skills for high-stakes moments like keynotes, sales pitches, major internal announcements, etc. One day, when they were co-leading a training on delivery skills, this conversation happened:

> **Maegan:** Don't you think it's weird that we offer "communication training," but we don't cover listening in any of those trainings?
>
> **Nicole:** Yes, I've been thinking that for years! People need both speaking and listening training.
>
> **Maegan:** I've noticed listening problems in our internal teams. I'll leave a client meeting and get together with the rest of the team afterward, and we'll each come away with entirely different interpretations of what needs to happen next. Or I'll read a statement of work someone else put together, but when I meet with the client for the first time, it's clear that the plan won't solve the client's problem.
>
> **Nicole:** Listening has come up with the clients I'm coaching, too. They want to know how to better connect with their teams. They always ask questions about what they can *say* to build trust and rapport. When I ask them if they're also *listening*, I either get blank stares or defensive responses like, "Of coooooourse I do!" But when I ask follow-up questions about their listening, they usually describe how they pay attention.

Paying attention is certainly a prerequisite for listening, but it's not synonymous with listening. You'll need to do better than "pay attention" if you're going to help your teams and organizations hit their ambitious goals. It's not enough to maintain eye contact, nod along, and look like you're listening while you're *really* thinking about another task on your to-do list or mentally rehearsing what you'll say next in the meeting.

In other words, paying attention can give your colleagues, leaders, direct reports, and customers the *impression* that you're listening, even if you're not. The people you work with deserve better, and so do you. If you only pay attention, you could limit your career growth and impact.

Another reason paying attention isn't enough is because it ignores the importance of responding as part of listening. Take these famous quotations you might have seen (or even shared yourself) on social media:

> "The quieter you become, the more you can hear."
>
> — ***Ram Dass***[8]

> "We have two ears and one mouth so that we can listen twice as much as we speak."
>
> — ***attributed to Greek philosopher Epictetus***

> "Most people do not listen with the intent to understand; they listen with the intent to reply."
>
> — ***Stephen R. Covey***[9]

These statements admirably draw attention to the fact that the world needs more (and better) listening, and these authors agree! But they also give the impression that speaking is the enemy of listening, and that's not true. In fact, responding is a critical part of listening, and in the workplace, if you're always "quieter," or you "listen twice as much," or you have no "intent to reply," you'll be doing yourself and the person speaking a disservice.

Try walking into a meeting with your manager, colleague, or top customer and saying, "I'm not going to respond today. I'm only here *to listen*." That's probably not going to go over well. Not only would that silence get awkward, but so much of your workday includes dynamic dialogue. You go back and forth, listening and responding. In a meeting with a customer, they may want you to reply with recommendations to solve their problem. In a one-on-one with your manager, they may want you to confirm that you understand the information they've shared. In a working session with your colleague, they may want you to scrutinize their idea.

Not only does listening include verbal responses, but it also includes the nonverbals you show while listening. Instead of eye contact and head nodding (signs that make it *look* like you're listening when you might not be), you can be more strategic about how you respond with your face, body, and voice.

Because great listening goes beyond paying attention, and it includes how you respond to the person speaking, this book won't tell you to sign out of email when you're about to jump into a virtual meeting or mute your notifications before joining a company town hall. Yes, those are good things to do. But we doubt you need an entire book to tell you that. Instead, this book will give you techniques to help you process and respond in a way that helps grow your influence. In the following chapters, we'll explore the art of Adaptive Listening in detail and provide practical, actionable strategies you can implement in your daily interactions.

## Even Active Listening Falls Short

One listening approach that's become common in the workplace is *active listening*. Psychologists Carl R. Rogers and Richard Evans Farson published the book *Active Listening* in the 1950s. As therapists, they wanted to know why some counselors were better than others at addressing their clients' problems. They found that counselors who listened for "total meaning" across both the patient's content and feelings had better results than counselors who judged or gave advice.[10]

Over the years, active listening has become synonymous with good listening, and active listening techniques have been incorporated into non-therapy roles.

Attributes of active listening, like giving the speaker your full attention and avoiding distractions, is solid advice. But active listening is limited.

**First, it wasn't purpose-built for the workday.** Active listening offers helpful tools for people who listen in a therapeutic setting, but it doesn't always consider the dynamic and interactive nature of people's jobs outside of that setting. For example, the active listening guidance to "avoid judgment" doesn't always apply at work. Sure, your internal judgments shouldn't distract you as your colleague tells you about their bad day, but many workplace interactions demand that you evaluate what people are saying. Across roles and industries, there are situations at work where people are asked to assess, critique, and poke holes in the information. Product managers question how a product might fit into the existing market. Consultants assess a client's organizational change efforts. Sales leaders pressure-test new collateral before using it with customers.

The authors of this book have made careers out of judging other people's communication skills and deliverables. They are primed to listen to clients and tell them when their presentation is unclear, their messages are redundant, and their delivery skills are distracting. There's a time and place to evaluate information, and with Adaptive Listening, you'll learn techniques that help you determine when and how to do it.

**Second, active listening doesn't account for the context of fast-paced, back-to-back meetings in a results-driven workday**. Active listening posits that you should "avoid jumping to conclusions." In the therapeutic context, this guidance makes perfect sense. Counselors and therapists work to give patients time to process information aloud, and they don't want to lead patients to an answer. Rather, they want to provide space for patients to uncover the answer.

In the workplace, jumping to conclusions and telling the other person that you're on the same page might be precisely what a situation demands. In building and testing the models for this book, the authors had many late-night, rapid-fire, clock-is-ticking interactions. Nicole would say energetically, "What if we move this second chapter to the end so we can—" and Maegan would interrupt with, "*Yes*! Do it!" This interruption wasn't a distraction or off-putting to Nicole. At this point, they were a #HiveMind, in a rhythm of building and moving forward while finishing each other's sentences. It was energizing and relieving to assess, adapt, and sync with each other, all in the name of progress. There are certainly places for thoughtful, methodical interactions in the workplace. But there are also agile working sessions, brainstorms, and meetings when someone is looking for you to make a decision—fast.

**Third, active listening certainly wasn't built for a distributed workforce** when sometimes you're listening to people who are physically in the room with you, sometimes listening to others through a computer screen or phone, or both simultaneously in a hybrid environment. A lot of workplace listening happens in group settings, small and large. Even though you can only listen to one person at a time, you likely listen to multiple people during a meeting, town hall, or breakout session.

Or what about listening to recordings? Does anything change when you're listening to someone live versus when you're listening to a presentation you couldn't attend? Or if you're relistening to a meeting where you had to step out in the middle? And what about the emojis, GIFs, and memes that pop up in the comments pane during a company-wide meeting or with a colleague via chat? Are those a distraction? A way to show you're listening? Both? These are valuable questions the authors wanted to consider, research, and test in developing a new model for workplace listening.

To be sure, active listening has made valuable contributions to the therapeutic setting and broader communication contexts. But it doesn't fully account for the intricacies of your workday.

## It's Time for Adaptive Listening

The authors had one more conversation about listening in the workplace that fueled the techniques you'll read in this book:

> **Maegan:** I spent almost a decade teaching communication courses to undergrads. Every biz comm, interpersonal comm, and organization

comm textbook has a chapter on listening. It was always a class favorite. Students would write in their end-of-semester evals that the listening chapter changed their life. One woman told me it saved her marriage!

**Nicole:** Ha! That's awesome. I've used my Speech-Language Pathology background to help speakers for years. There's a lot about communication disorders that relates to typically developing adults, and it can also be applied to listening. I'm curious about what you taught in your listening courses as a professor. Why do you think your students got so much out of the listening chapter?

**Maegan:** The chapters always included different listening styles,[11] and it was a big eye-opener to them that we don't all listen the same way. Then we talked about different listening goals, and again, they never considered listening as a goal-based activity. Listening seemed automatic to them before we covered it in class.

**Nicole:** I think we could build a training around that.

**Maegan:** Ya know what? I think we could, and we *should*! Even though some students took the new techniques home, most of the class needed help remembering them. They'd always ask me, "Dr. Stephens! Is this one a style or a goal?" The pieces were there, but it wasn't the most intuitive. And it wasn't specifically built for workplace listening.

Even though listening skills are often included in the standard curriculum for entry-level college communication courses, many professionals don't know they have a listening style, that they listen differently from others, or that they can change how they process and respond to the person speaking to them. Sure, organizations give lip service to the importance of listening in the workplace, and it doesn't seem like anyone is maliciously withholding listening training, but it was obvious to the authors that people needed a more memorable model.

The new model for great listening is Adaptive Listening: processing and responding in a way that meets the speaker's goals during the interaction. To break down that definition,

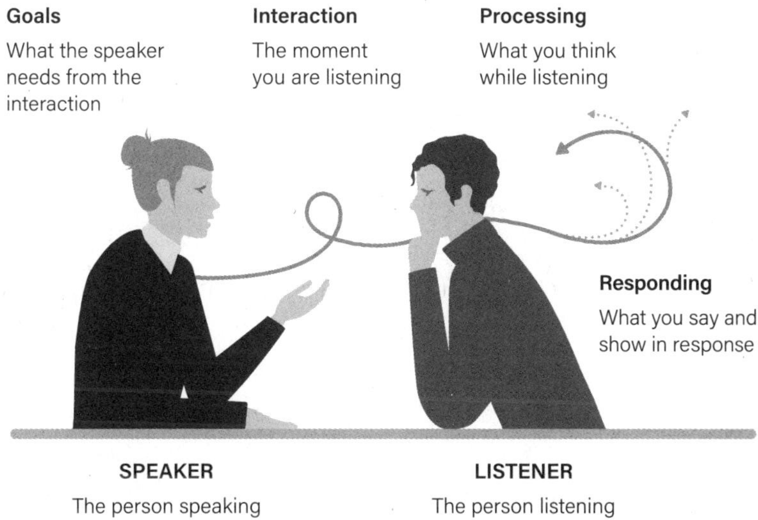


Adaptive Listening is a goal-oriented activity; you listen with the speaker's goals in mind. That can be a hard ask because you have a preferred way of listening (your listening style), you have your goals while listening (because you're a professional), you have barriers that prevent you from listening (because you're human), and other people aren't always clear on what they want or need (because they are also human). With Adaptive Listening, you'll recognize your preferences and goals, mitigate barriers that may get in your way, identify the other person's goals, and adapt the way you listen.

Adaptive Listening includes four listening styles and four listening goals. They map to each other, so instead of learning eight disparate terms, you only need to learn four: Support, Advance, Immerse, and Discern. Plus, **both styles and goals form the acronym S.A.I.D.** because, as a listener, you'll be listening to what's said (and even what's not said).

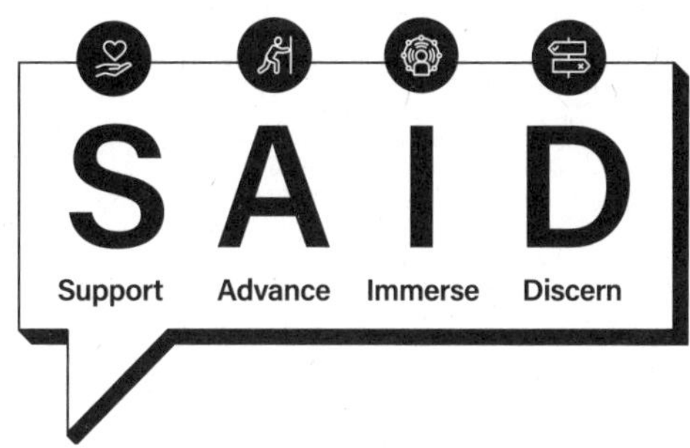

Each of these S.A.I.D. Listening Styles™ and S.A.I.D. Listening Goals™ have dedicated chapters with specific techniques you can integrate across various workplace situations and into your current workflow. For now, you can review the definitions of each in Table 1.1 below.

**Table 1.1. S.A.I.D. Listening Styles and Goals**

| S.A.I.D. Listening Styles | The Way You Prefer to Listen | S.A.I.D. Listening Goals | What the Speaker Needs from You |
|---|---|---|---|
| **Support Listeners** | Prioritize the speaker's emotions | **Listen to Support** | Meet their emotional need |
| **Advance Listeners** | Prioritize forward momentum | **Listen to Advance** | Move people, projects, or processes forward |
| **Immerse Listeners** | Prioritize the content | **Listen to Immerse** | Understand and remember the content |
| **Discern Listeners** | Prioritize evaluation | **Listen to Discern** | Evaluate the information |

At its core, Adaptive Listening is about bringing more empathy into the workplace. Empathy has various definitions, but many researchers agree that empathy is about sensing others' emotions and imagining what they're going through.[12] When you become an Adaptive Listener ™, you'll become more empathetic to every person speaking to you every time.

If the idea of being empathetic all the time sounds exhausting, consider this advice from actor-turned-communication expert Alan Alda. He found it hard to convince scientists to make their information more accessible to the public. When they pushed back, he told them, "The more empathy I have for others, the less annoying they are to me."[13] The scientists were convinced. They realized that using more empathetic communication wasn't only good for their audience, but they got something out of it, too. So, when you aren't sure you can muster the empathy to be an Adaptive Listener, remember that as a side benefit, it could make others less annoying to you.

You might already have listening techniques that work for you. Keep using them! As you read the following chapters, use Adaptive Listening to elevate or add to what you're already doing. You can also consider Adaptive Listening's potential to give your teams and organization a common language and toolkit for everyone to improve their listening. After all, just because you're already a good listener doesn't mean other people know how to be a good listener for you (yet).

If you're a die-hard active listening fan, approach Adaptive Listening as a more technique-driven, workplace-specific approach. Use the parts of active listening that bring you success in your workday and add Adaptive Listening techniques to help others meet their goals. Table 1.2 compares typical active listening advice to Adaptive Listening advice, so you can prepare for the nuances you'll read in the following chapters.

**Table 1.2. Active Listening and Adaptive Listening Comparison**

| Active Listening says: | Adaptive Listening says: |
|---|---|
| Pay attention. | Of course you should pay attention—that's what adults do at work. |
| Show you're listening. | There are different ways to show you're listening based on the speaker's needs. |
| Provide feedback/ask questions. | Yes, sometimes that's what the speaker needs, but not always. Plus, you still need to determine what type of feedback/questions are best for the situation. |
| Avoid judgment. | In the workplace, colleagues sometimes come to you specifically for your judgment, evaluation, or critique. |
| Respond appropriately. | Agree! But the appropriate response depends on the situation. |

| Active Listening says: | Adaptive Listening says: |
|---|---|
| Summarize. | Sometimes. But other times the information/next steps are so obvious, or the urgency to move forward is so great, that an in-depth summary or even paraphrasing the information can unnecessarily slow things down. |
| Share your experience and feelings. | Yikes. That can come across as selfish. Do so with caution and consider using alternative techniques. |
| Don't jump to conclusions. | Sometimes the speaker needs you to jump to conclusions. That's why they're speaking to you—for your ideas and expertise. |

## Become an Adaptive Listener

*Adaptive Listening* was written in two parts because there are two sides to communication: the listener's perspective and the speaker's perspective. Part I of this book focuses on knowing yourself as a listener. You bring your S.A.I.D. Listening Style to the interaction—how you prefer to process and respond to information. It's what you'd default to if you didn't have to consider who was speaking to you, what they wanted, or what the context was. Every interaction also includes your Listening L.E.N.S.™—a combination of internal and external influences that shape your ability to focus your listening on the speaker.

Part II of this book covers knowing how others need you to listen. Speakers bring their S.A.I.D. Listening Goal to the interaction. They aren't always aware they have a goal, but it's there. Otherwise, why would they be speaking to you? You'll learn how to identify their goal and how you can adapt how you listen to help them meet it.

Woven throughout both parts, you'll find examples and stories collected from "Adaptive Listeners in training." These listeners participated in interviews, focus groups, alpha and beta testing, workshops, and one-on-one coaching sessions to improve their listening skills. Their names have been changed with one exception: Nicole and Maegan have happily thrown themselves under the bus in the name of learning. You're welcome! May you be enlightened by our successes and entertained by our missteps.

Even though it's unlikely you need to be convinced that listening in the workplace matters, you're about to read techniques that can take you from a poor, average, or even good listener to a great listener. By the time you finish this book, you'll be on your way to becoming an Adaptive Listener who knows what other people need and how to give it to them. But if you commit to improving your Adaptive Listening skills, you won't just help others achieve their goals. You'll also have the power to cultivate trust and traction at work, which will help you meet your career goals (and maybe even your personal goals, too).

# Part One

## *Know How You Listen*

## Chapter 2

# Uncover Your S.A.I.D. Listening Style

If you've ever worked with a coach in any capacity—a sports coach, a fitness coach, a leadership coach, a communication coach (*cough cough* shameless plug *cough cough*)—your coach likely started by getting a baseline of your skills. They said something like, "Let me see your forehand," or "I'm going to time how long it takes you to run this mile," or "Give me the results from the last company feedback survey," or "Show me the recording from the presentation you gave last week." Any good coach wants to know where you're starting from so they know how to tailor their coaching.

Coaches also share that baseline information with you to build your awareness. A football coach doesn't spend hours watching gameday film and then destroy the footage. They curate clips to show their team how an undefended opponent can lead to a turnover, or how creating separation from a defender can help the offense to score.

Similarly, a leadership coach doesn't gather information on a leader's baseline skills and keep the results secret while jumping to an action plan. Before determining what a leader should do next, the coach thoroughly gathers data on the leader's behavior. Then, the coach helps the leader unpack which behaviors (or lack thereof) produce the results they're seeing and why.

The best way to develop any skill, whether you're an athlete or a leader, is to build awareness of your current performance. Listening is no different. Like sports proficiency or leadership, listening is a skill you can learn. You start by building awareness of how you currently listen.

## People Don't Listen the Same Way

Although hearing abilities are physiologically similar in typically developing adults, how they process, interpret, and respond to what they hear—their listening styles—varies. To further explore this idea, examine the following *morning update* scenario. As you read, ask yourself which of the four options following the scenario most closely resembles what would go through your head as you listened to an update from this project leader.

Before you read the scenario and options, know there isn't one right answer. Seriously, this is not a trick. Given the context provided, every one of the options is the "correct answer" as long as you pick the right answer for you.

*It's nine o'clock on a typical workday. You sit down at your desk and open your laptop. You've got your go-to beverage and are ready for your first meeting. It's a regular morning update where the project leader, someone you work with closely, provides information on revised goals, adjusted timelines, and progress reports. These updates are standard in your work, and the project leader usually shares information that's not particularly exciting or troubling. You're in this meeting with five other people.*

Ask yourself what would go through your head as you listened:

**Option 1:** I would appreciate how much work it took for this person to put the update together.

**Option 2:** I would highlight tasks that need to happen now that I've heard this information.

**Option 3:** I would crave more details about the information they've shared.

**Option 4:** I would evaluate the pros and cons of the information they've shared.

Now, if you're thinking, "Well, I'd do two out of four of those," or "I would choose option 1 in one situation, but I'd choose option 2 in a different situation," you're not alone. Thousands of people have answered this question. The responses vary across the four options, and many have said they wished they could have shared their rationale for their choice. (If you're also desperate to provide a rationale, feel free to email adaptivelistening@duarte.com, but rest assured, this scenario is not that deep.)

Given the various responses to this scenario, it's clear that people don't all listen the same way. Even if the person speaking is the same, and the listeners have the same context, people have listening preferences.

You've likely seen listening differences in action at work. Perhaps you've been in a small group meeting, a company-wide engagement, or other workplace interaction and assumed others were listening like you. After all, your fellow listeners were in the same room, listening to the same person deliver the same information. You watched your colleagues, leaders, or direct reports take notes and ask follow-up questions. You were sure everyone remembered the same key points, assessed the information the same way, and aligned on the same next steps—it was obvious!

That is...until it wasn't. Even if the speaker delivered a clear message, even if every person in that interaction swore they were absolutely, unequivocally paying close attention to the person speaking, people's listening differences can still lead to challenges. Often, these listening differences become apparent *after* the interaction when someone says something like:

- "Wait, I thought our strategy was X, but the rest of the group thinks it's Y? I'm confused."
- "Wait, everyone seems excited about this idea, but I have some concerns."
- "Wait, who's responsible for completing the next steps?"

When listeners leave an interaction with different interpretations of what happened, why it happened, and what needs to happen next, it might be frustrating, to be sure. But over time, and in a repeated pattern, these listening differences can cause significant problems with colleagues, leaders, direct reports, and customers. They create detours, double-backs, and delays that can damage company culture, causing people to look for positions elsewhere.[14]

Research shows that listening is critical to employee engagement and retention.[15] But culture isn't the only thing that mismatched listening might damage. Listening affects nearly every aspect of an organization, from addressing customer and client needs,[16] to improving agility,[17] to driving growth.[18]

The key to achieving listening alignment is first to accept that people listen differently; therefore, *you* don't listen in the same way as the people around you. Acknowledging those differences can help you dig deeper into some essential self-observations. It might help you recognize your listening preferences, how they can help you, and how they might prevent you from being a great listener. It might also help you build more awareness about listening and make you more tolerant of how others listen to you.

## The Four S.A.I.D. Listening Styles

In Chapter 1, you read that Adaptive Listening is a better way to listen at work. To become an Adaptive Listener, start by knowing how you prefer to process and respond to information. Then, ask yourself if your preferences will meet the goals of the person speaking to you. If your preferences don't match with what the speaker needs, then you'll need to adapt your listening.

You can learn more about how you currently listen by determining your S.A.I.D. Listening Style. **Your listening style is how you typically listen, regardless of who's speaking to you, what they want, or what the context is.** It's the type of listening that doesn't require much effort on your part. In fact, it's the type of listening you automatically default to, the kind of listening that's hard for you to stop doing, even if you realize the person speaking or the situation doesn't need that type of listening.

There are four S.A.I.D. Listening Styles: Support Listener, Advance Listener, Immerse Listener, and Discern Listener. Table 2.1 includes brief descriptions of the listening styles, and the following four chapters will dive deeply into each one.

**Table 2.1. S.A.I.D. Listening Styles and Description**

|  |  |  | 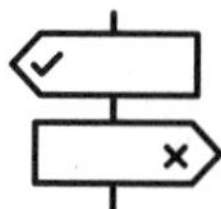 |
|---|---|---|---|
| **Support Listeners** | **Advance Listeners** | **Immerse Listeners** | **Discern Listeners** |
| Prioritize the speaker's emotions as they validate how the speaker feels and make space for others to contribute. | Prioritize forward momentum as they drive to next steps and link ideas across contexts. | Prioritize the content as they catalog the details and gain confirmation. | Prioritize evaluation as they embrace criteria and consider alternatives. |

As you explore each style, you might realize you're a great listener in situations that require a delicate hand. Or that you're a great listener when people need to get unstuck, fast. Or that you're a great listener when the interaction requires an accurate recall. Or that you're a great listener when people or projects need critical feedback.

You might also recognize which styles challenge you as a listener. You might realize it's hard to notice when others need compassion. Or that it's hard for you to keep track of all the details. Or it's hard for you to focus when there's no specific action for you to take. Or it's hard for you to figure out why you don't like an idea. When you're more aware of where you excel as a listener, and where you struggle, you can better prepare yourself to adapt your listening to help others meet their needs.

Although every listener has a primary S.A.I.D. Listening Style or a combination of styles, that doesn't mean you never use or are incapable of using the other styles. You will likely recognize yourself in all the styles. But know that no single S.A.I.D. Listening Style is better than another. **Each style is valuable when used at the right time, with the right person, and in the proper situation.** Industries, organizations, and departments need listeners across all four styles.

You can uncover your listening style by using the free S.A.I.D. Listening Style Finder ™. If you don't already know your listening style, stop what you're doing and visit www.duarte.com/adaptivelistening. It will take about ten minutes to complete the style finder, and your results will be emailed to you. You'll find that the structure is similar to the *morning update*—you'll read a brief scenario and select which of the four options sounds like how you'd prefer to process and respond. Only this time, you'll get to rank-order your choices to more fully account for your preferences. Like your answer to the *morning update*, there are no correct answers to the questions in the style finder, and there's nothing right or wrong with any of the styles. But know this: the results are only accurate if you answer honestly.

Keep in mind, although the S.A.I.D. Listening Style Finder tells you how you typically listen to others, it *does not* tell you how you always want others to listen to you. For example, if your S.A.I.D. Listening Style is Discern Listener, that doesn't mean you want everyone to be a Discern Listener every time you speak. Similarly, just because you know someone else's listening style, that doesn't mean they always want you to listen in the same way as their style. Rather, knowing your listening style will help you know exactly what situations come naturally to you (and where you excel), as well as when your listening style might be getting in the way. The more you know about how you listen, the more you can control it.

Just as you've grown and changed throughout your career, and will hopefully continue to do so, your listening style can change. Feel free to bookmark the style finder webpage so you can return to it if you ever notice a change in your listening preferences.

## Build Your Listening Awareness

In the following four chapters, you'll read more about the characteristics and cautions of each listening style. At least one of these styles will likely resonate strongly with you. The rest of the chapters will then offer deeper insights into how you listen some of the time.

Do you cheer people up when they don't need it? Do you rush the person or group because you're eager to get to the finish line? Does your "I'm concentrating" face look more like an "I'm not even listening to you" face? Do you call out problems or potential setbacks when others are ready to move on? Once you've read the chapter on your listening style, you'll probably start thinking differently about how you listen in your next interaction.

You might be wondering, "Can I only read the chapter corresponding to my style and just skip the others?"

Not if you want to become an Adaptive Listener. The goal of this book is to help you adapt to the other styles based on what the person speaking needs. As you read the chapters that don't correspond to your listening style, pay attention to which styles would take a lot of effort to adapt to and which ones seem within your current skillset. In Part II of the book, you'll learn techniques to help you adapt the way you listen to meet others' needs across professional situations.

There's another reason to read the style chapters that don't correspond to your listening style—to learn more about how the people you work with listen. You can share the S.A.I.D. Listening Style Finder with others to uncover their listening style (and the authors would greatly appreciate it if you did). However, you might not always feel comfortable or confident enough to send it to your manager, leadership team, or a challenging customer.

Luckily, after reading all the style chapters, you'll be able to make smart assumptions based on what you observe in others. Once you understand your colleagues' listening styles, you may become more tolerant of their listening preferences and even seek out the type of listener you need in different situations. Even if your assumptions about others' listening styles aren't always spot-on, the insights from the upcoming chapters will provide a solid foundation for understanding.

Prepare yourself for a journey of discovery, as you're about to gain profound insights into your listening preferences and the preferences of those around you.

## Chapter 3

# Support S.A.I.D. Listening Style

The "S" in the S.A.I.D. Listening Style acronym stands for Support Listener. This style refers to individuals who prioritize the speaker's emotions while listening. Support Listeners often actively create space for others to express their emotions, whether the speaker is explicit about their emotions or not. Support Listeners foster a connected environment where others feel included.

**Table 3.1. S.A.I.D. Listening Styles and Description**

| 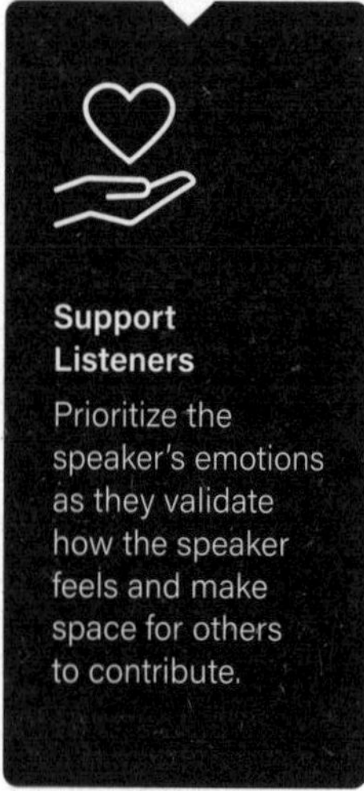 |  |  | 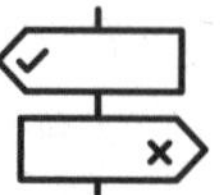 |
|---|---|---|---|
| **Support Listeners** | **Advance Listeners** | **Immerse Listeners** | **Discern Listeners** |
| Prioritize the speaker's emotions as they validate how the speaker feels and make space for others to contribute. | Prioritize forward momentum as they drive to next steps and link ideas across contexts. | Prioritize the content as they catalog the details and gain confirmation. | Prioritize evaluation as they embrace criteria and consider alternatives. |

In Chapter 2, you considered your listening preferences after reading the *morning update* (and hopefully after getting your results from the S.A.I.D. Listening Style Finder). In this chapter and the three that follow, that scenario offers a starting place to learn more about each listening style.

Here's the scenario again:

> *It's nine o'clock on a typical workday. You sit down at your desk and open your laptop. You've got your go-to beverage and are ready for your first meeting. It's a regular morning update where the project leader, someone you work with closely, provides information on revised goals, adjusted timelines, and progress reports. These updates are standard in your work, and the project leader usually shares information that's not particularly exciting or troubling. You're in this meeting with five other people.*

Support Listeners most often choose option 1 as their response.

**Option 1: I would appreciate how much work it took for the project leader to put the update together.**

Option 2: I would highlight tasks that need to happen now that I've heard this information.

Option 3: I would crave more details about the information they've shared.

Option 4: I would evaluate the pros and cons of the information they've shared.

Although a Support Listener can certainly highlight tasks that need to be completed (like an Advance Listener), seek more details about the information (like an Immerse Listener), or uncover the pros and cons (like a Discern Listener), a Support Listener focuses more frequently and consistently on how the person speaking feels in the moment.

As you read the following characteristics and cautions of Support Listeners, consider whether the descriptions and examples match how you usually prefer to process and respond. If they do, you'll find recommendations for how you can continue to strengthen your style. If, however, these characteristics sound nothing like you, reflect on why it might be hard for you to prioritize others' emotions while you're listening. Every Adaptive Listener needs to know the right time to offer Support Listening.

## Support Listener Characteristics

While listening to the project leader in the *morning update*, a Support Listener might think, "I bet it took this person a lot of time to prepare for this meeting. There are many moving parts, so it couldn't have been easy." A Support Listener might even respond during the meeting with something like, "Thanks for taking the time to put this update together. I appreciate it."

Here are additional examples of how a Support Listener might process information across different workplace scenarios:

- When listening to a vision keynote, a Support Listener might think, "My CEO put real effort into crafting this vision."

- When listening to a customer talk about their pain points with their current product, a Support Listener might think, "This poor customer. They're trying to run a company and shouldn't have to deal with all these issues."
- When listening to a direct report talk about how much they learned in a new internal training, a Support Listener might think, "I'm thrilled this person is growing in their career. Good for them!"
- When listening to a colleague vent about another coworker, a Support Listener might think, "Ugh, this sounds stressful!"

Some Adaptive Listeners in training initially pushed back on the value of emotions in the workplace. In fact, some people think emotions have no place at work. "We're here to get a job done—not to spend hours talking about our feelings," they might say. Understandably, some people want to avoid dwelling on, or being distracted by, emotions at work. You *do* have a job to complete, and you *do* have business objectives and goals to meet.

But the fact is, everyone brings emotions to work. People aren't robots. They have feelings about their work, what's going on at home, and what's happening in the world around them.[19] That doesn't necessarily mean emotions prevent people from getting their jobs done. Support Listeners accept that people bring their emotions to work—and embrace it.

To prioritize the emotions of the person speaking, Support Listeners often 1) validate how the speaker feels and 2) make space for others to contribute.

## Support Listeners Validate How the Speaker Feels

One reason Support Listeners are great at prioritizing a speaker's emotions is that they seem in tune with the current or anticipated feelings of others. They pick up emotional cues based on what the speaker says and how they say it. Support Listeners also look for emotional cues based on what the speaker *doesn't* say, intentionally or unintentionally. They read between the lines of the speaker's message, and pay close attention to their facial expressions, tone of voice, and body language.

Once the Support Listener knows how the speaker feels, they process and respond in a way that validates those feelings. Not only do Support Listeners use language that confirms what others are feeling, but they also mirror the speaker's vocal tone and body language. Mirroring is the process of emulating or copying another individual's behaviors, speech, and characteristics.[20] When you stand in front of a mirror and wave your hand, you can see your mirrored self waving back at you. If you smile, your mirrored self smiles back. If you dance, your mirrored self dances with you.

Now imagine your mirrored self wasn't you but a Support Listener. When a speaker looks sad, so does the Support Listener. If their speaking rate gets faster, a Support Listener increases their speaking rate, too. If a speaker's gestures are frequent and urgent, a Support Listener will use frequent and urgent gestures, too. Support Listeners use mirroring to show empathy, build rapport, and help others feel more comfortable.[21]

Mirroring is a common technique taught in therapy, persuasion, negotiations, and sales training, and has proven to positively impact trust-building. One study explored communication training in business-to-business persuasive selling situations. It found that those trained in mirroring were more successful in getting customers to commit to purchasing than those who didn't use the mirroring technique.[22]

There's a fine line between mirroring and mimicking, but Support Listeners often successfully use mirroring techniques without ever being trained. Take this situation between Shonda and Mario, for example:

Shonda, a project manager, and Mario, an account executive, were tasked with arranging a complicated timeline for a customer project. Four people were on their team to consider, all with other projects to juggle and upcoming vacations on the books. The timeline was further compounded by the customer's schedule, varied locations and time zones, not to mention a looming deadline for an upcoming event. Shonda and Mario were tasked with solving this tricky timeline puzzle and only had a half hour to do it before meeting with the customer.

To make matters more hectic, Mario had to hop on a flight to Tokyo to meet with another customer the next day. He still hadn't packed, checked in for his flight, or confirmed travel details. Shonda, a tried-and-true Support Listener, didn't know any of this. All she knew was Mario was acting differently from usual during their meeting:

> **Shonda:** Hey, Mario. Ready to tackle this timeline?
>
> **Mario:** (frowning, legs bouncing under, with a quick speaking rate) Yeah. Sure. Let's get to it.
>
> **Shonda:** (mentally thinking, "Mario isn't usually this abrupt, and he seems kind of agitated.")
>
> Is this project stressing you out?
>
> **Mario:** (using a loud volume, increased speaking rate, and a wide-eyed facial expression) Ha! How can you tell? Yeah, I *am* stressed. I have a million things to do before I leave for Tokyo tomorrow, and I'm worried we won't be able to figure out this timeline before I leave.
>
> **Shonda:** (mirroring Mario's wide eyes, increased volume, and speaking rate) Ugh, I hate this for you! You have so much on your plate right now! I bet all you wanna do is focus on your trip and not have to think about this scheduling problem.
>
> **Mario:** (cracks a smile) Yes, that's exactly right! (decreases his volume and speaking rate, stops bouncing his legs) But I know we've got to get this done.
>
> **Shonda:** (soft smile and nodding in agreement) I know. Just one more thing on the list. Hopefully, it won't be too painful. Here's what I'm thinking...
>
> *Mario and Shonda work together for the next twenty-nine minutes to finalize the timeline.*

This exchange didn't last long, but it accomplished a lot. Shonda immediately recognized and validated Mario's emotions using verbal recognition and mirroring. Because Mario showed exasperation, frustration, and urgency, Shonda did the same, both verbally and nonverbally. By doing so, she sent a message that she cared about Mario's feelings. Based on Mario's change in behavior at the end of the exchange, Shonda helped him feel less burdened and calmer using validating techniques. Then, both could move forward with the task at hand.

## Support Listeners Make Space for Others

In addition to validating others' emotions, another hallmark of Support Listeners is selflessness. They tend to put their ideas and contributions aside to make space for others to share. Support Listeners may remain quieter than other participants in team meetings, brainstorms, or other group communication interactions. When they speak up, it's likely to praise someone else's idea and make the original contributor shine. It's not that Support Listeners don't have great ideas to contribute or accomplishments to share with others. Of course, they do! But they often sacrifice their contributions in favor of others'.

Support Listeners' selflessness is valuable when making space for less dominant personalities. Support Listeners gravitate toward the person whose voice is not being considered. In the group setting, Support Listeners might work hard to bring the quieter voices into the interaction.

One Support Listener and director of HR, Jeri, shared a technique they use to make space for others in their workplace interactions: During a meeting, if Jeri senses that most ideas are coming from one or two participants, they are drawn to the quiet people.

"I want to be brave on their behalf and make way for them to be heard amongst the sea of other voices," Jeri shared. "I'm the person who often says things like, 'I'd love to know what our colleague has to say about this topic.' "

When asked why Jeri approaches interactions this way, they said, "When I bring people in, I can see the relief and appreciation on their faces. It makes me feel so good to be the leader focused on making space for everyone." Jeri further shared that when they make space for others in this way, they can feel a positive change in the group dynamic. There's more balance and harmony when all the voices, including the quiet ones, can contribute.

Support Listeners focus on speakers' emotions and pay special attention to those who don't naturally speak up or shine independently. These listeners enjoy bringing others into the spotlight and aren't afraid to silence themselves to give others space.

## Support Listener Cautions

After reading the characteristics of a Support Listener you might have thought, "Hey! Those listeners sound great! I want someone to validate my feelings and make space for me to contribute!" Maybe you even realized you *are* a Support Listener, and you're proud of how you use your listening skills to take care of others. You're right. Support Listeners are great. But these listeners must take caution, too.

Support Listeners run the risk of too much self-sacrifice for the sake of the speaker or group. They also need to watch out for overdoing their support. As you read more about these two cautions, ask yourself if you can recall times when you've done the same, all in the name of being a Support Listener.

### Support Listeners May Withhold Contributions

Support Listeners often spend their energy looking for ways to include others in conversations or meetings, like when they wait to state their ideas until others have contributed or invite a quiet participant to share with the group. But the gift of space that Support Listeners create for others can come at a steep price.

Corey is a Support Listener. She's also a dedicated and thorough logistics manager with a knack for creating efficient processes. She was part of a working group tasked with updating the training process for new employees. Corey was excited to dive into the work and potentially revolutionize the experience for new employees. Each person in the group spent time drafting a potential process, and then the group scheduled a meeting where everyone would share their ideas.

When it came time for the meeting, Corey was excited about her proposal. She thought her idea would benefit new employees and was eager to tell the group. Once the meeting got started, however, her excitement dwindled after another colleague presented their idea first.

Corey shared during an interview, "A colleague offered her idea before I could share mine...and the whole group loved it. They praised her and her idea, so I chose not to share my own and instead, offered my praise, too."

It's not that Corey was mad that another colleague went first. Nor did she believe her idea wasn't as good as her colleague's. Corey said, "I felt my idea would have been a more streamlined and clear approach." But when Corey saw how excited and aligned the group was, she decided to stay quiet.

Support Listeners may hold back in meetings, and they have the best intentions for doing so. They want to maintain group harmony, avoid confrontation, and foster a positive team environment. But when Support Listeners make a habit of withholding their contributions, it can have negative consequences.

In Corey's case, her colleagues missed hearing a potentially great idea. Even if they hadn't selected Corey's idea as the new process, the group could have benefited from looking at the problem from a new perspective. Or there might have been elements of Corey's idea that could have helped other processes in their organization. Unfortunately for Corey and the group, no one will ever know.

There are also potential long-term career consequences when Support Listeners neglect sharing. They can miss opportunities to demonstrate their expertise. How will peers and leaders learn about the breadth and depth of what someone can bring to the organization if no one hears or sees those contributions? When it comes time for promotions and succession planning, Support Listeners could make their career progression harder.

If you recognize this caution in yourself, try enlisting the help of an accountability partner. Seek out a trusted colleague who is often in meetings or working groups with you. Then, tell the person that you're working on contributing more during meetings.

- Ask them to invite you into the conversation with comments like "[insert name] and I were talking about this earlier, and they have some interesting thoughts," or, "I want to make sure we've heard from anyone who has an idea—let's pause for a few minutes so people can collect their thoughts before we move on."
- Request your accountability partner remind you to speak up with a ping or chat message during a virtual meeting.
- Invite your accountability partner to physically nudge you when you sit next to one another in an in-person meeting.

Support Listeners are often strong caretakers. **The warmth they bring to interactions doesn't have to override their goals.** It's okay for them to ask for what they need and be taken care of, too.

## Support Listeners May Excessively Cheerlead

At one point or another, everyone needs an encouraging boost at work:

- A "great work on that presentation" from a manager
- An "I know that was a tough meeting; I'm here if you want to talk" from a peer
- A "thanks for everything you did to get us back on track" from a customer

But there are times when excessive compliments or praise can turn others off. Support Listeners' enthusiasm can sometimes be too much for the person or group. Nicole witnessed this kind of over-the-top praise while she was part of a team working onsite at a Duarte client's event.

Nicole was at a large convention center with a presentation designer (Angela) and project manager (Mo). Nicole, Angela, and Mo were tasked with finalizing a forty-five-minute keynote presentation that their executive client would deliver on the main stage of a conference center. Nicole's main task was to make sure the keynote's content was engaging and persuasive, and that the on-slide copy matched what the executive would be saying when that slide was on screen. Angela's main task was to create stunning and relevant visuals that would appear on a stage behind the executive as he presented. Mo's main task was coordinating between the client and the Duarte team and ensuring the team completed the deliverables on time.

It was one in the morning, and the executive was scheduled to deliver the keynote in less than eight hours. As the executive and his team slept, Nicole, Mo, and Angela were hurriedly but confidently working on final edits to the presentation file. This type of "last minute, locked away in a conference room with no windows, ample snacks, and half-empty coffee cups" working style was familiar to the Duarte team. Executives have busy schedules, and they're rarely ready to make final edits to their presentations until it's almost showtime.

The three of them were collaborating on the working file, which was projected on a screen in front of the room. During this dynamic interaction, everyone was speaking and listening to each other. Nicole pointed out the changes that needed to be made, slide by slide, and Angela made them one at a time. A word tweak here, a color change there, nothing overly complicated or time-consuming for Angela, who was a tenured and skilled designer.

But despite the simplicity of Nicole's recommended changes, every time Angela made one design adjustment, Mo would commend her for doing it.

> **Mo:** (in response to Angela making a minor word tweak) Yes, that's so great!
>
> **Angela:** Thanks, Mo.
>
> <Two minutes later>
>
> **Mo:** (in response to the next change Angela made) Oh my gosh, I love that!

> **Angela:** (smiles in response to the praise but doesn't verbalize a response)
>
> <A minute later>
>
> **Mo:** (in response to another simple change) Angela, you're so good at this!
>
> **Angela:** (laughs in an uncomfortable, scoffing manner)
>
> <Two minutes later>
>
> **Mo:** This deck is looking amazing!
>
> **Angela:** (stops making edits and steals a side-eyed glance at Nicole)

The compliments Mo gave were lovely. (No, really, they were. The authors aren't scrooges and genuinely love praise! In fact, if you want to write a rave review for *Adaptive Listening*, that would be delightful.)

Given the late hour and the team's fatigue, some cheerleading made sense. But based on Angela's cues, Mo overdid the excessive compliments without realizing it. Angela didn't need a boost every time she made a simple yet valuable edit, and she also found the constant praise distracting. It slowed her down and was disruptive when she was trying to finish a job. Since the tasks weren't challenging for an experienced designer like Angela, she even felt slightly offended by being praised for completing menial tasks.

Support Listeners' unique ability to celebrate with peers, direct reports, leaders, and customers is a gift. But when overdone, it can not only cause disruption, but it can also irritate others. If you recognize that you tend to excessively cheerlead how Mo did, pay attention to cues a speaker might give off to show frustration. Look for facial expressions such as eye rolls or wide eyes. Pay attention to vocalic cues such as nervous laughter, scoffs, or throat-clearing. Notice if the person receiving your praise stops thanking you for your compliments. These are all signs that you might have overdone it and it's time to move on from Support Listening.

## Appreciating Support Listeners

Even though Support Listeners should be aware of the cautions associated with their listening style, they still bring immense value to teams and organizations. They leave others feeling taken care of personally, whether it's time to celebrate or commiserate. These listeners are go-to communication partners when the speaker needs a listener who won't give them unwanted advice (like an Advance Listener might), won't burden them with interrogating questions (like an Immerse Listener might), and won't judge them (like a Discern Listener might).

Figure 3.1. summarizes the characteristics and cautions of Support Listeners, as well as tips to maneuver the cautions.

**Figure 3.1. Support Listener Overview**

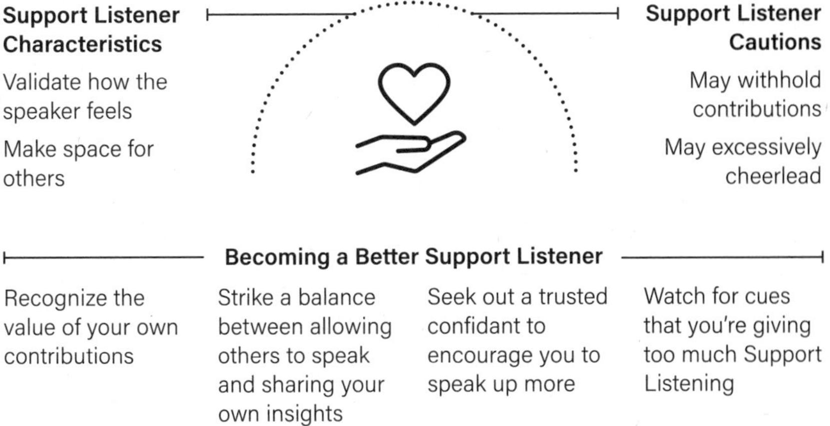


You might be a Support Listener if you read this chapter and thought, "Yep, that sounds like me." If you are, there's a chance some supportive thoughts are going through your head right now. You might be thinking, "These authors are great...they get me, and I get them," or, "I love how the authors are addressing the importance of emotions in the workplace, especially when it comes to listening." These authors thank you, Support Listener.

If while reading this chapter you thought, "Well, these authors sure are trying hard, but I'm not quite buying this yet." That's okay, Support Listener. But please stick with it. Your Support Listener characteristics and cautions may become clearer as you contrast them to the listening styles in the following three chapters.

If Support Listener isn't your primary S.A.I.D. Listening Style, you still might have recognized parts of yourself in the style. Maybe you already try to validate others' emotions, or you recognized that you're guilty of trying to cheer up and cheer on people, whether they need it or not.

Even if you're an Advance, Immerse, or Discern Listener, it's unlikely you never behave like a Support Listener, and that's good news. As you become an Adaptive Listener, you'll know how and when to act like a Support Listener to help others meet their goals. You'll learn how to develop or sharpen your Support Listening skills in Chapter 9: Adapt to Support.

Whether you're a Support Listener or not, think about your colleagues who might be.

- Have you noticed others who are great at validating your emotions or making space for you to contribute in meetings and conversations? If so, thanking them or reciprocating might make them feel just as good.
- Is there a go-to person you vent to? If so, consider the emotional toll your sharing could be taking on them.
- Can you think of people who don't tend to speak up often? If so, give them the benefit of the doubt. Perhaps they're quiet because they're selfless and busy thinking of others.
- Have you ever felt annoyed or agitated by someone's excessive cheerleading? If so, reframe your thinking. Know they have the best intentions when praising you.

The gift Support Listeners bring to teams and organizations is undeniable. Their listening style is a tremendous asset, particularly in emotionally charged or sensitive discussions. As you notice the Support Listeners around you, you'll have an easier time seeking them out when you need a cheerleader or a confidant. You'll also be more likely to appreciate them for the care they bring to you and your organization.

You'll likely notice a stark difference between this style and the next one, Advance Listener.

## Chapter 4

# Advance S.A.I.D. Listening Style

The "A" in the S.A.I.D. Listening Style acronym stands for Advance Listener. This style refers to individuals who prioritize forward momentum while listening. When other listeners might ask clarifying questions, want to gather more details, or need more time to analyze the options, Advance Listeners often think about suggestions, advice, or directives because they want to keep things moving. They often think, respond, and act with speed and urgency—even when the situation doesn't require speed and urgency.

**Table 4.1. S.A.I.D. Listening Styles and Description**

|  |  |  | 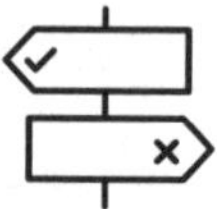 |
|---|---|---|---|
| **Support Listeners** | **Advance Listeners** | **Immerse Listeners** | **Discern Listeners** |
| Prioritize the speaker's emotions as they validate how the speaker feels and make space for others to contribute. | Prioritize forward momentum as they drive to next steps and link ideas across contexts. | Prioritize the content as they catalog the details and gain confirmation. | Prioritize evaluation as they embrace criteria and consider alternatives. |

Recall the *morning update* described in Chapter 2 where you chose which option most closely resembles what would go through your head as you listened to this project leader:

> *It's nine o'clock on a typical workday. You sit down at your desk and open your laptop. You've got your go-to beverage and are ready for your first meeting. It's a regular morning update where the project leader, someone you work with closely, provides information on revised goals, adjusted timelines, and progress reports. These updates are standard in your work, and the project leader usually shares information that's not particularly exciting or troubling. You're in this meeting with five other people.*

Advance Listeners most often choose option 2 as their response.

Option 1: I would appreciate how much work it took for the project leader to put the update together.

**Option 2: I would highlight what steps to take now that I have this information.**

Option 3: I would crave more details about the information they've shared.

Option 4: I would evaluate the pros and cons of the information they've shared.

Although an Advance Listener can likely validate the speaker's emotions (like a Support Listener), seek more details about the information (like an Immerse Listener), or uncover the pros and cons (like a Discern Listener), an Advance Listener prefers to treat the information as a springboard. They listen, and then they're ready to jump ahead.

If you see a bit of yourself in the characteristics and cautions of Advance Listeners, this chapter will cover ways you can get the most out of your listening style. If the descriptions don't sound like you, think of situations where it would be valuable for you to listen like an Advance Listener to can help others meet their goals.

## Advance Listener Characteristics

While listening to the project leader in the *morning update*, an Advance Listener might think,

"That adjusted timeline means I'll need to reach out for more resources," or, "Those revised goals need to get shared with everyone fast." An Advance Listener might even respond during the meeting with something like, "I have an idea about what we can do next."

Here are additional examples of how an Advance Listener might process information across different workplace scenarios:

- When listening to a vision keynote, an Advance Listener might think, "I know what I'm going to do to implement the ideas my CEO is describing."
- When listening to a customer talk about their pain points with their current product, an Advance Listener might think, "It's clear to me which solution in my product offerings will solve this problem."

- When listening to a direct report talk about how much they learned in a new internal training, an Advance Listener might think, "Great, now that this training is done, I'm going to recommend the next training this person should take."
- When listening to a colleague vent about another coworker, an Advance Listener might think, "Since I'm close with both of them, I should set up a meeting to find a solution to this conflict."

Some Adaptive Listeners in training have questioned, "If the Advance Listener is thinking all that, are they even listening?" The answer is yes. If they weren't listening, they wouldn't have been able to think about next steps. Sometimes this type of listening is exactly what the speaker needs. Other times, it's a distraction.

Advance Listeners often display these two characteristics: 1) they prioritize forward momentum by driving toward next steps, and 2) they link ideas across different contexts.

## Advance Listeners Drive to Next Steps

Regardless of what they're listening to, Advance Listeners' minds are often drawn to the steps or actions it might take to make things happen. While interviewing a job candidate, a hiring manager who's an Advance Listener might quickly decide during an interview, "I've got enough info to move this person to the next round." An engineer who's an Advance Listener might quickly interject during a meeting about switching vendors and say, "I'll need two months to get the new vendor up to speed." A realtor who's an Advance Listener might quickly realize while taking a client on a tour, "The next place I show them needs to have a bigger entryway or they're not going to even consider making a purchase." Across situations, Advance Listeners often have their ears tuned for what it'll take to drive toward milestones, deadlines, or finish lines.

Many Advance Listeners we interviewed attributed this characteristic of continually driving toward next steps as a contributor to their career success. They've been labeled as quick thinkers, problem solvers, and doers. Advance

Listeners' minds seem to naturally question, "What needs to happen next for this to be successful?" or, "What steps can I take to keep things moving?" Their focus on the end goal and how to get there can make them an asset on high-performing teams.

Advance Listeners are often among the first people to respond when a speaker says to a group, "Does anyone have any ideas about what we should do next?" One Advance Listener admitted, "I'm not saying my ideas are always *good*. But I almost always *have* an idea about what we could try or do next. Awkward silence feels like a waste of time, so I do what [the person asking the question] wants—I give them an idea." By meeting the speaker's needs in situations like this, an Advance Listener is an Adaptive Listener.

Sometimes Advance Listeners listen for ways to take on the next steps themselves. Other times, they listen for steps and tasks they can relay or delegate to others. Then there are times when they don't know who should complete the next steps, but they know the steps need to be done. The Advance Listener might even respond with an action plan or checklist that others can use so there's no confusion or wasted time.

If you have a reputation for being a momentum maker or can't stop yourself from thinking and responding with next steps, you might be an Advance Listener.

## Advance Listeners Link Ideas Across Contexts

Not only do Advance Listeners drive toward next steps while they're listening, but they also recognize how the information they're currently listening to might be applied to different situations. They might notice the benefits of a solution to one problem and think, "That could also solve this other problem." They might listen to a guest speaker and think, "I know how we can apply the lessons in this talk to the issue we're having on the team." They might listen to customers talk about their pain points and think, "Ah, I bet that's the concern my other customer has, too." Can listeners with other styles find these connections? Sure they can. But Advance Listeners' brains often do it without even trying.

Advance Listeners get inspired while listening and see a new opportunity, recognize a repeatable pattern, or envision how positive results in one context could be duplicated or multiplied in another.

Maegan is an Advance Listener who leads a department of communication strategists, speechwriters, and speaker coaches at Duarte. Given her leadership position and decades of experience in the communication field, colleagues often ask her to join working groups, roundtables, and cross-functional teams so she can share her expertise.

Maegan attends a monthly roundtable hosted by a product lead. In these roundtables, the product lead gives updates, talks about challenges with the product, and asks the group to brainstorm potential product enhancements. During one roundtable, the product lead gave this update:

> **Product lead:** We're piloting a new process to train people how to use the product. I've been testing it internally, and I think it will make onboarding and the user experience smoother. I want to walk you all through the process at a high level now.

Maegan knew it was time to soak in the details (and once you read Chapter 11: Adapt to Immerse, you'll know, too). She sat up straight and kept her eyes on the speaker. About two minutes into the product lead's remarks, Maegan immediately recognized the benefit of the new process. In fact, the process sounded so great that she couldn't help herself from thinking how this process could improve *another* product at Duarte. With each new detail the product lead shared, Maegan envisioned how the other product could use the same process to streamline onboarding and the user experience.

Before working on her Adaptive Listening skills, Maegan would have jumped into the conversation to ask a follow-up question that related to her product. She had a habit of spotting links across context and bringing it up to the group, all in the name of progress. But when she looked back on those interactions, she felt embarrassed every time she made an interaction about *her goals* and not the *speaker's goals*. That's why with this product lead, Maegan didn't speak up.

Instead, she grabbed a sticky note (which she always has at the ready) and wrote a reminder: *Meet with product lead to dive into new process for other product.* Once she got her thought down, she returned her attention to the speaker. She forced herself to stop thinking about the other product and focus on the product the lead was reviewing.

After the roundtable was over, Maegan scheduled a meeting with the product lead. In the end, the process wasn't the right fit for Maegan's product. But if it wasn't for her Advance Listening characteristic of linking ideas across contexts, she might never have considered this process a viable solution.

While looking for ways to optimize, avoid mistakes, or take advantage in other contexts can benefit Advance Listeners and their organization, it's possible that, like Maegan, they can get distracted when they start linking ideas between contexts. When the distraction becomes too much, they're not listening. If this characteristic sounds like you, don't worry. You'll learn techniques to help you refocus your listening in future chapters (like Maegan used when she wrote down her distracting thoughts).

## Advance Listener Cautions

While reading the characteristics of Advance Listeners, you might have thought, "I'd like to have a coworker who keeps us moving forward!" Or maybe you thought, "I *am* that coworker! I'm pretty great." There's no question that, with a focus on driving toward next steps and applying information from one context to another, Advance Listeners bring value to the workplace.

But as great as Advance Listeners can be, there are cautions to consider. With their speed and quick thinking, Advance Listeners could inadvertently exclude others. Plus, their verbal and nonverbal action-based behavior might also come across as impatient, potentially damaging professional relationships and their reputation over time. As you read the following cautions, ask yourself if you engage in this behavior. If so, is it always serving the people around you?

## Advance Listeners May Exclude Others

Since Advance Listeners are often focused on the end goal, they sometimes inadvertently cut others out of the process. They may exclude others from contributing to the plans or decision-making because they're ready to move ahead.

In the *morning update* revisited at the start of this chapter, assume that after the meeting, the project leader approaches an Advance Listener and unloads more concerns that weren't shared in the meeting. The project leader expresses sheer anxiety over the seemingly impossible deadlines, inevitable late nights, and resource constraints. Staying true to their characteristic of creating momentum and driving toward next steps, the Advance Listener outlines a plan on the spot to take on three action items that will create timeline and resource efficiencies. The project leader is so relieved that someone has offered to move things forward and says, "That's a great plan. Thanks for offering to take that on." Within the hour, the plan is emailed out to the rest of the team.

Now, if you're thinking, "This Advance Listener is an awesome coworker! They just helped the group push things toward the finish line," you're right...but only partially. The focus of this example is not on the Advance Listener or the project leader but on how the Advance Listener made the rest of the team feel.

When the rest of the team opens their emails and sees that this plan has already been outlined, they feel a mixture of confusion, concern, and even outrage. One team member who was excluded from the post-meeting planning session messages another team member on the organization's internal chat:

> **Team member 1:** (frantically typing) Did you see this email?! What just happened? How is there a plan? None of us were consulted.
>
> **Team member 2:** (quickly responds) I'm just as surprised as you are. (sends GIF of someone shrugging shoulders and looking annoyed)
>
> **Team member 1:** (quickly responds) I thought we were still in a brainstorming phase! Now it looks like several decisions have been

> made without us, and [Advanced Listener] is doing the bulk of the work without us...
>
> **Team member 2:** (quickly responds) I guess so...I mean, I was still processing all the details of the project during that update. I didn't know it was time to create a plan! I would have jumped in if I had known! But I guess they don't need us anymore...

Even though the Advance Listener had good intentions, their conversation and post-meeting planning session with the project leader left the other team members feeling neglected. This tension could make it harder for the team to work together in the future.

Not only could the Advance Listener's preferences harm this specific group dynamic, but if the Advance Listener keeps acting this way, it could lead to a decline in team culture over time. Suppose this new plan works well, so the Advance Listener and the project lead get into their groove. Without realizing it, they continue to create plans and don't check in with the rest of the team. Others might start to feel inadequate or obsolete. People who constantly feel that way might throw their hands in the air and think, "I don't even get a say anymore," or, "Forget it; my voice doesn't count here."

In scenarios like this, the Advance Listener could have included additional messaging in the emailed plan, opening the door for others to contribute. Instead of dictating or announcing the plan, the email could have included an explanation about why the plan was created without consulting the rest of the team ("We chatted after the meeting and organically generated some ideas") and invited comments and questions ("I'd love to know what you all think of this plan," or, "Are there any questions/concerns about this plan?").

If you're an Advance Listener who tends to bypass others in favor of speed and efficiency, remember that inclusion also matters. Include all relevant parties from the beginning or invite other team members to weigh in on plans instead of dictating what will be done. **It's possible to create momentum *and* collaborate.** If you've got an idea, or want to create action steps, that's great! Just make sure you notify others of your plan and ask for their input or work to gain their buy-in. When you do, you'll balance the strength of your quick actions with the warmth of including others.

Do Advance Listeners get things done? Yes! But doing so with tunnel vision or in a way that alienates others poses risks. Even if they have good intentions for creating momentum, Advance Listeners may create an unhealthy dynamic if they cut others out.

## Advance Listeners May Come Across as Impatient

In addition to inadvertently cutting others out, Advance Listeners may come across as impatient. While their fast-thinking and fast-acting are valuable, those processing and responding behaviors can make colleagues and customers feel rushed or irritated.

Ernie and Briella are both customer success managers who make sure existing customers are happy with their purchase and are getting the most out of it. They're having a one-on-one virtual meeting because Ernie is about to go on vacation and Briella is tasked with temporarily managing his customer caseload while he's away.

Briella is an Advance Listener. She's always ready to quickly intake information and move on to the next task. Ernie comes to the meeting prepared with all the context, details, and "what ifs" Briella might need as she covers his customer caseload for the next two weeks:

> **Ernie:** (medium energy, slower speaking rate) Thanks for taking on my caseload with everything else you have going on! I really appreciate it.
>
> **Briella:** (high energy, faster speaking rate) No problem!
>
> **Ernie:** Okay, so let me give you a rundown of each customer. I want to tell you what I know they need and give you context in case they reach out with questions about anything else.

**Briella:** (eyes wide with a surprised facial expression) Oh! I didn't realize we were going one by one through all the possibilities. Okay. Let me have it.

**Ernie:** This is the first customer who needs a follow-up while I'm out. They're still having some issues with their product, and—

**Briella:** uh-huh, mm-hmm, uh-huh.

**Ernie:**—I promised them I'd look into it and get back to them by Tuesday. Of course, there's a chance the customer figures it out themselves before Tuesday. They have an eager team who can usually come to the answer if they get a few days to problem-solve.

**Briella:** (furiously nodding) Okay, yep, got it.

**Ernie:** (gets a bit frazzled) Yeah...so...okay, in terms of additional context, I've updated all my notes in the system. You'll see they've been with us for two years, and they've loved every update we've put out. I have a list of additional requests they've made, but they know it will be some time before we can act on them.

**Briella:** (quick speaking rate) Sure. Makes sense.

**Ernie:** Okay, onto the next one. This customer just received their product, and it would be great to follow up with them to see how—

**Briella:** (more intense head nodding) Oh yeah, totally.

**Ernie:**—to see how they're doing so far—

**Briella:** Okay, and what about this third client? What's going on with them?

**Ernie:** (startled) Well, hang on. I still have more to say about this second one.

**Briella:** (moves hands to suggest they speed it along) Oh yeah, okay. Keep going.

As the conversation unfolds, Ernie is frustrated with Briella's verbal and nonverbal responses. Although she's being an Advance Listener to help Ernie move things forward while he's away, her intense nodding and excessive interjections (uh-huh, mm-hmm, okay, and yeah) aren't giving Ernie what he needs. Plus, given that this is a virtual meeting, there's an additional complication.

If you're routinely in virtual meetings, you might already know the issue. It can be tricky when two people speak at the same time. The software isn't always designed to handle overlapping voices. Those extra stutters can cause delays and disruptions. Sometimes you end up with the awkward, "You go—no, you go—no, it's okay, you go" back and forth.

If you see yourself in Briella, ask, "Am I an Advance Listener who unconsciously rushes speakers?" Subtle nods and the occasional "mm-hmm" or "got it" can help the speaker feel confident that you'll help them create momentum, but too much can work against you.

To monitor this behavior, watch a recording of yourself during an interaction. Observe the amount, frequency, and urgency of your nods. Watching yourself, a kind of biofeedback, can help you build awareness so you can minimize or prevent impatient behaviors.[23] If self-regulation doesn't work for you, or you're unaware of your verbal and nonverbal responses, find an accountability partner who can monitor your behavior and help you build awareness.

## Appreciating Advance Listeners

Even though Advance Listeners need to be aware of the cautions associated with their listening style, they bring value to teams and organizations by driving forward momentum. They leave others feeling confident that what needs to get done *will* get done by either the speaker, the listener, or someone else. An Advance Listener can also be helpful when other listeners are too focused on emotions (like a Support Listener), being too methodical (like an Immerse Listener), or being too critical (like a Discern Listener).

Figure 4.1 provides a summary of the characteristics and cautions of Advance Listeners, as well as tips for maneuvering the cautions.

**Figure 4.1. Advance Listener Overview**

If you're reading this chapter, nodding and thinking, "Yep, that's me, all right!" then you might be an Advance Listener. If you are, there's a chance you've been reading this book at a quick pace. You might be thinking, "I get it. Let's keep moving!" Or you might be thinking, "Oh, I can't wait to tell my team about this book! I know how they can use it." These authors thank you for the referral, Advance Listener.

Or maybe you're thinking, "I don't yet see how this information will help me, my teams, or my organization move forward..." Don't worry, Advance Listener. Chapter 10: Adapt to Advance covers techniques to help Advance Listeners like you sharpen their skills. Chapter 10 will also help all listeners become Adaptive Listeners by knowing when and how to use Advance Listening techniques.

If Advance Listening isn't your primary S.A.I.D. Listening Style, you might already be incorporating some of the characteristics in your workday. Maybe you already drive to the next steps, either because your role demands it, or you've learned it's a useful way to close out a meeting and make sure everyone knows what's happening next. Chapter 10 will guide you when and how to prioritize forward momentum to ensure you're meeting others' needs.

Whether you're an Advance Listener or not, think about your colleagues who might be:

- Is there a colleague who's great at helping you move forward? If so, think about how they've made a positive impact on a project or situation and thank them.
- Have you noticed someone who connects the dots from one idea to another? If so, consider the value this person unlocked and how you can replicate it.
- Can you think of people who move so quickly that they sometimes overlook the opinions and contributions of others? If so, reframe your thinking: they mean well, even if those intentions are sometimes misguided.
- Have you ever felt annoyed or agitated by someone's energy or forcefulness? If so, remember they're trying to help get you across the finish line and improve productivity.

Advance Listeners bring organizations the gift of "unsticking the stuck" and moving others forward. Once you start spotting the Advance Listeners in your organization, you'll know who to go to when you need a push. You can also reframe any perceptions you might have of their "impatience." Instead, you'll start appreciating their "eagerness."

The Advance Listener's desire to speed up the interaction contrasts with the next listening style, the Immerse Listener.

## Chapter 5

# Immerse S.A.I.D. Listening Style

The "I" in the S.A.I.D. Listening Style acronym stands for Immerse Listener. This style refers to individuals who prioritize the content while listening and often crave more information. They might not be ready to move on from the content as quickly as other listeners because of their curiosity and desire to know more. When other listeners merely skim the surface to understand the gist or main points of what's being said, Immerse Listeners seek a deep, comprehensive understanding of the speaker's message, craving the nuance and depth that lies beneath the surface.

**Table 5.1. S.A.I.D. Listening Styles and Description**

**Support Listeners**
Prioritize the speaker's emotions as they validate how the speaker feels and make space for others to contribute.

**Advance Listeners**
Prioritize forward momentum as they drive to next steps and link ideas across contexts.

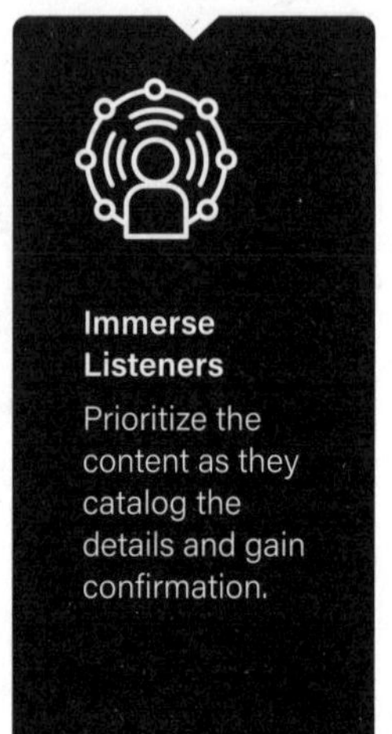

**Immerse Listeners**
Prioritize the content as they catalog the details and gain confirmation.

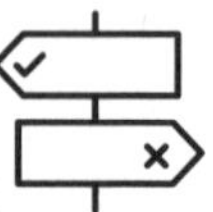

**Discern Listeners**
Prioritize evaluation as they embrace criteria and consider alternatives.

Recall the *morning update* described in Chapter 2, where you chose which option most closely resembles what would be going through your head as you listened to this project leader:

> *It's nine o'clock on a typical workday. You sit down at your desk and open your laptop. You've got your go-to beverage and are ready for your first meeting. It's a regular morning update where the project leader, someone you work with closely, provides information on revised goals, adjusted timelines, and progress reports. These updates are standard in your work, and the project leader usually shares information that's not particularly exciting or troubling. You're in this meeting with five other people.*

Immerse Listeners most often choose option 3 as their response.

Option 1: I would appreciate how much work it took for the project leader to put the update together.

Option 2: I would highlight what steps to take now that I have this information.

**Option 3: I would crave more details about the information they've shared.**

Option 4: I would evaluate the pros and cons of the information they've shared.

Although an Immerse Listener can certainly prioritize the emotions of the person speaking (like a Support Listener), act on the information (like an Advance Listener), or evaluate the information (like a Discern Listener), an Immerse Listener prefers gathering details and deeply understanding the information.

If the following characteristics and cautions sound like you, then you might be an Immerse Listener. If they sound like how you listen sometimes but not always, then maybe you have more than one primary listening style. If they don't sound like you at all, consider situations where you think this type of listening may benefit the people speaking to you (and even benefit you in the long run) because every Adaptive Listener needs to use Immerse Listening at times.

## Immerse Listener Characteristics

While listening to the project leader in the *morning update*, an Immerse Listener might think, "I wonder what the breakdown of that revised timeline looks like," or, "I'm curious what the teams will think once this updated process is implemented."

Here are additional examples of how an Immerse Listener might process information across different workplace scenarios:

- When listening to a vision keynote, an Immerse Listener might think, "These updates from my CEO are important, and I want to know even more about the initiatives now."
- When listening to a customer talk about their pain points with their current product, an Immerse Listener might think, "There's probably more nuance to this problem that they haven't told me yet. I need to learn more about what this customer is going through with their existing partner."

- When a direct report talks about how much they learned in a new internal training, an Immerse Listener might think, "I wonder what the training activities look like. I want to understand what this training is all about."
- When listening to a colleague vent about another coworker, an Immerse Listener might think, "I need to ask questions to gather more information about this situation."

Immerse Listeners often prioritize the speaker's content by 1) cataloging the details while the person is speaking and 2) gaining confirmation that what they absorbed is precisely what the speaker intended to convey.

## Immerse Listeners Catalog the Details

Regardless of what's said, Immerse Listeners often mentally or physically take notes to catalog the details the speaker is sharing. As they listen, they're filing the information into the right folder in their brain or directly into their notebooks or laptops. They might think, "Okay, this first piece of information is a recap of something I already know. I'll put it in this part of my brain/on this page in my notebook/in this digital file. The second piece of information is an update, so I'll put it in another spot. The third piece of information is entirely new to me. I need to set this aside and revisit it later."

Cataloging the details using mental or physical note-taking makes Immerse Listeners feel confident that they're prioritizing the speaker's content. One Immerse Listener, a message strategist, described their note-taking this way: "My note-taking looks a lot like a stream of consciousness, and I tend to write everything down verbatim. I'll break out those spiral-bound notebooks from my college days when I want to make sure I collect all the necessary details." Now, Immerse Listeners aren't the only type of listeners to take notes while listening, but an Immerse Listener's goal is to take notes so that later, they can make sure everything has been documented and retained.

Immerse Listeners often have a more thorough record of previous projects, plans, strategies, successes, failures, etc., compared with other S.A.I.D.

Listening Styles. This historical memory can help an Immerse Listener, and those who work with them, build on prior efforts and avoid repeating past mistakes.

One Immerse Listener, a tenured attorney, said that lawyers in his position must remember many niche cases and recite them off the top of their heads when interacting with clients. He described how cataloging the details of these cases, both mentally and physically, has worked to his advantage.

"Clients often ask me if we can make a particular argument," he shared, "and I have to tell them whether or not that argument will work and why." Good attorneys need an almost encyclopedic knowledge of past cases so they can justify to their clients why an argument will hold or won't, based on previous court decisions. As an Immerse Listener, this attorney has found his listening style particularly valuable when building credibility with hyper-critical clients.

"Remembering names, problems, and short pieces of obscure evidence helps me do my job well and creates trust with my clients," he said, "and it makes me a great resource for my colleagues when they need case details."

By cataloging the details, Immerse Listeners gain confidence that they've got all the information they need. When others might be listening to "get the gist," Immerse Listeners treat all the details as critical and want a mental or written record of it. These listeners know that obtaining critical information is not only helpful for them, but it's kind to others. It helps teams stay focused and can complement other listening styles who may wish to bypass nuances in the information.

## Immerse Listeners Gain Confirmation

Immerse Listeners don't only mentally catalog, write down, or type information as they're listening. They also seek confirmation that they understand the information how the speaker intended. They might do so in the middle of a conversation as a check-in to ensure they're tracking along with the message. They might gain confirmation at the end of a conversation, listing the key points they absorbed to make sure they got it all. They might email after a meeting to double-check that nothing was missed. They want to ensure they're on the same page as the speaker.

One Immerse Listener, Lee, shared how gaining confirmation in all types of meetings helps him feel confident that he interpreted the information correctly. When he's in a one-on-one meeting and dynamic dialogue with another person, Lee uses a topic change, pause, or lull in the conversation to check in.

He'll say something like, "Before we move on, I want to make sure I got everything so far." He'll quickly and succinctly summarize the discussion and ask, "Did I get that right?" or "Do I understand this correctly?" This response allows the speaker to confirm that "Yes, that's right" or, "Not quite," and reframe their talking points differently. By seeking confirmation, Lee walks away from the conversation knowing he fully understands the speaker's intention. He also offers empathy to his colleagues—by asking these questions, they feel confident that Lee wants to get it right for *them*.

But that's not the only time Lee seeks confirmation about what he heard. He finds this technique particularly helpful in a group setting when several speakers are communicating back and forth with one another, debating or building on an idea.

"When people talk over each other, talk in circles, or share inarticulate thoughts and opinions, it's hard for me to focus on all the content...that's my worst nightmare. I want *all* the information and ideas being shared, but it's hard to find the individual contributions in a sea of chatter." In this situation, Lee often seeks confirmation of everyone's ideas or opinions once the heat cools off.

He'll say something like, "Okay, Person A, your opinion is this, right? And Person B, you disagree because of X reasons. You think Y instead, correct?" Lee continues to go down the line with each person who expressed their opinion and double-checks that he's grasped each person's contribution individually, which gives him a clearer picture of the entire conversation.

Lee notes an added benefit from this characteristic. "Sometimes when I confirm what I heard, the rest of the group realizes they weren't on the same page after all," Lee said. "Or they know they're not on the same page and when I confirm what I heard, I bring clarity to the discussion or help others realize we have more debating to do."

Not only does seeking confirmation help him gain a complete understanding of the information, but it also helps fast-moving groups slow down and regroup. The group can pause from their rapid-fire, shoot from-the-hip dialogue and gain clarity. You might have experienced the benefits of this type of confirmation-seeking behavior from someone else, or maybe you just realized this is a characteristic of yours.

## Immerse Listener Cautions

After reading the characteristics of an Immerse Listener you might have thought, "I listen like that all the time! Go me!" Or you might have thought, "Those listeners can help us keep track of the details. We need them!" That's true. Organizations *do* need Immerse Listeners. But these listeners also need to be cautious.

Sometimes, with the best of intentions, Immerse Listeners end up stalling the interaction with all their immersing. They can also appear disengaged, even when they're not—it's just their listening face. As you read the following cautions, see if you can recognize these behaviors in yourself. If so, you can start building awareness and, ultimately, avoid the cautions altogether.

### Immerse Listeners May Stop Momentum

As Immerse Listeners prioritize the content, taking time to process the information and ask questions to confirm they have all the details, it might not always serve the person or group. This might be especially frustrating for listeners who are eager to move on to next steps (like an Advance Listener) or ready to evaluate ideas, options, and alternatives (like a Discern Listener). If Immerse Listeners aren't careful, they can run the risk of stalling the interaction.

One member of a cross-functional team felt the strain of a stalled interaction when working with a colleague. The team included two people, Clara and Brooks. Clara was responsible for finding meaning behind the data. Brooks, an Immerse Listener, was responsible for designing visuals to bring the data and its meaning to life.

Once the survey data was in, the two came together for a working session:

> **Clara:** (buzzing through her notes and feeling the pressure of a tight deadline) Okay, as I said in my email, the main takeaway from this part of the data is that there's a big difference between how chief marketing officers view the role of owned media versus paid media. Let's show this difference creatively. I have some preliminary ideas, but we don't have a lot of time before this report is due, so I'd love to land on an idea for this part of the data because we have a lot of other parts to cover.
>
> **Brooks:** (looks at the takeaway intently and squints his eyes while his hand is on his chin) Hmm...
>
> **Clara:** So, I was thinking we could maybe use color to emphasize the difference, or maybe we could use contrasting images to show a comparison...
>
> **Brooks:** Hmm...yeah, I see what you mean. We could use color to emphasize the difference or photography to show the difference. Those are good ideas!
>
> **Clara:** Thanks! So, which one should we go with? Color or photography?
>
> **Brooks:** Hmm. I don't know yet. Talk to me more about the difference between these views.
>
> **Clara:** (internal monologue: "I'm starting to feel frustrated. I don't have much more to say about this difference. I already wrote my thoughts in the email.") Yeah...sure...okay... (speaking at a quicker pace, as she's becoming more agitated) So these leaders have a much more favorable view of

> owned versus paid media. They think owned is better because they have a lot more control for a lot less cost.
>
> **Brooks**: Hmm. Okay. Let's play around with this. I'd like to explore this further and dig deeper into our options. Here, I'll share my screen (initiates screen share). Which color do you like here and why?
>
> **Clara**: (furrows her brow in irritation) (internal monologue: "Uh, oh. This data point is one of the easy ones! We don't have time for an in-depth discussion on each part of the visualization.") Um, (sighs heavily) sure. If that's what you think is best, then I defer to your expertise.
>
> **Brooks**: Let me keep thinking about it. I'll play around with a few different ideas and do some more research.
>
> **Clara**: (sighs heavily and drops her shoulders in defeat) Okay, keep me posted. Let me move on to the next finding...

It can be hard for an Immerse Listener to move on when they desire a deep understanding and want to take their time processing the information. But ignoring the needs of the speaker or group can lead to tension, concern, and even animosity.

If you're not sure whether you tend to stall the group, you can start paying more attention to the cues others give you—consciously or unconsciously—that tell you they're ready to move on.

- Do they increase their speaking rate or use an exasperated sigh as they answer your follow-up questions or reexplain a point?
- Do they bounce their legs, tap their pen, or shake their head in an agitated manner?

Of course, cues like increased speaking rate and bouncing legs could mean something different in a different situation. The goal here is to be aware of these cues and ask yourself, "Am I stalling the speaker or group?" If you realize you're holding up progress, check in with yourself. Could you live without knowing more details?

If you decide that you unequivocally need the additional information, but you know it may stall the speaker or group, you can call attention to that fact with a statement like, "Hey, I know I'm asking us to take some extra time here. Bear with me for another minute or two." A simple phrase like this shows that you're taking ownership of your behavior and you realize the impact it may have on others. Your admission might make it easier for people to empathize with you and potentially feel less tension or frustration toward you. But Immerse Listeners can also try to accept that they might have enough information to move forward, even if it doesn't feel complete.

## Immerse Listeners May Appear Disengaged

In addition to potentially stalling the group, Immerse Listeners may give the impression they're distracted or disengaged while they're listening. Immerse Listeners have shared with the authors that they're often focused on getting all the information down or concentrating on what's being said. Their focus is so intense they sometimes forget about the person speaking to them. It's like their brain is a computer with one job: process the bits and bytes.

If an Immerse Listener is diligently taking notes to catalog everything being said, it can prevent them from maintaining a connection with the speaker. Suppose an Immerse Listener is in the audience of an in-person company meeting. A company leader takes the stage to share celebratory news about an excelling initiative. An Immerse Listener might find it easier to concentrate on the details by writing down the information the leader is sharing, point by point.

But when that leader looks into the audience and sees an Immerse Listener scribbling away (or typing notes on their laptop or phone), this leader might think, "Why would anyone be taking notes right now?" or, "What are they *really* working on instead of listening to me?" The leader might not confirm their suspicion or say anything about it to the Immerse Listener, but that doesn't mean the perception isn't there.

An Immerse Listener might also come across as disengaged if they're looking away from the speaker, off into the distance, or out a window. This technique often helps Immerse Listeners center themselves and ignore any potential distractions as they're listening. But it can also have unintended negative consequences.

Jack, an Immerse Listener, had a routine one-on-one with his manager.

> **Manager**: Hey, Jack. I've noticed that you've been checked out in our team meetings. I'm not the only one. Other people have noticed that you're not paying attention. Is something wrong?
>
> **Jack**: Oh, wow. I don't know what to say. I can tell you that I am absolutely paying attention in our team meetings.
>
> **Manager**: Well, take yesterday's meeting, for example. You barely spoke; you were pretty far away from the camera, leaning back in your chair. And you weren't even looking into the camera for most of the meeting. You were looking off to the side...
>
> **Jack**: I promise, I know what the meeting was about. I know the progress everyone is making on their projects. I know the changes you want us to make. I know what's ahead next quarter.
>
> **Manager**. I'm so glad something isn't wrong! I was getting worried. I don't want the rest of the team to think you're phoning it in.

When Jack recounted this interaction to the authors, he shared that he was frustrated after this one-on-one. At the same time, he could see where his manager was coming from. Yes, Jack looked off to the side and not directly at the computer screen while his colleagues talked. He realized that even though that technique made it easier for him to focus, it probably didn't look great to the rest of the team. He decided to be more mindful of how he showed up in future meetings.

If you think you may appear disengaged due to your diligent note-taking, facial expressions, or even body positioning, try setting expectations for the people speaking to you:

- If you're meeting with a new colleague, customer, or partner, you could tell them, "I'm going to be taking notes today" or, "I tend to write down a lot of notes, just as a heads up."
- If you're part of an audience where it would be awkward or inappropriate for you to tell a presenter or leader about your tendency, you can be intentional about pausing your note-taking, making eye contact, and showing engaged nonverbal behaviors like nodding or smiling.
- The colleagues you work with regularly might already know about your habits, but it can't hurt to call out your behavior or flash them a smile during a routine meeting, too.

## Appreciating Immerse Listeners

Even though there are cautions associated with Immerse Listeners, their deep thinking and curiosity are valuable to organizations. Immerse Listeners make space to listen to the details and confirm what's been said, which gives them confidence they understand the full picture. These listeners can even help the group gain that same confidence. This is especially important when other listeners are prioritizing emotions over content (like Support Listeners), moving forward quickly (like Advance Listeners), or are hyper-focused on what's not working (like Discern Listeners).

Figure 5.1 summarizes the characteristics and cautions of Immerse Listeners, as well as tips for maneuvering the cautions.

**Figure 5.1. Immerse Listener Overview**

**Immerse Listener Characteristics**

Catalog the details

Gain confirmation

**Immerse Listener Cautions**

May stop momentum

May appear disengaged

**Becoming a Better Immerse Listener**

Let go of the desire for more depth if the speaker is agitated and you can live without the details

Contextualize your asks for more information if you notice the speaker is ready to move on

Use nonverbal cues (like eye contact and smiling) to show the speaker you're invested in them as much as you're invested in the content

Prime the speaker to be prepared for any distracting nonverbal cues you might give off

You might be an Immerse Listener if you read this chapter and thought, "Yep, that sounds like me." Right now, you might be mentally checking in with yourself to make sure you understand the S.A.I.D. Listening Style descriptions. Or maybe you took a reading break to ruminate on what you just read. Perhaps you even reread sections, paragraphs, or individual sentences to ensure you absorbed everything.

Or maybe you're an Immerse Listener thinking, "I don't know if I've gotten enough information to be all-in..." You might be eager to ask more questions and gather more details. If you're craving more, consider attending Duarte's Adaptive Listening workshop, where you can participate in facilitator-led exercises, assess examples with a group of listeners, and get answers to your burning questions.

If you're not an Immerse Listener, these characteristics and cautions might still resonate with you. Maybe you also take transcript-like notes or look away from the speaker or group as you process the information. In Chapter 11: Adapt to Immerse, you'll learn how to identify the right times to engage in Immerse

Listening and how to do it effectively so you can continue to build your Adaptive Listening skills.

Whether you're an Immerse Listener or not, think about your colleagues who might be.

- Is there a go-to person you consistently ask for details you might have missed? If so, think about the burden you might be placing on them and reconsider how often you approach them.
- Have you noticed someone who asks a lot of questions during meetings to gather more information? If so, thank the person for helping the group learn and grow!
- Can you think of people who consistently double-check what was said and potentially slow momentum? If so, reframe your thinking. See the good intentions and the value their approach brings.
- Have you ever felt annoyed or agitated by a colleague you thought was "disconnected" from the conversation? If so, recognize that this colleague might have been trying to focus.

Immerse Listeners bring a thoroughness to teams and organizations. These are likely the listeners you turn to when you need clarity or confirmation. The more you become aware of the Immerse Listeners around you, the more you'll appreciate the depth and completeness they can bring to interactions.

Immerse Listeners are sometimes known to slow down a group. So are Discern Listeners, the style covered in the next chapter. But as you're about to read, their motivation for doing so differs.

## Chapter 6

# Discern S.A.I.D. Listening Style

The "D" in the S.A.I.D. Listening Style acronym stands for Discern Listener. This style refers to individuals who prioritize evaluation while listening. Regardless of what's being said, Discern Listeners are drawn to the information with a critical ear. Their top priority is making sure the idea, plan, or project is set up for success.

**Table 6.1. S.A.I.D. Listening Styles and Description**

**Support Listeners**
Prioritize the speaker's emotions as they validate how the speaker feels and make space for others to contribute.

**Advance Listeners**
Prioritize forward momentum as they drive to next steps and link ideas across contexts.

**Immerse Listeners**
Prioritize the content as they catalog the details and gain confirmation.

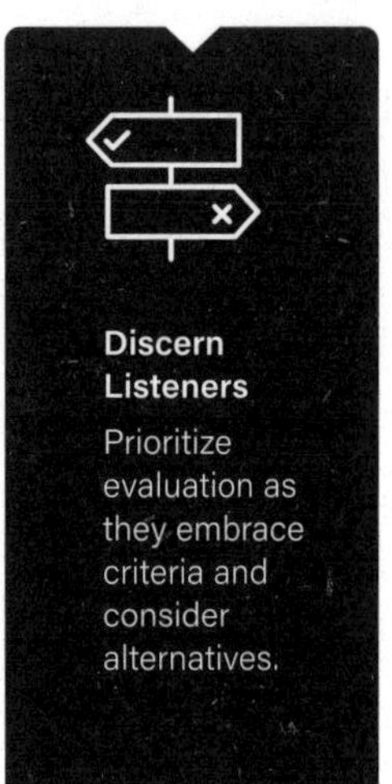

**Discern Listeners**
Prioritize evaluation as they embrace criteria and consider alternatives.

Recall the *morning update* described in Chapter 2, where you chose which option most closely resembles what would be going through your head as you listened to this project leader:

> *It's nine o'clock on a typical workday. You sit down at your desk and open your laptop. You've got your go-to beverage and are ready for your first meeting. It's a regular morning update where the project leader, someone you work with closely, provides information on revised goals, adjusted timelines, and progress reports. These updates are standard in your work, and the project leader usually shares information that's not particularly exciting or troubling. You're in this meeting with five other people.*

Discern Listeners most often choose option 4 as their response.

Option 1: I would appreciate how much work it took for the project leader to put the update together.

Option 2: I would highlight what steps to take now that I have this information.

Option 3: I would crave more details about the information they've shared.

**Option 4: I would evaluate the pros and cons of the information they've shared.**

A Discern Listener may still validate the emotions of the person speaking (like a Support Listener), move people and projects forward (like an Advance Listener), or seek more details about the information (like an Immerse Listener). But a Discern Listener's difference, though, is that they're often primed to listen for what could go wrong or what might have been left out of consideration.

As you read the following characteristics and cautions of Discern Listeners, you might notice these behaviors in yourself. You'll be able to leverage your listening style correctly with the recommendations in this chapter. If while reading the descriptions you think you'd struggle to listen this way, pay close attention to the value these listeners bring to workplace interactions.

## Discern Listener Characteristics

While listening to the project leader in the *morning update*, a Discern Listener might think, "How can we be sure that this new plan won't create the same problems as the old plan?" They might even say, "Have you considered alternatives to the revised goals you've mentioned today?"

Here are additional examples of how a Discern Listener might process information across different workplace scenarios:

- When listening to a vision keynote, a Discern Listener might think, "I can see the upside in the new goals, but there are some implementation risks I haven't heard my CEO mention yet."
- When listening to a customer talk about their pain points with their current product, a Discern Listener might think, "I know exactly what's working and what's not working with their current approach, because I've seen situations like this with other customers."

- When listening to a direct report talk about how much they learned in a new internal training, a Discern Listener might think, "This training has two elements I always look for: short and actionable. It sounds like a good training to me."
- When listening to a colleague vent about another coworker, a Discern Listener might think, "Yep. It sure sounds to me like they messed up."

Some Adaptive Listeners in training question the difference between Discern Listeners and Advance Listeners. In fact, some listeners share Advance and Discern as their co-primary styles. Listeners with both styles are often quick to evaluate "what's working and not working" and then jump ahead to "what should be done about it."

But for listeners who only have one primary style, this is the key difference between the two: **Discern Listeners are *problem finders* who are motivated to double-check an idea and ensure it was evaluated from all angles.** Advance Listeners, on the other hand, are *problem-solvers* who are motivated to put solutions or next steps into motion.

Imagine two marketing managers are listening to a product pitch for a new application that claims to make it easier for marketing team members to collaborate on content creation. These marketing managers work at the same organization, on the same team, and are peers. The difference is that one of the marketing managers is a Discern Listener and the other is an Advance Listener. Figure 6.1 compares how each listener might process and respond to the product pitch.

**Figure 6.1. Advance Listener vs Discern Listener Example**

**What they might think**

I know exactly which team members could become power users for this app.

I've heard enough to make a decision.

**The Way They Prefer to Listen**

Prioritizes forward momentum

**ADVANCE LISTENER**

**How they might respond**

"Walk me through an example that shows the collaboration in action."

"If we move forward with the basic plan, how do upgrades work?"

**vs.**

**What they might think**

This product might not actually meet our needs.

I'm skeptical that this sales rep will be a good partner.

**DISCERN LISTENER**

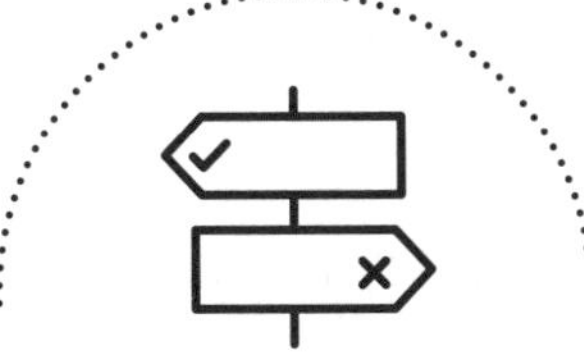

**The Way They Prefer to Listen**

Prioritizes evaluation

**How they might respond**

"I haven't heard you mention anything about how artificial intelligence is used in this application"

"I noticed your app contains a different feature than the app we use. Why is this feature better?"

Just because a Discern Listener is skilled at finding problems doesn't mean they always know how to solve them. Conversely, just because an Advance Listener is ready to move forward with a solution doesn't mean they always evaluate that solution properly before moving forward. Of course, an Adaptive Listener needs to know how to act like both a Discern Listener and Advance Listener in the right situations.

Discern Listeners often prioritize evaluation by 1) embracing criteria and 2) considering alternative ideas or approaches.

## Discern Listeners Embrace Criteria

Discern Listeners are expert evaluators because they're always considering a set of criteria. Instead of listening without preconceptions, they compare the new information against existing norms. Sometimes these criteria already exist, like when an organization has established benchmarks, a project has parameters, or a person has standards. Then, the Discern Listener uses these criteria to judge the incoming information accordingly.

Here's a deeper look at Nicole's experience as a Discern Listener. As an executive speaker coach, Nicole works one-on-one with leaders to help them build their speaking skills and prepare for upcoming high-stakes moments. There's never a question in her mind as to what a great speaker looks like because she uses Duarte's established criteria to evaluate a speaker: A great speaker is comfortable, dynamic, and empathetic. Each one of those characteristics has a list of observable actions that Nicole can evaluate on a five-point scale.

But what happens when she's in a situation where an established set of criteria doesn't exist? For instance, when a friend asks for feedback on the examples they want to share during an interview, or a leader asks for feedback on a report they need to present to the board. In these situations, Nicole quickly tries to align criteria with questions like, "What does success look like for you?" or, "What kind of feedback are you looking for?"

When everyone agrees on the criteria, it's more likely that people will accept the feedback. Sometimes, Nicole makes suggestions for criteria. If she's listening to a friend's interview responses, for example, she might ask for a copy of the job description and compare her friend's answers. She wants to make sure her friend's responses reflect the skills described in the job posting. Her feedback will be based on the criteria that "my friend's answers need to show they're more than capable of excelling at this job."

Discern Listeners understand the importance of establishing criteria. In an ideal world, they make sure everyone understands and agrees on these criteria because feedback is more helpful when everyone involved is prepared to receive it. But even in the absence of agreement, Discern Listeners establish those criteria in their heads to guide their evaluation or critique.

## Discern Listeners Consider Alternatives

Discern Listeners not only embrace criteria to help them evaluate but also think about and suggest alternative ideas to ensure the speaker or group has considered the best option. Sometimes these listeners get labeled as the "devil's advocate" because they push back on an idea or plan, even if they aren't against it. They may even be perceived as confrontational or arrogant. But the Discern Listener's goal isn't to suggest their idea or plan is better. Instead, they simply want to ensure all possible options have been explored.

This characteristic can be particularly valuable when the speaker or group is quick to act without exploring or brainstorming other ideas. While writing this book, there were several moments when Maegan (an Advance Listener) was full steam ahead on an idea. A theory or a story would pop into her brain, and she'd immediately start implementing it into the chapter only to have Nicole (a Discern Listener) say something like, "Wait, wait, slow down. Are we sure that's the best option?"

Other times, even if Nicole didn't have an alternative option to offer, she would still challenge Maegan's idea by asking, "Is there another idea we haven't thought of yet?" or, "Should we brainstorm alternatives?" Even with fast-approaching deadlines and a seemingly good idea, Nicole frequently had the innate desire to interrogate the decision to make sure it was right. The two authors often had engaging back-and-forth discussions, and there were plenty of times when Maegan pushed Nicole to keep things moving when Nicole wanted to critique and evaluate ideas, so it all worked out!

Discern Listeners know that the fastest or easiest way forward isn't always the best. They're not afraid to play devil's advocate to make sure the most appropriate solution has been identified.

## Discern Listener Cautions

While reading the characteristics of Discern Listeners, you might have thought, "I wish I had a workplace sidekick like this! I could use someone to critique my work and help me explore alternative ideas!" Or maybe you thought, "I do that all the time, and it seems my team is lucky to have me." (They sure are!) With a focus on evaluating, Discern Listeners protect and improve projects, processes, and programs by uncovering risks and finding rewards. But like the other styles, Discern Listeners can run into trouble.

Discern Listeners' eagerness to identify potential issues can sometimes disrupt progress, especially when the rest of the team is ready to move forward. These listeners might also frustrate the speaker or other group with repeated criticism that comes across as harsh or persistently negative. If the descriptions in the following cautions sound like you, you might be a Discern Listener who could benefit from holding back at times.

### Discern Listeners May Stop Momentum

Just like Immerse Listeners may stop momentum by remaining fixated on gathering details and seeking confirmation, Discern Listeners may also stop momentum if they fixate on evaluating when others are ready to move on. Even with the best intentions, too many critical comments can irritate others, especially if the time for critique or judgment has passed.

In a group of advertising creatives, Ari, a Discern Listener and graphic designer, is speaking with colleagues Ula, a copywriter, and Matt, an art director. The team is working on a campaign for a long-time client who manufactures high-end cleaning equipment. They've made multiple rounds of edits and are completing a final review of their work before they present it.

> **Ula**: Let me walk you through the final copy I wrote for this campaign. As we discussed, the messaging now reflects a lighter tone, just like the client requested: "Sure, the '90s are back. But that doesn't mean you want

> a *grungy* home. So put the retro on pause, and get the next generation of at-home cleaning with Turbo X."
>
> **Ari**: Ula, I'm sorry to interrupt, but do we really think this opening is in a light enough tone like the client wanted?
>
> **Ula**: I think so, yeah. But let me read some more....
>
> **Matt**: Yeah, we all agreed that opening would grab their attention in our last meeting, but let's keep listening to what Ula wrote. Then we can decide.
>
> **Ari**: Yeah, yeah. Totally. Keep going.
>
> **Ula**: (finishes reading the copy) "The Turbo X redefines style and function. Our sleek, modern design seamlessly complements any décor, while the powerful suction and advanced features ensure your home stays pristine and polished, no matter the era."
>
> **Ari**: I'm not sure about this generations/era theme...what other ideas do we have?
>
> **Ula**: (confused facial expression) I mean, we went over three other ideas last week and all landed on this one.
>
> **Ari**: Oh yeah! There were three other ideas! Can you pull those up?
>
> **Matt**: (hesitant) Well, uh, ya know, I don't think we really have time to rehash all those ideas again.
>
> **Ari**: (eager) I just think if we spend a bit more time on the concept, we'll land on a better choice.
>
> (Ula and Matt glance sideways at each other with raised eyebrows and sigh heavily)

Ari likely has good intentions for wanting this ad campaign to be the best it can be for their long-time client. But it's also clear that his evaluating habits have stopped the group's momentum, maybe even burst their bubbles! Discern

Listeners can be great checks-and-balances partners because they pressure test ideas to make sure they're viable. Poking holes at an idea or deliverable can help colleagues and partners filter out the good ideas from the bad ones.

But there's a time and place for evaluating. If the speaker or group believes an idea will work, it can be frustrating for a Discern Listener to say things like, "But wait, what about this?" or, "Has anyone considered this?" or, "I like (or don't like) this and here's why," especially when everyone else is ready to take action. Plus, if a Discern Listener keeps evaluating, timelines might get pushed or missed entirely.

If Ari's behavior sounds like yours, it's important to consider whether the moment for evaluation has passed. Ask yourself,

- Has the person or group already reached a final decision?
- Has the team already come to a consensus?
- Was there already a brainstorming/ideation step?

It's probably no longer time to evaluate if the answer to these questions is yes. Unless the agreed-upon idea or deliverable is in danger of failure or harm, it's time to accept that the majority rules, move forward, and act on the decision.

## Discern Listeners May Come Across as Negative

In addition to stopping momentum, Discern Listeners may come across as negative or even overly critical. Even when the speaker is seeking feedback, the critique might go deeper than the speaker was expecting. It's also possible that the Discern Listener's delivery could feel jarring or harsh. Finding red flags, considering alternatives, and uncovering areas for improvement can come across as negative if the Discern Listener doesn't deliver it the right way.

Bayani, Delroy, and Lily, members of a senior leadership team, held monthly meetings where each leader would share ideas for upcoming initiatives they wanted to tackle. These leaders had a friendly dynamic and resolved conflict in a healthy way, but Delroy's Discern Listening Style was agitating to Lily.

> **Bayani**: All right, who wants to share their initiative idea first?
>
> **Lily**: I'll go. I was thinking we could do a re-org and combine three teams into one.
>
> **Delroy**: Hmm...I don't know about that. People are comfortable in their teams now, and a re-org would take a lot of cross-training. We don't have time to deal with that.
>
> **Lily**: I hear you. I'm not sure about it myself. But if we need to streamline the management layer, this could be one way to do it.
>
> **Bayani**: There could be some potential here.
>
> **Delroy**: (with furrowed brow) I don't know if it's even possible. Where are we going to find the time to do this?
>
> **Lily**: All right, (heavy sigh) does anyone else have an idea they want to share instead?

When recounting this interaction, one of the leaders on this team described Delroy as an "optimism killer" because he came across as a downer every time the group met, draining the energy from the rest of the leaders. Discern Listeners need to be aware of their potential to come across as harsh or critical. Even if their evaluations are helpful, they may be interpreted as negative or pessimistic.

To counter potential negative perceptions, Discern Listeners can soften their criticism in two ways:

1. **Use a warm vocal tone.** Avoid loud volume or a fast-speaking rate. Loud and fast voices can come across as aggressive or harsh. Instead, aim for a neutral volume, slower speaking rate, and even slightly elongated words to come across as kind and curious.
2. **Be mindful of facial expressions often associated with judgment or negativity,** like a furrowed brow or pursed lips. If you're regularly in recorded virtual or hybrid meetings, go back and review your nonverbals. If your expressions are skeptical most of the time, work on forming a

more neutral expression. Reserve your skeptical face for the times when you'rc truly skeptical.

Discern Listeners may need to be thoughtful about *the way* they deliver their feedback. Although their red-flag finding can protect teams and organizations, critical feedback that comes across as excessive or harsh could damage the listener's reputation or harm team culture, especially if it occurs repeatedly.

## Appreciating Discern Listeners

Although Discern Listeners can stop momentum and give the impression they're overly critical or negative, these listeners help organizations by spotting risks and encouraging people and groups to think through ideas from multiple sides. A Discern Listener's critical ear can leave a group feeling confident that the idea or plan has been pressure-tested. They can be particularly helpful when others are too focused on emotions (like Support Listeners might be), are ready to go full steam ahead (like Advance Listeners might be), or have taken the information at face value (like Immerse Listeners might do).

Figure 6.2 provides a summary of the characteristics and cautions of Discern Listeners, as well as tips for maneuvering the cautions.

**Figure 6.2. Discern Listener Overview**

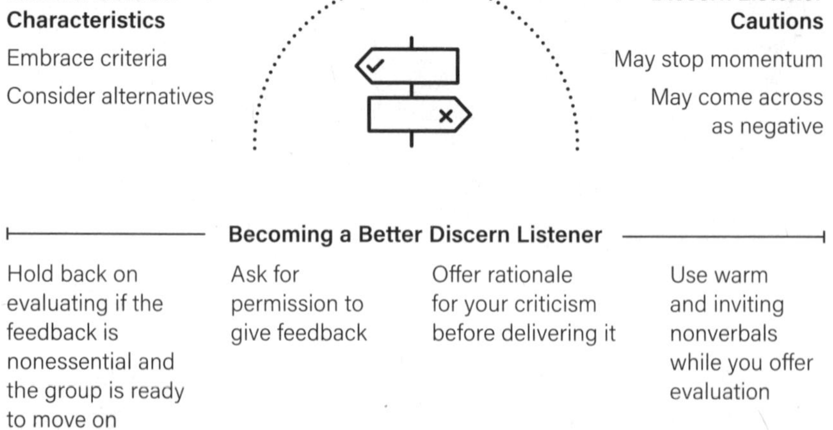

If you read this chapter and thought, "Yep, that sounds like me," you could be a Discern Listener. There's a chance you've been reading with your criteria for what makes a good professional or communication skills book or what makes someone a great listener at work. At this point, you may already have your list of strengths and weaknesses you'd like to share with the authors. Maybe you're even skeptical about *everything* you've read so far. You likely wouldn't be afraid to share your critique. The authors look forward to listening to you, Discern Listener.

If Discern Listening isn't your primary S.A.I.D. Listening Style, you still might recognize elements of the style in yourself. Maybe you also use criteria when evaluating a situation or idea, just not as often or directly as a Discern Listener might. Or maybe you've received feedback that you come across too negative or critical at times. You'll learn more about how to build your Discern Listening skills in Chapter 12: Adapt to Discern. Then, you'll have the techniques to act like a Discern Listener when the speaker needs that type of listening from you.

Whether you're a Discern Listener or not, think about your colleagues who might be:

- Have you noticed colleagues who can spot potential problems before others? If so, consider praising them for the value they bring to your role, team, or organization.
- Is there a go-to person who you know will pressure test your idea and make it stronger? If so, thank them or reciprocate by helping them in the same way.
- Can you think of people who pull the group back and insist they think through potential consequences? If so, remember these people likely have good intentions for slowing things down.
- Have you ever felt annoyed or agitated by a colleague who often makes negative comments about an idea or plan? If so, reframe your thinking. This person is likely trying to help you avoid risks.

Once you know who the Discern Listeners in your organization are, you can seek them out when you need someone to find the red flags or look at your idea differently. You'll also be more open to appreciating the critical ear they bring to you, your team, and your organization—even if it means more work for you in the end.

Understanding your S.A.I.D. Listening Style means you're already on your way to becoming an Adaptive Listener. You now have more awareness about how you process what people say to you at work and how you respond. This baseline knowledge will help you grow your listening skills.

In the next chapter, you'll learn about one more set of influences that can impact how you listen.

## Chapter 7

# Focus Your Listening L.E.N.S.

In addition to your listening style, other influences shape your ability to process and respond. These influences can create an ideal listening situation for you and the person speaking to you, or they can create barriers that inhibit you from being an Adaptive Listener.

To highlight these influences, return to the *morning update* from Chapters 2 through 6.

*It's nine o'clock on a typical workday. You sit down at your desk and open your laptop. You've got your go-to beverage and are ready for your first meeting. It's a regular morning update where the project leader, someone you work with closely, provides information on revised goals, adjusted timelines, and progress reports. These updates are standard in your work, and the project leader usually shares information that's not particularly exciting or troubling. You're in this meeting with five other people.*

But this time, as you think about the *morning update*, consider this additional context:

*Although this meeting is routine and typically low stress for you, imagine today you're joining after a rough morning. A family member called you last night with an emergency. You spent hours in urgent care, chatting with doctors and helping your loved one get the necessary medication. You insisted on spending the night at their house to ensure they were okay. You slept on their twenty-five-year-old pullout couch in a hot room. Of course, in the chaos of the evening, you forgot to charge your phone. It inevitably died while you were sleeping, so you woke up late and had no time to shower. Luckily, your family member feels 100 percent better, but now you feel rushed and gross!*

Given all that additional context, if you had to attend the *morning update*, how would you feel? What might be going through your head? How might the situation with your family member influence how you listen in that meeting?

Switch contexts for a moment. Pretend you aren't joining the *morning update* after a rough night and morning. Instead, you wake up refreshed! You just had your best night's sleep in months. Before bed, you had a yummy early dinner with close friends and watched a funny movie you've had on your must-watch list. Miraculously, you shut off all screens before nine o'clock, took a reinvigorating shower, and fell asleep in your freshly washed sheets. You awake with plenty of time to get ready for your day.

Given this change in context, if you had to attend the *morning update*, how would you feel? What might be going through your head? How might the situation influence the way you listen in that meeting?

In comparing these two contexts, you would likely feel different and therefore listen differently during the *morning update*. You might not realize it, but the context likely influenced your Listening L.E.N.S.

Your Listening L.E.N.S. is a collection of components, beyond your listening style, that influence how you listen. Each letter in L.E.N.S. stands for a different component:

> **Listener** refers to your state of mind.
>
> **Environment** refers to the conditions surrounding your listening.
>
> **News** refers to the information you're receiving.
>
> **Speaker** refers to the person communicating with you.

Each component can cause you to dial in or tune out while listening. Figure 7.1 previews each L.E.N.S. component, detailed further in this chapter.

**Figure 7.1. The Listening L.E.N.S.**

Just like changing the lens on your camera can put the object you're shooting in or out of focus, your L.E.N.S. can put your listening in or out of focus. If your L.E.N.S. is focused, you're more likely to adapt your listening to meet the speaker's goal (you'll read how to adapt your listening in Chapters 9 through 12). If your L.E.N.S. is unfocused, you'll likely find it hard to meet the speaker's goal. You might even be tempted to stop listening altogether. The good news is there are three tactics you can use to help you focus your L.E.N.S.

## Focus Your L.E.N.S.

Based on the situation, you'll use one of three tactics to focus your L.E.N.S. You'll either accept it, voice it, or change it. It might seem counter-intuitive to review these tactics before you've read the in-depth description of each L.E.N.S. component, but previewing the tactics first will help you see each in action as you read the rest of the chapter. Once you can focus your L.E.N.S., you'll have a better chance of adapting how you listen to meet the speaker's needs.

### Accept Your L.E.N.S.

In work and life, it's sometimes hard to accept the things we can't change. If it were possible to control every influence standing in the way of being a great listener, you'd listen perfectly, 100 percent of the time. Alas, sometimes the only thing you can do to build awareness of these influences is to accept your current reality.

Recall the additional context to the *morning update* at the beginning of the chapter. You had a family emergency and a loved one needed your help. You slept on their awful pullout couch in a hot room. Your phone died, so your alarm didn't go off, and you didn't have time to shower.

Now, you can't change the fact that your family member needed you during an emergency. You can't change how uncomfortable that old mattress was. You can't go back in time, charge your phone, wake up on time, and shower before your meeting. You also can't change the fact that you have a meeting to attend.

All you can do, prior to starting your workday, is prime yourself to accept your situation. Research shows that your psychological health improves when you accept a situation instead of ruminating about it. Acceptance helps you experience less negative emotion in times of stress.[24]

Accepting an unfocused L.E.N.S. includes four steps: **state the cause**, **use "and," acknowledge reality**, and **own what you *can* control**. In the context of the *morning update*, accepting an unfocused L.E.N.S. might look like this:

"I didn't sleep well. I didn't wake up on time. I didn't get to shower. *And* I can't do anything about that right now. What I *can* do is show up to my meeting today and do the best I can." Figure 7.2 highlights the steps in this example.

**Figure 7.2. How to Accept an Unfocused L.E.N.S.**

| ACCEPT STEPS | State the cause | Use "and" | Acknowledge reality | Own what you can control |
|---|---|---|---|---|
| ACCEPT EXAMPLES | I didn't sleep well. I didn't wake up on time. I didn't get to shower. | AND | I can't do anything about it right now. | What I can do is show up to my meeting today and do the best I can. |

You'll notice that the cause statement and the acknowledge statement are connected with the word "and." There's a good reason you will **use "and"** as opposed to "but."

Jennifer Stoops, a marriage and family therapist based in the New York Metro area, says, "I often hear people say things like, 'I'm trying my best, but I'm not good enough,' or, 'I try my hardest at work, but I still feel like a failure.' Using the word 'but' negates the first part of those sentences. The fact is you can try your best *and* still not feel good enough. The power of allowing yourself to think more than one distinct thought allows you the freedom to problem solve and prevent yourself from feeling stuck and powerless."

You can state the cause *and* acknowledge reality (see what we did there), so try using "and" instead of "but" and see how that makes you feel. It might help you accept the situation and move on.

After you've connected the cause and your reality, it's time to **own what you *can* control.** You can still attend your meeting, which is a choice. Will you be tired? Most likely. Will you feel dirty? Probably. But stating that you do have control over attending is empowering. By doing so, you'll increase your focus and the chance that you'll help the speaker meet their goals.

You can also pair your mental reframe with physical calming techniques like taking a deep breath. It's normal to feel anxious when you believe you have no control over what happens to you. Perhaps your heart rate goes up, your palms sweat, your face gets flushed, or your jaw clenches. Taking a deep breath is a *physical* way to accept the things you can't control.

Stoops says that mindful breathing helps ground people in the present moment.

"Our minds are built to navigate many different directions, and the breath can be a stabilizing force," says Stoops. "A deep breath will help you refocus on the current moment and allow your mind to return to the goal. This is rooted in biology, and our breath is integral to regulating the nervous system. A deep breath will help lower blood pressure and help you gain awareness of your current mental and emotional state so you can focus on the present."

When you combine accepting thoughts (**state the cause**, **use "and," acknowledge reality,** and **own what you *can* control**) with calming techniques like breathwork, you're effectively taking ownership over your unfocused L.E.N.S. The "accept it" tactic is an empowering way to manage your listening even in challenging circumstances.

## Voice Your L.E.N.S.

Sometimes the tactic of accepting your L.E.N.S. isn't enough. There will be times when you simply can't focus your L.E.N.S. by letting go. If you did have an emergency-filled evening before your *morning update*, you might experience such extreme fatigue that the thought of listening to anyone at work seems impossible.

In that case, try the second tactic: voice it. Tell the speaker that you may have trouble focusing. You might do this before the interaction via a ping, email, or pulling the speaker aside for a quick chat if you're about to be part of a group. You might also use this tactic during an interaction if you notice your L.E.N.S. went out of focus, despite your best efforts. In either case, you can **share your regret**, **state the cause**, and **offer your best efforts**.

In the *morning update*, and given the family emergency context, you might have been able to reach out to the project leader before the meeting with a message that said, "Hey, I'm sorry for reaching out like this, but I wanted to give you a heads up that I had a rough night. I was up late with a family emergency. Everything's okay now, and I'm going to make it to the meeting and try my best. But if I seem distracted or don't participate as much as usual, that's why."

When you start by **sharing your regret**, you signal to the speaker or group that you respect their time. You also take the initiative to create a culture of mutual understanding.

After you share your regret, you can also **state the cause**, just like you would if you were using the accept tactic. Only this time, you'll state *why* you might have trouble focusing. Many people in the workplace are reasonable and understanding once they've been given all the information. (If you just raised your eyebrows in suspicion of how reasonable others are, you might save yourself some grief if you concede that many people are, in fact, trying their best.) When you state the cause, you invite people to be reasonable and understand your rationale.

To close out the voice tactic, you can **offer your best efforts**. After all, you are still going to attend the meeting. When you tell people you're trying, you make it easier for them to give you the grace and space you need. They might even give you permission to bow out of the interaction entirely, although that's not your goal with this tactic. Like the accept tactic, the goal is to bring more awareness and control to your unfocused L.E.N.S. The more aware you are of your listening barriers, the more likely you can find your focus.

Voicing an unfocused or potentially unfocused L.E.N.S. is a great option in a psychologically safe workplace relationship. If you think someone would use your admission as ammunition against you, it's probably better for you to use the first tactic of accepting your unfocused L.E.N.S. Similarly, if the stakes are too high for you to **share your regret, state the cause**, and **offer your best efforts**, then accept it and move on.

## Change Your L.E.N.S.

In rare cases, you might have the power to make a change, so you don't have to force yourself to focus when it's too challenging. In some situations, with some speakers, you can postpone your listening or change the listening environment to be the best listener you can be. When you think it's appropriate to use the change tactic, you'll **share your regret, state the cause, request the change,** and **offer an alternative.**

If you experienced the family emergency context before your *morning update*, you might recognize that because you're so tired, it would be unsafe for you to drive to work. Even if you could make it to the office safely, you'd be too exhausted to focus. In that case, you could reach out to the project leader and say, "Hey, I'm sorry to reach out like this, but I had a rough night with a family emergency. Everything's okay now, but I can't make it into the office safely. I'd appreciate it if you could let me miss the meeting today. If you record it, I can promise I'll watch it before tomorrow so I'm up to speed."

**Sharing your regret** and **stating the cause** are similar to the voice tactic. The difference is that you'll also **request the change** you want. For the *morning* *update*, the request for change is you skipping the meeting. In other situations, the change might be rescheduling the meeting day and time or sending someone else to attend in your place.

Instead of a request, you could demand the meeting be changed, but that's not a collaborative way to interact with your colleagues and customers. A request is more inviting and puts the speaker in a position to help you. It also allows them an opportunity to decline your cancellation request if the interaction must happen as scheduled. But chances are, your colleagues and customers will grant your request.

If suggesting such a change seems forceful or aggressive, remember that you're doing so for the sake of your safety and to better prepare yourself to listen the way the speaker needs. If you aren't in the position of power or authority to "change it," then you'd likely want to use the accept tactic to help you focus your L.E.N.S.

If you feel comfortable using the change tactic, then you'll also want to **offer an alternative** for your absence, like watching the recording or scheduling a follow-up to learn what you missed. Just make sure you do so when your L.E.N.S. is more focused.

These three tactics can work regardless of which L.E.N.S. component is out of focus. Now that you know how to accept, voice, or change your unfocused L.E.N.S., you can read more about each component.

## Listener: The "L" in L.E.N.S.

The first component of your L.E.N.S. is the listener. In other words, you. Influences in your personal or professional life can impact your ability to listen. You have other responsibilities, people, and activities inside and outside of work that can sometimes cause your L.E.N.S. to be less focused than you'd like. When assessing the listener component of your L.E.N.S., consider the mood you're bringing to the interaction and the amount of time you have to dedicate to listening.

## Listener: Consider Your Mood

Many factors can impact your mood and prevent you from listening with a focused L.E.N.S. Perhaps you just came from a rough meeting, or your kid is home sick from school. Maybe you have anxiety about interacting with a new person at work and worry about how you'll show up. Or perhaps, like in the *morning update*, you had a rough night's sleep and you're exhausted. All those factors might cause you to be in a less-than-ideal mood.

For example, many of the authors' colleagues felt anxious and stressed amid the unexpected rain and mudslides in the Pacific Northwest in early 2023. Those based in Seattle and the Bay Area had downed powerlines and trees in their yards and roads, leaking roofs, and flooded garages, not to mention closed schools. Many had to contend with childcare adjustments, home repairs, and unreliable Wi-Fi.

One of the authors' colleagues, an Adaptive Listener in training, shared that he knew it would be hard for him to listen in meetings that day from the moment he woke up with flickering lights. He felt worried and his thoughts were preoccupied, making it difficult for him to do his job and meet deadlines. That unfocused L.E.N.S., while entirely understandable, might have caused a cascading effect for everyone he interacted with that day. If he couldn't bring his whole self to his work interactions, it might have caused slower meetings and delayed timelines.

Luckily, this person made the smart decision to focus their L.E.N.S. by voicing it. At the start of every meeting that day, he shared his regret, stated the facts, and offered his best efforts. He said to the speaker or group, "Hey, I've got to tell you that I'm distracted by our storms today. And my daughter is home with me because her school is closed. I must admit, I'm distracted. I will do my best to listen, but I might need some grace."

This listener not only gave themselves a feeling of relief by telling colleagues what was going on for him, but he also gave his colleagues a gift: others felt permission to share that they, too, were distracted by the storms and the impact they had on their homes, families, and coworkers. Getting his feelings and thoughts off his chest and out in the open allowed everyone to bring their whole selves to each interaction.

But your mood doesn't have to be bad to cause an unfocused L.E.N.S. Maybe you're amped up because you just got a promotion or closed a major deal. Maybe you have a date tonight or leave for a much-needed vacation tomorrow.

For example, in a coaching session with a global sales leader, Nicole was surprised that her client started the session in a vastly different way. This leader often brought a straight-to-the-point, all-business, no-small-talk, let's-get-it-done mood to their interactions. But this time, the client shared that his daughter had secured a teaching job at an elementary school in Nicole's small hometown in New Jersey.

This proud dad was so excited about this opportunity for his daughter, and Nicole's connection to the location, that he had to get it out before they could start the session. Sometimes it's hard to listen when you're too thrilled, eager, or jazzed. If the client had kept his emotions inside, it might have impacted his ability to listen to Nicole's coaching and implement her feedback. Instead, by using the voice tactic, the client could focus his L.E.N.S. and be present.

## Listener: Consider the Amount of Time You Have

Ahh, time. The one resource there's never enough of. You might think, "Umm, when do I *ever* have enough time to be a fully focused listener?" That's understandable. It seems people are constantly being asked to do more with less time. You likely feel rushed, anxious, or preoccupied when you don't have enough time to give a speaker your full attention.

That lack of time can be a creeping, nagging feeling in the back of your brain. When those feelings surface, not only are you in danger of making the speaker think they—and what they have to say—don't matter to you, but you're also in danger of missing out on important information. That's why it's critical to consider how much time you can dedicate to a speaker before you listen.

Picture this: You open your work calendar for the first time today and notice that you have a meeting at four thirty in the afternoon with a longwinded direct report. This person is the most junior member of your team, and they're energetic and eager to learn from you. Nearly every one-on-one meeting turns into a teaching-learning moment. You admire their enthusiasm and hunger for professional development, and when your schedule allows, you're more than happy to coach them.

Today, however, you know you must sign off right at five o'clock because your best friend needs a prompt airport pickup. Your direct report is unlikely to end promptly at five, and you already feel anxious about listening.

You have a choice to make:

- You can **accept** that your direct report might continue the meeting beyond five o'clock. If and when that happens, you'll say to yourself, "This meeting is running late, and I will be late to pick up my friend, *and* I can't do much about that at this point." Then you'll say to yourself, "What I *can* do is be present for my direct report who's craving my advice and guidance."
- You can **voice** at the start of the meeting that you're heading right to the airport as soon as this meeting ends at five o'clock. That way you've alerted your direct report about your potentially unfocused L.E.N.S., which means you'll be less preoccupied by it. As a bonus, you've reinforced your boundaries for when this one-on-one will end today.
- You can **change** the meeting. If you're pretty sure your direct report will want to go past your scheduled one-on-one time, and you want to ensure you can give them what they need, change it. Reschedule the meeting for a time when you can dig deeply and be fully focused.

## Environment: The "E" in L.E.N.S.

The next component of your L.E.N.S. is the environment you're in while listening. Your environment includes the setting, how many other people are listening along with you, and the time of day. As you read these descriptions and stories, remember that knowing and controlling the influence the environment has on your listening can help you give speakers what they need.

## Environment: Consider the Setting

Do you work in a busy, bustling office? A ghost town where only a few people show up on random days? Have you cultivated the ideal work-from-home space? Or have you tried to carve out space amidst your hectic household? Do you finish work on planes, trains, and automobiles? Maybe a combo of it all? The physical setting of your environment could make it easier or harder for you to focus your L.E.N.S.

Jen is a chief of staff in a hybrid environment. Tuesday through Thursday, she's in the office with the executive she supports. On Mondays and Fridays, Jen works from home. That is, unless she's traveling to an offsite event or meeting with the executive, which happens about once a month.

As much as Jen appreciates the collaboration she has with her executive when they're in the office together and the flexibility of working from home, she listens best when she's in an airport lounge or flying in the skies. Jen saves a stash of recorded meetings, presentations, and voice memos to review while she's traveling, because that's the only time she's not distracted by other work. For others, the presence of disgruntled travelers and unexpected turbulence might be a distraction. For Jen, these settings help her get in the zone.

Across industries, employees have varied opinions and reactions to their listening setting. Some people listen much better face-to-face because they find it easier to be present when another person is sitting directly across from them. Others shine in a virtual setting. They find comfort in being in a space they can control, like a home office, and that makes it easier for them to listen. Plus, in a virtual meeting, they might only need to be "on" from the waist up. Still, others like to listen when they're on the go, whether traveling or taking a walk around the neighborhood.

It's probably easier for you to be an Adaptive Listener in some places more than others. But you're likely required to listen in a variety of settings. If you prefer in-person interactions, but you're listening during a virtual meeting, you might be preoccupied with thoughts like, "I hate being virtual. This would be so much better if we were in person." If you've been asked to turn your camera on even though you aren't camera-ready today, you might be annoyed. If you prefer being virtual but have to drive into the office for a presentation, you might get distracted and think, "Wait, did I remember to brush my teeth before this morning's in-person meeting? It's been a while since I've had to check that."

If you find yourself in a nonideal setting, try the tactic that works best for you:

- **Accept** that it's not an ideal setting for you and focus your listening anyway.
- **Voice** that this setting isn't your favorite. Be honest and ask for the speaker's patience.
- **Change** the setting or ask the person speaking if you can make a change.

Regardless of the tactic you choose, you'll be taking control of the situation and setting yourself up to be a better listener.

## Environment: Consider the Number of Listeners

You've probably heard the phrase, "Laughter is contagious." Well, for some people, so is listening. Some situations outlined in this book are one-on-one, speaker-and-listener interactions. Other situations involve listening groups when you are one of many listeners. Some listeners thrive when there are other listeners around them. Suppose you're sitting in a large auditorium listening to a guest speaker deliver a keynote on her treacherous climb up Mount Everest. The listeners on every side of you are fully focused and intently listening.[25] In that case, you might feel like Janey.

Janey was in this guest speaker's audience. She finds it easier to fully focus her L.E.N.S. when she's part of a large group because she doesn't feel pressured to respond. She gets nervous in one-on-one settings, and that pressure tends to cause anxiety and pull her out of focus. But when she's one listener in an audience of many, Janey finds it easier to listen.

The opposite was true for Ben. He was listening to the same keynote, but because he was one of many audience members, he felt inconspicuous. When he's hidden amongst others in the crowd, Ben finds it easy for his L.E.N.S. to go out of focus. He's sure the speakers won't notice if he checks his phone or starts daydreaming. Ben prefers listening in one-on-one settings where his listening is more focused because he's the only listener.

Then there's James. When he's in the audience, he notices everything. The person to his left is bouncing their leg and sneaking some glances at their social media account on their phone. The person to his right is checking their email on their laptop while *appearing* to take notes. The person behind him is whispering to the colleague next to them. Even though James wants to focus on the information being presented, he finds it difficult to do so because the listeners around him are distracted. He's impacted and influenced by the behavior of other listeners.

Perhaps you're like Janey and feel completely focused and at ease when part of a listening group. Or maybe you're like Ben and are easily distracted when you're one of many listeners. Or perhaps, like James, you like listening in a group, but you get easily distracted by others. Take notice of the influences the number of listeners has on your listening, and then use the accept, voice, or change tactic that works best for you.

## Environment: Consider the Time of Day

For the listener component of L.E.N.S., it's important to consider how much time you need to dedicate to the speaker because a time crunch can cause an unfocused L.E.N.S. For the environment component, you'll need to consider a different time-centric influence: *when* you listen.

Both authors of this book thrive in the morning. They're often energetic, alert, and perfectly capable of focusing their listening during early working hours. Maybe you're like the authors, or maybe morning chipper-ness sounds like your worst nightmare. Unfortunately, everyone must listen at work regardless of the time of day.

As global communication consultants, Nicole and Maegan often coach clients in different time zones. US-based clients are often easy to accommodate. At most, they're usually three hours ahead or behind, which is a manageable difference to work around. But for several months, Nicole had a series of coaching sessions with a client based in Japan, and due to time zone differences (Nicole is based in New York), she had to hold that session at eight o'clock in the evening in the eastern time zone. You might be a person who thrives at night, but as a morning gal, Nicole knew her L.E.N.S. would be unfocused that late at night.

In this situation, Nicole couldn't use the change tactic to adjust the meeting time due to the client's calendar. It wasn't professionally appropriate for her to use the voice tactic, either. Nicole wasn't about to tell a senior leader at a major tech company that she couldn't be a great listener because of the time of day. Her best choice for these coaching sessions was to use the accept tactic.

Before each coaching session, Nicole told herself, "It's late for me. I'm tired. I'm not an evening person. *And* there's nothing I can do about that. I still have a job to do. So, I'll take a deep breath, make a shot of espresso, and be the focused coach this leader is expecting!" The simple act of accepting that unfocused L.E.N.S. helped Nicole be present and have a great coaching session.

Whether you focus better in the morning, afternoon, evening, or when the rest of your colleagues are fast asleep, you'll inevitably need to listen during a time of day that's not ideal for you. If it's appropriate, you can change the time of the interaction so you're primed to be an Adaptive Listener. If you can't change it, or even voice it, then accept the reality so you can focus your L.E.N.S.

## News: The "N" in L.E.N.S.

The next component of the L.E.N.S. is news. The news is the information or content the speaker is sharing with you. The news can have a different influence on your listening depending on how new or familiar it is, how complicated it is, and how relevant that information is to you. Think about how the news component of your L.E.N.S. might be focused or unfocused as you read these descriptions and stories.

## News: Consider the Novelty

You might not have noticed it before, but as a listener, you don't treat all news equally. You likely listen differently depending on how novel or new the information is to you.

Think about a time when you flew to a city you've never been to before. You were probably hyper-focused, looking for signs, walkways, and trams. "Where is baggage claim?!" "How do I get there?!" "How do I call a rideshare, and where do I get picked up?" "Oh no, do they even have a rideshare at this airport?!" Because this airport and this city were entirely new to you, you were probably primed to intake new information.

But what about when you flew home from the trip and landed at the airport you know so well? You probably strode through the terminal, made a beeline for the exit, had your rideshare booked before you even arrived at baggage claim, and headed directly to the pickup location. You were on autopilot.

Your brain has a schema for familiar information.[26] When listening to familiar words and ideas, you can quickly connect the dots in your brain. For some, your listening will be *less* focused because when you consciously or unconsciously tune out, your brain doesn't have to work hard to comprehend what's being said. For others, you'll be *more* focused because it's easy to dial in to familiar information.

Your brain doesn't have the same schema for novel information. In these situations, some listeners are hyper-focused to make sure they don't miss anything. Others feel anxious when listening to novel information, worried they might not understand or remember it. That anxiety and pressure can cause an unfocused L.E.N.S.

Think about how you listen to familiar versus novel information. Are you more likely to lose your focus in one situation than another? If so, do the work to focus your L.E.N.S.

## News: Consider the Complexity

The news component of your L.E.N.S. can also impact your ability to focus when the information is complex. News complexity varies from person to person based on their expertise on that subject matter. Some listeners feel anxious when they hear complex information and fear they can't comprehend it. Those listeners might need to work hard to focus their L.E.N.S. in these situations. Other listeners are excited by complex news because complexity is like a fun puzzle to solve.

But for other listeners, if the information is too complex, they might lose focus and tune out because the content feels beyond their ability to fully comprehend.

Vera, an enterprise software salesperson, is meeting with a brand-new customer, a chief technology officer (CTO). The CTO tells Vera about a seemingly ordinary and straightforward problem: their company's current software doesn't have the capability they desperately need to automate their processes. This situation isn't too complex for Vera to understand. She's helped dozens of companies, with the same problem, successfully switch to her company's product.

The CTO's needs are simple for Vera to understand because she's a senior and experienced salesperson. She doesn't realize it, but she's not as focused as she should be because this information isn't complex enough for her.

But suppose the CTO adds details about the problem that Vera wasn't expecting. The CTO shares that their company needs specific functionality given their current systems. Suddenly, Vera realizes she might have been less focused than she thought. She wants to be sure her product can provide what the CTO is looking for, but it might require customization. She needs to focus her L.E.N.S. to get more details from this customer because their problem sounds more complex than she originally thought. So, she uses the voice tactic.

"Would you mind giving me additional information on the functionality you're looking for? What I originally heard you say sounded like a simple problem, but I want to tune in to your specific needs and make sure we can meet them. Tell me more about your current systems." This was a subtle but effective way for Vera to share that she missed some critical information and why, while also creating an opportunity to listen better the second time.

L.E.N.S. focused. Potential crisis averted.

As you become more mindful of how you listen to complex information, you can use the accept, voice, and change techniques to ensure your L.E.N.S. is focused.

## News: Consider the Relevancy

The third and final consideration for the news component of your L.E.N.S. is relevancy. Some people struggle to listen when the information doesn't impact them directly or immediately. But you could miss relevant details in the workplace if you multitask or tune out.

Some Adaptive Listening in training have pushed back on the need to focus during these situations. They've asked, "Do I have to listen when the information is irrelevant to me and my role?" It's a fair question. You have limited time in your workday, especially if you're a busy leader. Why worry about focusing your L.E.N.S. on speakers who aren't giving you relevant information? Why bother listening to these speakers at *all*?

You should still listen for two reasons. First, when you don't listen, you're not being empathetic. Second, you could miss something important if you stop listening.

Viktor, a social media manager, shared a time he got into trouble when his L.E.N.S. became unfocused. He was a new employee attending a company-wide meeting. He was initially looking forward to learning more about the marketing and social media topics on the agenda because those were directly related to his role.

"When the leadership team talked about things that didn't seem to apply to me or my new role," he said, "I was mentally off in a different place. I thought, 'I don't need to care about this part.' " But then Viktor met with the CEO days later, and she brought up a topic he had tuned out, assuming it wasn't relevant. Viktor admitted, "I thought, 'Oh man, I wasn't paying attention to that part!' I froze out of fear and hoped she would change the subject."

Do your best to avoid tuning out when the news isn't relevant to you. If you notice your focus slipping, consider which tactic would help you get back to being an Adaptive Listener. Should you accept that this information isn't relevant and listen anyway because it's the empathetic thing to do? Should you tell the speaker that you tuned out and need them to repeat themselves? Should you request a change, like asking the speaker to reframe the topic so it *is* relevant to you or telling them you aren't going to continue listening? It might seem rude, but maybe that candor is what's best for the speaker at that moment.

## Speaker: The "S" in L.E.N.S.

The final letter in L.E.N.S. stands for speaker. Whether there's a hierarchy or power difference between you and the speaker, or you've formed biases about them, the person speaking to you can impact your ability to focus while listening. It might not be easy for you to admit that the speaker component of your L.E.N.S. is unfocused. You might believe (or want to believe) that you give the same focus to every person speaking to you. But that's probably not true unless you've done the work to focus your L.E.N.S.

### Speaker: Consider Their Role

Like the other L.E.N.S. components, the speaker component will impact listeners differently in each interaction. The relationship between your role and the speaker's role is one significant factor that may contribute to your focus (or lack thereof). Do you always give the same focus when you're listening to a boss? A direct report? A customer? A peer? An investor? Probably not.

Your L.E.N.S. may be focused when listening to your supervisor, a member of your organization's leadership team, or even a customer or client with the buying power because the stakes feel high when interacting with them. But there's also a chance you become nervous about the hierarchy between you and the speaker, so your L.E.N.S. becomes unfocused.

Hakob, a marketing associate, felt the impact of the speaker L.E.N.S.:

Hakob was in his role for more than two years when the CMO of his company asked him to collaborate on a project. He admired this leader. In fact, this CMO's leadership style was a major reason he joined the organization in the first place.

"When she finally asked me for my input on a project, I was flattered and excited but also awestruck and nervous," Hakob said. "I recognized this opportunity as flattering—the CMO wouldn't have asked me to be involved if she didn't think my skills were up to the task—but I was also feeling the pressure."

Hakob feared that if he didn't get this project right, at best the CMO would never ask for his help again. At worst, she might think he was awful at his job and fire him (admittedly, that would be an extreme reaction by the CMO and perhaps not the healthiest workplace environment, but the possibility still scared Hakob). Not only was he distracted by the pressure, but he also wanted to make his CMO happy.

"So, throughout our first meeting, I nodded and said yes to everything she asked. We were in the zone," Hakob shared. "I was eager and excited during the meeting, but I walked out of there confused about what I would do next. I was so distracted by her power, seniority, and the pressure of getting things right that I wasn't nearly as focused as I thought I was in the moment."

It's important to consider how the speaker component of your L.E.N.S. might be unfocused when listening up. But it's also important to think about your L.E.N.S. when listening to peers, direct reports, or external stakeholders. The power distance between you and the speaker could change the stakes, which could in turn change your ability to focus.

As you become more aware of how a speaker's role impacts your listening, you might also find it helpful to use the change tactic like Hakob did for future meetings. Knowing that the speaker component of his L.E.N.S. would likely be unfocused every time he collaborated with his CMO, Hakob requested a change: He asked permission to record future virtual meetings so he could go back and listen if needed. Knowing that the recording was available helped him feel less anxious about missing something. Hakob had a more focused L.E.N.S. moving forward, and hopefully you will, too.

## Speaker: Consider Your Impression of Them

You might not always recognize the impact your impressions can have on your ability to listen to someone, but it's essential to build awareness about what you think and how you feel about the people you interact with at work. Your impressions of others form fast. Your impression of a speaker can affect your focus through cognitive biases like the halo effect and the horn effect.

Suppose Armen, a senior marketing leader, meets a newly hired sales leader, Emmylou, for the first time. Emmylou was brought in from another organization to revamp the company's sales strategy and collaborate with Armen and the rest of the marketing team on new sales enablement materials.

In the first meeting, Emmylou impresses Armen with her researched data, action plans, and creative ideas on how sales and marketing can collaborate. This new sales leader is brilliant, optimistic, and inclusive. Armen has formed a great first impression of Emmylou, his new partner, and looks forward to working with her. Until or unless she proves otherwise, Emmylou is now in Armen's good graces.

In the 1920s, psychologist Edward Thorndike named this phenomenon the "halo effect." He published an article titled "A Constant Error in Psychological Ratings," in which he asked commanding officers in the US Army to rate their soldiers based on physical, intellectual, personal, and leadership qualities. Thorndike found that if officers rated soldiers highly in one area, they were also likely to apply that favorable rating to other attributes. The same pattern was discovered with soldiers rated low on the scale. If rated low in one area, there was a high correlation that they would also be ranked low in the other areas. In

Thorndike's words, "Ratings were apparently affected by a marked tendency to think of the person in general as rather good or rather inferior and to color the judgments of the qualities by this general feeling."[27]

Think about someone at work who you like and get along with extremely well. Picture that person with a symbolic golden glowing halo around their head. Now, imagine that person made a small error. Chances are, your brain would discount that negative experience. You might brush it off. "It was just a small mistake! Not an indictment on their character!" But you want to be careful of letting the halo effect cause you to give others more benefit of the doubt than they deserve.

The opposite of the "halo effect" is the "horn effect." Can you think of someone you don't like to work with, who makes your day harder, who you avoid interacting with? If you form a negative impression of someone, you might not be able to unsee devil horns on that person moving forward. Now, imagine that person committed the same small mistake as your halo-wearer. You probably wouldn't brush it off.

Suppose Armen's first interaction with Emmylou went differently. What if she arrived with no data, action plan, or creative ideas? What if she made an insensitive or degrading comment? Armen might have thought she was completely unprepared and unqualified as a partner. Or, if she brought lots of data and ideas to the meeting but wasn't interested in any feedback, Armen might have formed the impression that Emmylou doesn't value collaboration. Even if she eventually acted in a diligent and creative way, it might be hard for Armen to let go of that initial impression.

Now, if you're thinking, "But that sales leader wasn't collaborative. They weren't inclusive. They didn't show up prepared. They're *not* a good partner," that's understandable. But if Armen walked into his next interaction with that mindset, he wouldn't be an empathetic Adaptive Listener. He might miss out on good ideas and the potential for future collaboration, all because of his impression.

Past experiences can offer valuable information about your colleagues and customers, and it would be unwise to ignore that information completely. But try not to give those past experiences and impressions absolute power. If you do, you might not give the speaker what they need, and you might even damage a workplace relationship.

## The Cumulative L.E.N.S. Effect

If more than one component of your L.E.N.S. is out of focus, then it might have a cumulative effect on your listening. If you're not in a great mood, *and* you don't have time, *and* you're not a morning person, *and* the news isn't novel to you, *and* the speaker has a horn effect with you, then it can become extremely challenging for you to be an Adaptive Listener who helps the speaker meet their goals.

Before and during your interactions, mentally check each L.E.N.S. component. Ask yourself, "Could something about me (the listener), this environment, this news, or this speaker make it harder for me to be an Adaptive Listener?" If the answer is yes, use the accept, voice, or change tactics.

If you continue to struggle with meeting a speaker's goals, especially after you've read the techniques in Chapters 9 through 12, then you might have a lingering unfocused L.E.N.S. See Figure 7.3 and assess which component of your L.E.N.S. could be impacting your Adaptive Listening.

**Figure 7.3. Check Your L.E.N.S.**

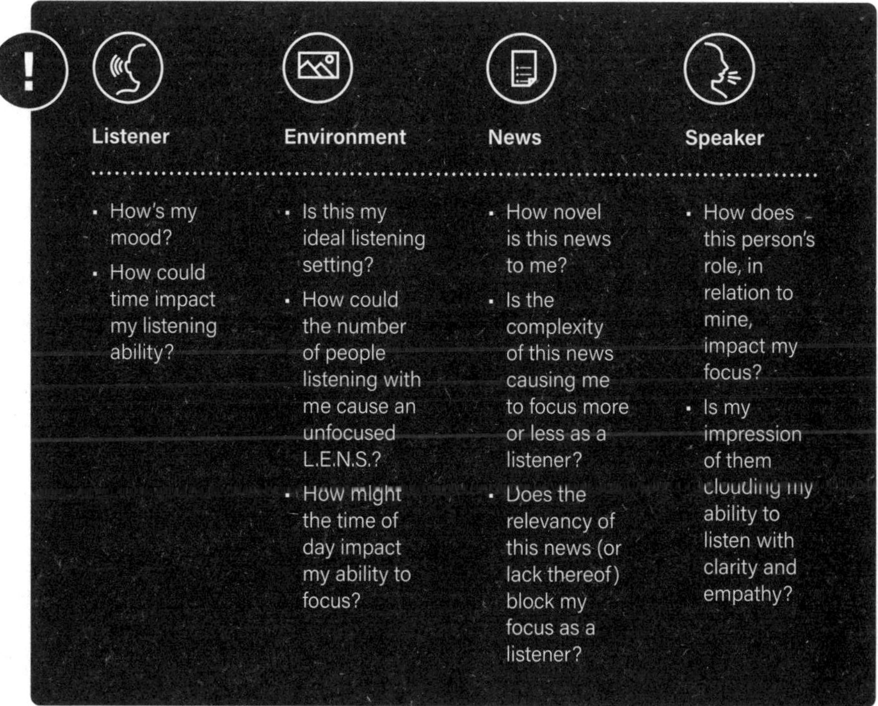


Remember, the more awareness you have about your L.E.N.S., the more you can control it. Some of the components of L.E.N.S. might never impact your ability to listen. Some components might impact your listening some of the time. Others might be constant or repeated barriers. Awareness is power. Check your L.E.N.S., focus it, and continue adapting how you listen to help speakers meet their goals.

# Part Two

# *Know How Others Need You to Listen*

## Chapter 8

# Meet the S.A.I.D. Listening Goals

Now that you have more awareness about the way you currently listen, Part II of this book will help you approach listening as a goal-oriented activity in which you play a crucial role. Neuroscientists have found that people like having goals because it gives them a clear path forward.[28] That clarity provides comfort because, as a species, humans don't love uncertainty. In the early days of human survival, uncertainty could mean being eaten by a predator or not having enough food. Today, some people are more comfortable with uncertainty than others. Still, your workday is more complicated when you don't know what's next or what to do about it. A lack of identifiable goals can lead to anxiety and frustration for you and lost productivity for your organization.[29]

There's a good chance you already have a goal while listening. The problem is, that goal is probably about what *you* want to get out of the interaction. You might think:

- "Oh, my manager wants me to listen to an update about the team? I'm here to determine how that information impacts me and my job."
- "Oh, I'm meeting an existing customer? I'm here to convince them our newest solution is the right one for their organization so I can make the sale."
- "Oh, I'm in a team meeting? I'm here to contribute ideas that make me stand out from my peers."

It's not that those thoughts are horrible or even wrong, but they aren't particularly empathetic to the person speaking to you. You can be an empathetic Adaptive Listener when you treat each listening interaction as an opportunity to help the speaker meet their goal.

## The S.A.I.D. Listening Goals

Every time a leader, peer, direct report, customer, vendor, analyst, or advisor speaks to you, they have a goal they're trying to achieve. Yes, every time.

For example, when a direct report has a big win and tells their manager, the direct report's goal might be to make their manager proud, to get recognized for their efforts and achievement, or to demonstrate that they're ready for more high-stakes projects. When a customer tells a salesperson about their current problems, the customer likely wants the salesperson to offer solutions. Even when a colleague shares a story about their weekend with a peer, the colleague might have a goal to build a connection, create a moment of fun and levity, or seek an outsider's opinion about a personal situation.

If you're wondering how you'd *ever* identify the goal of *every* person you listen to at work, recall from Chapter 1 that this book will make it easy for you.

The good news: There are only four possible listening goals for each workplace interaction.

The even better news: The four goals map directly to the four S.A.I.D. Listening Styles (Support Listener, Advance Listener, Immerse Listener, and Discern Listener), so you don't have to learn the goals from scratch.

The great news: Sometimes your S.A.I.D. Listening Style will align perfectly with the S.A.I.D. Listening Goal, so you might not have to adapt at all. Just by using the listening style that comes naturally to you, you'll help the person meet their goal.

And perhaps the best news: You can use the techniques in the following four chapters to know when and how to adapt your listening to help someone meet their needs, whether their goal is the same as your listening style or not.

When someone speaks to you at work, they either need you to **Listen to Support**, **Listen to Advance**, **Listen to Immerse**, or **Listen to Discern**. You'll find a brief description of each goal in Table 8.1.

**Table 8.1. S.A.I.D. Listening Goals**

| S.A.I.D. Listening Goals | What the Speaker Needs from You |
|---|---|
| Listen to Support | Meet their emotional need |
| Listen to Advance | Move people, projects, or processes forward |
| Listen to Immerse | Understand and remember the content |
| Listen to Discern | Evaluate the information |

The S.A.I.D. Listening Goals apply to every workplace interaction where you're asked to listen, whether in a one-on-one, a small group, or part of a larger audience. They apply when you're listening to colleagues and coworkers, customers, clients, and vendors. They apply when you're listening to leaders, peers, and direct reports. Sometimes you know the person speaking well and other times, you've just met them. Sometimes you're expected to participate in a back-and-forth dialogue with the person. Other times you're expected to stay silent (but likely still express nonverbals like eye contact, nodding, or smiling).

The goals are what the person speaking needs from your listening. Sometimes the type of listening the speaker needs will be obvious and you'll meet those needs easily. Like when a leader needs you to take the next steps on a project, and you have the time and expertise to do it, you'll Listen to Advance.

Other times, the person might know precisely what they *want* from you, but you'll know it's not what they *need*. For example, when a direct report wants you to tell them the answer to their problem (Listen to Advance), but you know it's better for their development if you help them find the answer themselves (Listen to Discern). Or when a colleague is having a bad day and is rambling about it. Your colleague might not realize it, but you'll know they need you to Listen to Support more than they need you to Listen to Immerse.

Given your fast-paced and dynamic workday, people often need you to meet more than one goal before the meeting, conversation, or presentation is over.

- A peer might need you to give them feedback on their upcoming pitch or presentation (Listen to Discern), offer them direction on how to fix whatever you think isn't working (Listen to Advance), and keep their confidence high before they deliver the pitch (Listen to Support).
- A direct report might show up stressed about how many projects they have to complete. They need you to give them space to offload their mental strain (Listen to Support) and then tell them how to prioritize their workload (Listen to Advance).
- A leader might need you to know about a program that won't launch for a few months (Listen to Immerse) and value their efforts (Listen to Support).

You might be thinking, "Wait! How am I supposed to know what they need?!" Don't worry. You'll have all those answers by the time you finish reading Chapters 9 through 12.

## Take on the Burden

Adaptive Listeners in training have asked, "Why is it my responsibility as a listener to identify the speaker's goals?" They've also challenged, "Can't I just ask the speaker what they need? We're not supposed to make assumptions about others, right?" These are fair concerns.

But remember, you likely spend more than half your day listening to other people, and managers spend even more time listening.[30] Plus, business communication moves fast. Do you have time to start every interaction with, "Wait—before you start speaking, what do you need from me, your listener?" Are you going to interrupt the presenter on the stage, the CEO speaking at your department meeting, or the customer you're meeting with for the first time to ask them how they want you to listen?

Even if you thought, "Yes, I'm fully comfortable asking someone how they want me to listen before they start speaking to me," what about in the middle of an interaction? What would you do if your leader, direct report, colleague, or customer's goal changed from Listen to Support, Listen to Immerse, or Listen to Advance? Would you stop them every few minutes to ask, "Okay, and what do you want from me as your listener now?" "Wait, pause there—how would you like me to listen now?" "All right, and what about now?" Not only could your double-checking be inefficient and even cringeworthy, but it's also unnecessary once you learn Adaptive Listening techniques.

Great listeners take on the burden. You can do the hard work of figuring out what your leaders, direct reports, colleagues, and customers need from your listening. By doing so, you'll create fluid interactions that leave them feeling satisfied. Plus, until everyone you work with is more familiar with Adaptive Listening, asking someone, "What do you need from me as a listener in this interaction?" can be a tricky question for them to answer.

Taking on the burden doesn't mean you need to memorize all the situations and techniques you'll read in the following chapters. At the highest level, you want to train yourself to ask, "What does the speaker need from me in this interaction?" Then, your answer will be one of the four S.A.I.D. Listening Goals.

Once you've made that question-and-answer a routine part of your workday, you'll be practicing Adaptive Listening.

When you're ready to grow your skills even further, each chapter covers how to adapt the way you listen in common and complex situations specific to each listening goal. Common situations are ones where it's usually obvious or expected that you'll listen a certain way. In complex situations, it's often harder to spot the listening goal. These chapters will help you identify the goal and teach you how to process the information and respond in a way that helps the speaker.

You'll likely gain a lot of value from reading the chapters that don't map to your listening style, since that type of listening comes less naturally to you. As you're reading, note the situations in which you'd struggle to adapt your listening. Then, return to that specific chapter and section when you want to prepare for an upcoming interaction or assess how strong your listening was afterward. But a piece of advice: don't skip the chapter that maps to your S.A.I.D. Listening Style! Even if you're thinking, "I already know how to listen to meet that goal," you'll likely read techniques for common and complex situations you haven't tried yet.

Get ready for the "how" of Adaptive Listening. The following chapters give you practical tips you can try immediately, maybe even in your next meeting. After reading when and how to Listen to Support, Advance, Immerse, and Discern, you'll be well on your way to becoming an influential and empathetic Adaptive Listener. You might just influence the way others listen to you, too.

## Chapter 9

# Adapt to Support

To become an Adaptive Listener, understanding the four S.A.I.D. Listening Goals—Support, Advance, Immerse, and Discern—is critical. This chapter, and the three that follow, will delve deeper into *how* to listen the way a speaker needs. But first, it's important to call out the difference between Support Listening and the other listening goals.

When you need to Listen to Advance, Immerse, or Discern, you'll generally listen in a way that's directly related to the job you were hired to do. You'll listen to the directions you need to move the project forward (Listen to Advance), or you'll listen to remember the details and be prepared when the topic comes up again later (Listen to Immerse), or you'll evaluate if the output from another team is hitting the mark (Listen to Discern). But when you need to Listen to Support, you'll listen and respond in a way that helps meet the speaker's emotional needs.

Now, unless your job description clearly states that you're responsible for the emotional well-being of others in your organization, you might question why you need to Listen to Support at work. The reason is that people experience emotions before, during, and after their workday (and because you're also a person, you feel emotions at work, too). Even if people hide or mask their emotions in the workplace, they're still there.

If dealing with other people's emotions at work sounds like it will make your job harder, you're not wrong. Not only do you need to know and implement Support Listening techniques, but being empathetic to others takes effort. It can be emotionally draining for you to prioritize other's emotions.[31] But if you ignore or avoid emotions, you're missing an opportunity to build trusted relationships that help you accomplish your professional ambitions and have a more enjoyable workday. Instead, you can be an Adaptive Listener who knows how to recognize emotions in others and yourself so you can address them appropriately.

Recognizing how others feel can be challenging, but it's an important skill. You must be able to recognize those emotions to validate them, an important step in Support Listening. The following sections will teach you how to process and respond in a variety of common and complex Support Listening situations, and it all starts with learning how to read emotions.

## Emotions in the Workplace

Before diving into how to read emotions, here's some Emotions 101. Whether at work or at home, most researchers agree that humans have six basic emotions: joy, sadness, disgust, fear, anger, and surprise.[32] These emotions are universal, meaning people from different cultures and backgrounds experience the same six emotions even though they may express those emotions differently.

The United States is a more expressive culture than other national cultures. Imagine an American employee who's angry about a project setback. That person might express their anger with direct statements about why they're angry. They might use facial expressions, tone, and body movements that communicate their anger. They could have a clenched jaw, a raised voice, or a drastic change in the physical distance between themselves and the other person.

In China, on the other hand, people are often more reserved with their anger expressions. They might maintain a more neutral expression and choose not to vocalize their anger.[33] Of course, there are nuances to every culture. As you work to identify the emotions of those around you, it's wise to keep your cultural context in mind.

Technically, emotions and feelings are different. Emotions are triggered in the brain, form fast based on a response to a stimulus, and can leave just as quickly. Feelings are interpretations that stem from emotions or physical sensations (like "feeling hungry"). They're more specific and longer lasting than emotions.[34] For example, joy is an emotion. When experiencing joy, you might feel "excited" or "fascinated" or "accepted" based on the situation and your interpretation of it. Despite the distinction between emotions and feelings, many people use the terms interchangeably. For the sake of simplicity, the authors chose to do the same (so please don't @ us).

Both emotions and feelings can be categorized as comfortable or uncomfortable. You probably know almost instinctively if an emotion is comfortable or uncomfortable. You know you like feeling joy and you don't like feeling sadness. Comfortable emotions are emotions that you could sit in all day, every day. They might even be emotions that you're chasing (e.g., "I just want to be happy") or emotions you're trying to hold onto (e.g., "I don't want this amazing night to end!"). Uncomfortable emotions are emotions most people want to move beyond, like extreme sadness or stomach-churning disgust.

But it's not that emotions are good or bad. Even uncomfortable emotions are valuable, but they get a bad reputation in the workplace. If you've ever heard someone say, "Let's not get emotional," they're usually talking about uncomfortable emotions like anger or sadness. They don't usually mean, "Let's keep that joy to a minimum," even though anger, sadness, and joy are all emotions. Still, uncomfortable emotions can be hard for people to express and potentially harder for listeners to know how to handle, especially at work. But people must experience both comfortable and uncomfortable emotions to grow.[35]

Adaptive Listeners know that embracing and sharing emotions with others can be powerful. One study found that when healthcare workers shared their authentic emotions with coworkers, it helped alleviate burnout and fostered a workplace climate of authenticity.[36] Emotion-sharing also allows people to build community and deepen professional relationships. When employees believe their emotional needs are being met, organizations report less turnover and higher job satisfaction scores.[37]

To hone your Support Listening skills, start by recognizing emotions in yourself and others. Refer to Table 9.1 for a list of comfortable and uncomfortable emotions commonly experienced in the workplace. As you review it, reflect on how you'd identify these emotions in others and yourself.

**Table 9.1. Comfortable and Uncomfortable Emotions**

| Comfortable Emotions | | Uncomfortable Emotions | |
|---|---|---|---|
| Amazed | Included | Annoyed | Jealous |
| Appreciated | Inquisitive | Anxious | Loathing |
| Awe | Inspired | Bitter | Lonely |
| Brave | Optimistic | Bored | Melancholy |
| Comfort | Proud | Critical | Mortified |
| Composed | Reassured | Disappointed | Nervous |
| Confident | Relieved | Discouraged | Pressured |
| Content | Renewed | Disgust | Rejected |
| Curious | Secure | Enraged | Revolted |
| Delighted | Thankful | Gloomy | Stressed |
| Eager | Useful | Guilty | Timid |
| Empowered | Valued | Hesitant | Worried |
| Encouraged | Vindicated | Humiliated | Uneasy |
| Excited | | Inferior | |

Just because you need to Listen to Support doesn't mean you have to fill your calendar with long, drawn-out emotion-sharing interactions that neglect your organization's other priorities. Adults can experience emotions *and* get their jobs done. Even when people are in heightened emotional states, they can often regulate their emotions and return to the job. As you become an Adaptive Listener, you can listen in a way that helps meet the speaker's work needs (usually through Advance, Immerse, or Discern Listening) and their emotional needs (through Support Listening).

## How to Validate Emotions

Now that you have a baseline for emotions in the workplace, it's important to explore the art of validating emotions—a technique essential to all Support Listening situations.

Imagine someone at work is talking to you about how angry and frustrated they are with a current project. You *could* use Advance Listening techniques to help them fix the situation. You *could* use Immerse Listening techniques to gather more information about the problem. You *could* use Discern Listening techniques to evaluate why they're angry and whether you think they should be. You *could* even be a Support Listener who rushes to cheer them up (because you forgot about the caution of excessive cheerleading in Chapter 3).

The best option, though, would be for you to **validate their emotions**. You can validate someone's emotions by giving them space to feel and letting them know that whatever they're feeling is okay. When you validate someone's emotions, you communicate empathy, assuring them that their feelings are understandable. You'll validate people's comfortable and uncomfortable emotions, but you'll usually spend more effort validating the uncomfortable ones. It's often harder for people to return to a neutral or comfortable emotion during a heightened uncomfortable emotion.

Researchers have found that when you validate a coworker's emotions, that coworker is more likely to trust you.[38] That's why, even when you need to help the speaker meet a different listening goal, you'll still want to validate their emotions using these three techniques: **determine their emotion**, **acknowledge their emotion**, and **justify their emotion**.

First, you'll observe what they say, how they say it, and even what they don't say to **determine their emotion**. You'll do this mentally while you're listening. Sometimes it'll be easy for you to determine how they feel because they'll tell you directly or display an obvious emotional cue, like smiling when they're happy or crying when they're sad. Or perhaps you work closely with the speaker, and you've consciously or unconsciously made mental notes about how they usually act when they feel a certain way. Maybe the person is smiley 90 percent of the time, so when they show up with a frown, you know they're experiencing a different emotion than usual.

But not all emotional displays are as obvious as smile = happy or cry = sad. It can be hard to figure out what someone else is feeling if they don't offer clear cues. One way to determine a speaker's emotion is to watch for micro expressions. A micro expression is a facial expression that only lasts a fraction of a second. Then, the person's face goes back to their previous expression. Instead of a macro expression, like holding a smile, a micro expression would be a quick upward turn in the corners of the mouth and then a return to a more neutral expression. If you blinked, you might miss it. But if you're vigilant, you might be able to determine the speaker's emotions before they even realize they're experiencing it.

Although word choice, tone, and body language cues often vary across cultures, evidence indicates that micro expressions associated with basic emotions are universally recognizable.[39] The Paul Ekman Group, a leading emotion research firm, even offers quizzes and trainings to improve your ability to read micro expressions.[40] For now, Table 9.2 includes a list of common facial movements, which correspond to the basic six emotions, so you can practice reading others' emotions.

**Table 9.2. Micro Expressions for Basic Emotions**

| | | | |
|---|---|---|---|
| |   |  |  |
| **Emotion** | **Joy** | **Surprise** | **Sadness** |
| **Micro Expression** | Pushed up cheeks<br>Movement around corner of eyes | Raise eyebrows<br>Open mouth | Drooping uper eyelids<br>Downturn corners of mouth |
| |  |  |  |
| **Emotion** | **Anger** 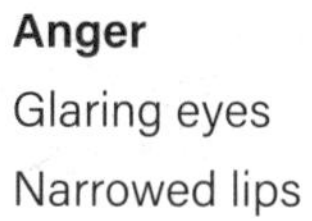 | **Fear** | **Disgust** |
| **Micro Expression** | Glaring eyes<br>Narrowed lips | Stretched lips<br>Tense lower eyelids | Wrinkled nose<br>Raised upper lip |

Once you've determined the speaker's emotion, either through overt cues or subtle micro expressions, you can move to the second step: **acknowledge their emotion.** If you stop at the first step of determining their emotion and choose not to acknowledge it, you'll be unlikely to get the benefits of validating their emotion. Instead, tell them what emotion or feeling you believe they're experiencing by naming it aloud, directly to the speaker.

While this might seem challenging initially, it will undoubtedly become more intuitive with practice. You'll improve your ability to determine their emotion, gain confidence as you state what you've noticed, and seek the benefits of letting others know you understand what they're feeling. You'll often combine this step with the next step, **justify their emotion.**

You can justify a speaker's emotions by letting them know their emotion can be viewed as an objective truth. Some people think that emotions aren't as valuable as rational thoughts, but an Adaptive Listener knows better. They know that emotions have a relevant role in the workplace. By telling a speaker that their reaction makes sense or that it's an emotion you would also feel in the same situation, you're telling them their reaction is reasonable and not out of control.

Although a simple "wow" or "aw" might show the speaker that you're picking up on their emotion or feeling, pairing the acknowledgment with a justification can be more genuine. The sample phrases in Table 9.3 give you a starting place for validation responses until you have your own list.

**Table 9.3. Phrases to Acknowledge and Justify Emotions**

| COMFORTABLE | UNCOMFORTABLE |
|---|---|
| *In each blank, insert relevant comfortable/uncomfortable emotion or feeling* | |
| That *is*_________news! | |
| I would be_________, too! | |
| It *is*___________that it happened even after you did *xyz*! | |
| It makes *sense* you feel_________. | |

The power of validation is clear in this example of Sam and their manager. Sam had recently joined a new organization and attended their first all-company meeting. The meeting started with the CEO stating there would be substantial layoffs in one part of the company, and that the people directly impacted by the layoffs had already been told. Still, the CEO wanted to talk to the entire company about why the layoffs were made and what it would mean for the company's outlook. After the meeting, Sam joined a one-on-one with their new manager.

> **Manager:** Hey, how's it going?
>
> **Sam:** Well...I'm kind of rattled by the layoff news. I know it's not about our department, but I just wasn't expecting that.
>
> **Manager:** It's normal to feel scared by this, especially as a new employee.
>
> **Sam:** Yeah, and I've never worked at a place that's had layoffs...
>
> **Manager:** It's definitely an unfortunate part of the job. If I were you, I'd be a bit shaken, too, walking into my first company meeting to hear that news.

During an interview with the authors, Sam shared that they weren't just rattled by the layoff news—they were freaking out. But luckily, their manager's response calmed their fears and made them feel less alone. Sam was direct about how they were feeling, which made it easy for the manager to determine the uncomfortable emotion. Then, the manager could acknowledge the emotion (e.g., feeling scared) and justify it (e.g., *it's normal*). With that validation, Sam could get through the workday and saw their manager as a trusted resource.

Some Adaptive Listeners in training have expressed reservations about justifying a speaker's emotional reaction when they don't agree with it. You might think a peer, direct report, leader, or customer is overreacting or wildly misinterpreted a situation, which has wrongly led them to this current emotion. But here's the hard truth: You can't argue with how another person feels. You can't tell someone they aren't feeling what they are, in fact, feeling in that moment. Plus, when you try to correct their feeling before you validate it, you're setting the stage for hostility and resentment. Even when you disagree, you can still justify the emotion they're feeling without condoning their behavior or reaction.

In addition to what you say to validate a speaker's emotions, you can also use your voice, face, and body to mirror those emotions. In Chapter 3 you read that strong mirroring skills is a common characteristic of Support Listeners. In the context of emotional validation, mirroring works like this: if the speaker exclaims in joy or anger using increased volume or pitch, your response can also be an exclamation with an increased volume or pitch. If they smile or frown, you can smile or frown as you respond. If they get big with their body posture in excitement or slump their shoulders in defeat, you can do the same.

If you're in person with the speaker, appropriate physical touch is another form of validation if you have consent or know the person speaking will accept it. A hug, a pat on the back, or a high five can show the speaker you're prioritizing their feelings and experiencing the moment with them. When you're listening to someone in a virtual or remote group setting, you can show your acceptance of their emotion or feeling by using a relevant emoji, meme, or GIF, if that's within the norms of your organization's culture or team dynamic.

After the interaction, or if you're listening to a recording of a meeting, presentation, or voice memo, you can also follow up with the speaker. Even in written form, expressing sentiments like, "Hey, just wanted to check in on you. How are you doing after we spoke?" or, "I'm thinking of you and your situation. Know I'm here for you if you need to talk more," can show them you care. When you **determine**, **acknowledge**, and **justify their emotion**, you give the speaker the type of Support Listening they need.

## Adapt in Common Support Situations

Common Support Listening situations routinely happen throughout your workday and where the speaker needs Support Listening *only*. They don't need you to Listen to Advance, Immerse, or Discern. They're solely looking for you to listen to celebrate a work win, commiserate about a work worry, or support them with a personal situation. If you've ever struggled to listen or respond during one of these common situations, the following techniques can make it easier for you and more effective for the people speaking to you.

### Support to Celebrate Work Wins

Celebrating work wins is one common situation where Support Listening is warranted. Hopefully, joy-filled opportunities are abundant in your workday. Your colleague closes a deal. Your team meets or exceeds their targets. Your direct report finishes a high-stakes project. Your manager receives accolades for their thought leadership. Your customer has a big win. From the small victories to the big ones, when people share celebratory news with you (or even when you learn about the information from someone else), you can Listen to Support.

In her Netflix special *A Call to Courage*, Brené Brown says that the most vulnerable emotion people express is probably the one you'd least expect. It's not shame, like when someone makes a mistake at work and has deep fears or anxieties about their value on the team or in the organization. No, the most vulnerable emotion is *joy*. Here's why...

When something good is happening in your life, or everything is going great, have you ever paused and thought, "I wonder how long this will last?" or "Let's wait for the other shoe to drop"? According to Brown's research, people often protect themselves once they experience joy and put up armor in preparation for the moment when their joy might be ripped away.

Given the vulnerability that can come with expressing joy, Adaptive Listeners can use four techniques to offer support during these workplace wins: **Hold the space** for the speaker to celebrate as long as they'd like, **validate their emotions**, show you're happy and excited for them by **inviting them to gush** over their win, and **offer kudos**.

When you know someone is coming to you with news they're excited about or proud to share, you can **hold the space** for them to celebrate as you Listen to Support. Holding space means giving the speaker as much time as they need to tell their work win story without rushing them or pushing them to finish. By doing so, you're telling the speaker, "I care as much about your work win as I do about getting our work done today" or, "I'm just as excited as you are about your work win." Adaptive Listeners hold space for their colleagues to celebrate, even if that celebration temporarily halts business. They know that colleagues who celebrate together can form powerful connections with one another. When it's time to respond to the speaker, Adaptive Listeners make sure to **validate their emotions** as covered in the previous section.

Gina, a property manager, recalled a time when her coworker held the space for her to celebrate her work win. She had applied for a promotion to be a manager in her organization twice before and, on her third try, she finally got the promotion. When she received the exciting news, she immediately told to her close colleague and friend François.

> **Gina:** (typing) I got the promotion!
>
> **François:** (typing) OMG, I knew you could do it. You must be so excited! Hang on...I'm gonna pause this project I'm working on and video call you. I want to hear all about it!
>
> **François:** (now on screen in a video call with Gina, leans forward to show interest, smiles, and uses an animated voice) So, tell me more! How did the interview go this time?
>
> **Gina:** Well, after interviewing twice already I was ready for potential questions they might ask, so I felt more prepared. I also practiced answering questions ahead of time, so I felt more confident this time.
>
> **François:** (claps) Yay! And you interviewed with a different senior leader this time, right? How were they?
>
> **Gina:** Yeah, they were friendly and made me feel comfortable. I had to give lots of specific examples from my past experience.
>
> **François:** Well, you obviously did great since you got the job! What did they say when they offered you the role?

François knew how hard Gina had worked to get to that next level and wanted to show her how proud and excited he was by holding space for her to celebrate. He stopped what he was doing to make room for his friend and colleague.

But holding space doesn't mean you'll remain silent as you listen to the good news. In addition to making time for the speaker to tell their win story, you can further show your support in how you respond. Instead of a quick "Yay!" or "Congrats!" you can do more by **inviting them to gush**. Ask the speaker follow-up questions that let them expound on why they're celebrating, just as François did for Gina when he called her on video and asked, "How were they?" and "What did they say when they offered you the role?"

But Support Listening doesn't have to stop with the interaction. Speakers often appreciate it when you **offer kudos** even after the interaction is over. Sometimes smiling, clapping, or giving verbal accolades in the moment doesn't feel like enough. In these cases, consider approaching the speaker hours or even days later and saying, "I wanted to congratulate you again on your news" or, "I can't stop thinking about your accomplishment. I think it's so great!" You might also send an email to offer kudos after the interaction.

Offering post-engagement kudos is also a great option when you're sitting in an audience and it's not appropriate to verbalize words of congratulations. When all you can do in the moment is smile or clap, consider reaching out after the interaction. Walk up to the presenter and or email them after to give them kudos.

Your workday might be hectic, and it might seem like you don't have time to celebrate work wins. But as you become a better Adaptive Listener, you'll notice how Support Listening in these situations can build camaraderie. When you **hold the space** for the speaker to talk about their work win, **validate their emotions**, **invite them to gush** by asking questions, and **offer kudos**, you're being intentional about how you communicate with others. They may even realize when they interact with you at work, they feel their best. That might come in handy when it's time for peer reviews, promotion reviews, or contract renewals.

## Support to Commiserate Work Worries

As great as it is to celebrate workplace wins, work is not all sunshine and rainbows. Your colleagues need Support Listening when they're going through hard times, too. A colleague might confide in you about a difficult meeting or a less-than-stellar review they received. A new hire might be nervous about joining your team or worried they won't remember all the onboarding information. A customer might be upset about the way your product performed or how poorly your services were delivered. When the person speaking to you is experiencing a work worry, you can Listen to Support by commiserating with them.

Sometimes it's hard to know what to say or do when others share their uncomfortable emotions because you can't relate to what they're going through. Maybe your work experience is positive, so it's difficult to understand why the person speaking is sad, angry, or frustrated; you're perfectly content with your job. Or maybe you're concerned that if you chime in and corroborate their negative talk, it will reach your leadership and result in reputational damage. While this rationale is understandable, avoiding these work-worry situations is a missed opportunity to build trust with colleagues, direct reports, leaders, and customers.

Even if it feels challenging, do your best to step outside your comfort zone. You can use these techniques to commiserate with the person speaking: **practice patience, validate their emotions, don't fix their problem, don't jump to cheer them up**, and **don't pile on your misery**. Note that three of the five techniques for commiserating workplace worries are more about what *not* to do rather than what to do. The fact is, if someone is coming to you because they're experiencing a workplace worry, they probably have a close relationship with you, trust you, or think highly of you.[41] That's why getting these situations right as an Adaptive Listener is more about avoiding common mistakes.

First, if you sense the person speaking needs you to commiserate, you can show you're listening to support by **practicing patience**. Your direct report, peer, or customer might need longer than they realize to express their worries. Before you validate their emotions, remain comfortable with your silence, and let them talk, get loud, cry it out, or otherwise express their uncomfortable emotions for as long as they need.

Practicing patience can be particularly challenging for Immerse, Advance, or Discern Listeners. If your S.A.I.D. Listening Style is Immerse, you might already be comfortable allowing others to speak without chiming in, but you're likely more comfortable listening to information rather than emotions-based content.

If your S.A.I.D. Listening Style is Advance or Discern, you might feel an urge to offer comments or suggestions. An Advance Listener might want to advise them on how they can get out of their uncomfortable position. A Discern Listener might want to offer critical responses that dissect how they ended up in this situation in the first place and how they could have avoided it. Even if you don't verbalize these thoughts, they can occupy your mind and distract you from being present with the speaker.

If commiserating is challenging for you, consider posing a question to the speaker that will give them the floor and encourage you to practice patience. You might say, "I'm here for you if you want to vent," or, "Do you want to talk about it?" You can use these prompts in addition to **validating their emotions**.

You'll want to avoid some common mistakes when it's time to commiserate a work worry. First, **don't fix their problem**, even if you have the power to do so. Just because someone is telling you about a problem doesn't mean they're asking you to solve it. Read that sentence again. Restricting yourself to only Support Listening can be challenging for Advance Listeners who are prone to offering advice. It can also be challenging for leaders who consider it their job to problem-solve. In Chapter 10: Adapt to Advance, you'll learn how to identify complex situations where the speaker needs both Support and Advance Listening. But in work-worry situations like these, focusing on Support Listening will help you give the speaker some emotional relief.

Maegan and Nicole experienced this situation during one of their routine one-on-one meetings. Maegan is Nicole's manager, and Nicole was coming out of a unique client meeting.

> **Nicole:** (slumped shoulders, a worried facial expression, shaky voice) Well, I've got *quite* a story for you!
>
> **Maegan:** (makes mental note that Nicole is both visibly and audibly upset) Uh-oh. Tell me...
>
> **Nicole:** Ya know that client I've been working with? The CEO of that real estate development company? I just presented him with three creative

> options for his upcoming presentation, and do you know what his response was?
>
> **Maegan:** Oh my gosh...what?
>
> **Nicole:** He said, "Nicole, it's not that I don't like them; it's that I *hate* them. They're all tied for last place." (increased speaking rate and volume) I was shocked and mortified! That's never happened to me before!
>
> **Maegan:** (matching Nicole's volume) Wow, you must have felt so thrown! I don't blame you for being shocked and mortified. That's some very tough feedback on creative options I *know* you worked so hard on!

As a manager, it might have been appropriate for Maegan to jump in and solve the problem or dissect what went wrong. But in this case, Nicole needed Support Listening based on her words ("I was shocked and mortified!"), body language (slumped shoulders, worried facial expression), and voice (increased speaking rate and volume). So instead, Maegan forced herself to practice patience.

Maegan commiserated with Nicole without rushing to fix her problem. This was particularly difficult for Maegan, whose S.A.I.D. Listening Style is Advance. But Maegan has learned over numerous failed attempts at listening that her Advance Listening Style isn't always what the speaker or group needs. In this case, Maegan knew that Nicole needed Support Listening.

If a similar situation happens to you, and a colleague approaches you to vent, you might genuinely want to help them fix their problem or offer advice. Instead, remind yourself that all they may need is Support Listening. Then, respond with an exclamation that validates their emotion and commiserates with them. Some version of, "Ugh, that's awful!" is often a safe bet. (And in case you're wondering, Nicole revised the deliverable and the client was happy in the end. Maegan knew better than to rush in with Advance Listening because she knew Nicole was a pro who can handle tough client feedback.)

Rushing to fix a speaker's problem isn't the only mistake to avoid while commiserating a work worry. You also want to make sure you **don't jump to**

**cheer them up**. It's true that listening to someone express a workplace worry is not always fun. Most people want their close colleagues, direct reports, leaders, and customers to feel good instead of uncomfortable. To get them to a comfortable place quickly, listeners sometimes try to make the speaker feel better before the speaker is emotionally ready. Common responses include, "It'll all work out," "It'll get better," or "Don't be sad."

If you're currently embarrassed at the realization you've rushed to cheer someone up, don't fret. You've got great intentions in trying to be empathetic, which is the right thing to do. But the best Adaptive Listeners commiserate with their colleagues and don't force others to feel comfortable emotions prematurely. Uncomfortable emotions can be cathartic. Allowing a speaker to express their anger or sadness might even help them overcome it. Although it might seem helpful and inherently supportive to cheer them up, try to commiserate and sit in the uncomfortable emotion *with them*. If you don't, you might run into trouble like this senior manager at a Fortune 100 tech company...

This senior manager was responsible for firing someone, and she felt awful about it. She liked the person she was letting go and it wasn't her decision. But it was part of her role, and it had to be done. As she explained why she had to let this person go, she delivered the news with a smile. She wanted to soften the blow and let the person know everything would be all right. She wanted to make the person feel better by balancing the bad news with some warmth. It didn't go over well.

When it was the fired employee's turn to respond, she said, "F*%# you and your smile!" Yikes. By smiling, the senior manager pushed a comfortable emotion on the person being fired—someone who wasn't ready for the warmth. That person didn't want to be cheered up. Instead, they might have benefited from a facial expression that conveyed sadness or frustration, the uncomfortable emotion they likely felt. Commiserating would have given the impression of solidarity and empathy much more than the smile. Lesson learned!

Finally, a well-intentioned but counterproductive technique some people use when trying to commiserate is to talk about their experiences in similar situations. They say something like, "I know how you feel," or, "Ugh, I know!

Me, too." Sometimes the listener might even jump in with a personal story to show just how much they understand what the speaker is going through.

You might think this approach is a great way to validate and empathize with the speaker's emotions. The problem with this technique is that it pulls focus away from the speaker who needs you to Listen to Support and, instead, makes the situation all about you. So, please **don't pile on your misery**.

The truth is no one can know how someone else feels. Even if you've been in a similar situation with similar (or the same) people, you're not on the same journey as the person speaking to you. Their background and context could mean they feel slightly or vastly different in this situation than you.

Even if you're sharing your misery comment or story to show connection and understanding, it can minimize the feelings of the person speaking to you. You may never articulate words like, "I know how you feel, so you're not special," but sharing your emotions and experiences might unintentionally convey that sentiment. As a result, the speaker might shut down or not share with you in the future.[42]

When you need to Listen to Support, the other person wants to know that you're there for them. Sure, they likely already know this because they went to you in the first place, but you can reinforce that trust by giving them what they need (and avoiding what they don't need) when it's time to commiserate a workplace worry.

## Support When It's Personal

Common Support Listening situations aren't always work-related. Not only do people bring their emotions about *work* to work, but they also bring their emotions about their *personal life* to work. And it's a good thing they do. When people are given the space and encouragement to bring their whole selves to work, they're happier and report higher job satisfaction.[43]

Personal topics include anything outside of work, like home, family, and friends. However, personal topics can also include feelings about non-work-related issues, including political, social, environmental, or economic matters. These personal situations often require you to Listen to Support at work. The person speaking to you might need you to celebrate or commiserate like they do when there's a workplace celebration or worry, but because these situations are personal, they're more nuanced.

With many people working in a virtual or hybrid environment, sometimes the celebratory or worrisome situation they're experiencing is happening at home *while* they're working. It can be challenging for remote workers to ignore those emotions when they log in for the workday.[44] As they're working from home, those move-in boxes could be piled up outside the camera's view, or that sick family member is on the other side of the wall, or their adorable new pet is giving them puppy dog eyes. It can be challenging for remote workers to manage their heightened emotions when they can't physically distance themselves from the triggering environment.

That's why, when someone comes to you with a comfortable or uncomfortable emotion based on a personal situation, you can use the same techniques you'd use to celebrate or commiserate a workplace situation. If they need you to celebrate a personal win, you'll hold space for them, validate their emotions, invite them to gush, and offer post-engagement kudos. If they need you to commiserate about a personal worry, you'll practice patience, validate their emotions, avoid fixing their problem, avoid jumping to cheer them up, and avoid piling on your misery.

In addition, you'll need to remember one more thing when you're listening to someone share a personal worry: **Don't pry**. If you press the speaker to reveal more about their personal situation, they might perceive it as intrusive. Instead, be comfortable with any silence, validate their emotions, and that's it. If they want to tell you more, they will.

If you choose to reach out to check on the speaker after the interaction, consider sticking to "I'm thinking of you," or, "Thank you for trusting me with this." These statements tell the person you're there for them without prying.

Whether virtually or in person, when the boundaries between work and personal life blur, you need to Listen to Support, even if the topic isn't work-related. That's true for both personal wins and personal worries. In these situations, you can be an Adaptive Listener by using the appropriate techniques and not overstepping your boundaries.

**Table 9.4. Adapt in Common Support Situations**

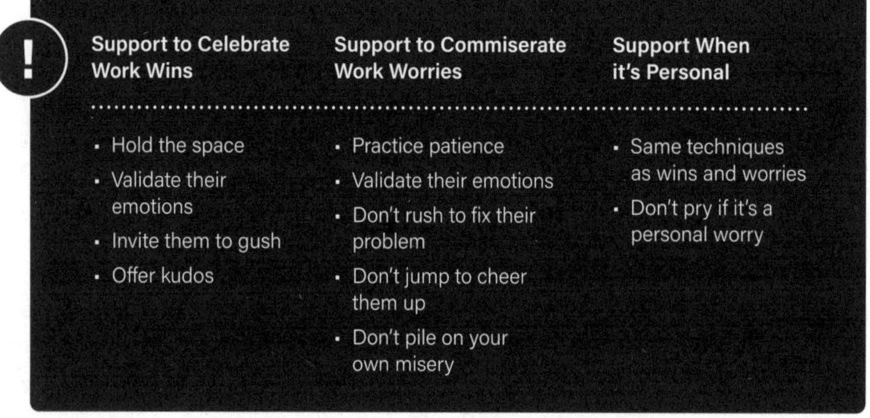

| Support to Celebrate Work Wins | Support to Commiserate Work Worries | Support When it's Personal |
|---|---|---|
| • Hold the space<br>• Validate their emotions<br>• Invite them to gush<br>• Offer kudos | • Practice patience<br>• Validate their emotions<br>• Don't rush to fix their problem<br>• Don't jump to cheer them up<br>• Don't pile on your own misery | • Same techniques as wins and worries<br>• Don't pry if it's a personal worry |

## Adapt in Complex Support Situations

Unlike common Support Listening situations, complex situations are when you know the primary goal isn't Listen to Support but rather one of the other S.A.I.D. Listening Goals: Listen to Advance, Listen to Immerse, or Listen to Discern. But **Adaptive Listeners work to give speakers some amount of Support Listening in every interaction** because they know it builds strong relationships and makes collaboration easier in the future.

You might not have thought about it before, but speakers often have emotional needs based solely on how their role relates to the person listening to them. Think about how you might want to feel when talking to a leader. Now, what if you were talking to a peer? What about a customer? Or a vendor/supplier?

Direct reports often want to feel acknowledged and valued when talking to their leaders or managers. Leaders often want to feel helpful and assured when talking to direct reports. Peers and partners often want to feel trusted and relieved when speaking to one another. Even clients, customers, and vendors want to feel a certain way when talking to the person selling to them or the person they're selling to.

When you consider how someone might want to feel based on their role in relation to yours, you can include Support Listening to potentially strengthen your relationship.

While it's not an exhaustive list, Table 9.5 can help you think about how someone might want to feel, given their role in relation to yours. This insight can help you meet their emotional needs using Support Listening, even when you also need to help the speaker meet another listening goal.

**Table 9.5. Sample Emotional Needs by Role**

| Direct Reports | Leaders | Peers & Partners | Clients | Vendors, Suppliers, Consultants |
|---|---|---|---|---|
| Accomplished | Assured | Confident | Assured | Accomplished |
| Acknowledged | Composed | Connected | Delighted | Admired |
| Empowered | Confident | Empowered | Impressed | Helpful |
| Proud | Helpful | Relieved | Proud | Irreplaceable |
| Useful | Inspirational | Trusted | Relieved | Respected |
| Valued | Respected | Useful | Satisfied | Unique |

These Support Listening situations are complex because you have to determine how much Support Listening you'll provide on top of meeting the speaker's primary goal. When the situation calls for it, you'll approach Support Listening as either a nice-to-add or a need-to-add.

## When Support Is a Nice-to-Add

Support Listening is a nice-to-add when the speaker's current emotional state isn't getting in the way of the work or task they ultimately what to complete—meaning the primary S.A.I.D. Listening Goal you will help them meet (Listen to Advance, Listen to Immerse, or Listen to Discern). Still, the speaker also has emotional needs that you can help them meet. In these situations, you'll **confirm they're comfortable**, **validate their emotions**, **meet their primary goal**, and then **briefly add Support Listening**.

Suppose you get a message from a peer saying, "Hey, can I get your advice on this project before I submit it to leadership?" You think, "I've got some time today, and I'm an awesome colleague, so sure." You respond with, "Happy to help! When and where?" The two of you plan to connect.

Just before you meet, you check in with yourself to confirm how you'll listen. Given that your peer directly asked you for advice to help move their project forward, you're confident this person wants you to Listen to Advance (if you're not yet confident, you will be by the time you read Chapter 10: Adapt to Advance).

Now that you've identified the primary goal, you need to determine how much Support Listening you'll include. When the meeting starts, you look for cues to **confirm they're comfortable**. Sure enough, you notice your peer seems calm. They smile at the start of the meeting and have a relaxed yet engaged posture. As they tell you why they need your advice, you notice their speaking rate, volume, and tone all seem typical based on your past interactions. You **validate their emotions** by showing up just as calm and ready to work as they are.

You do a quick calculation: because your peer appears to be in a comfortable emotional state (calm), you **meet their primary goal** (Listen to Advance). But because you also know this is a peer who will present to leadership, you want to help them feel empowered. That's why you **briefly add Support Listening** near the end of your interaction with a response like, "Yeah, I think once you do the things we discussed, it'll be ready to submit. But hey, it was strong already! I think they'll like it."

Across workplace interactions, you can briefly add Support Listening with simple responses or quick nonverbals. A kind word, a reassuring nod, a warm smile, or a thumbs-up emoji can all satisfy a speaker's emotional need without derailing the interaction.

When you use Support Listening as a nice-to-add, you'll leave the interaction knowing you helped your colleagues and customers meet their primary goal and emotional need, even if they didn't realize they had one. By the end of the interaction, they'll know that 1) you helped them get their job done, and 2) they feel good about themselves after meeting with you.

## When Support Is a Need-to-Add

When the person speaking to you is experiencing an uncomfortable emotion, Support Listening is no longer a nice-to-add. It's now a need-to-add. Someone feeling uncomfortable needs more Support Listening than someone who feels comfortable. If they don't get their uncomfortable emotion under control, they could become preoccupied or overwhelmed, making it more difficult for you to successfully meet their primary goal. In these situations, you'll **confirm their uncomfortable state**, **validate their emotions**, and then **adapt to their primary goal**.

A simple way to **confirm their uncomfortable state** is to take a quick inventory of what they're saying and how they're saying it. Is this person behaving differently from the way they usually do? And do they seem uncomfortable emotionally? There are typical behavior changes that alert you when someone is feeling uncomfortable:

- They're typically a clear speaker, but now they're over-explaining or repeating themselves.
- They're speaking at a higher pitch than usual.
- Their voice is usually steady, but now it's shaky or quivering, like they're driving over a bumpy road or can't quite catch their breath.
- Their speaking rate is faster than usual, and it sounds frantic or anxious, rather than excited.

- They increase or decrease the volume of their voice to show anger, sadness, or fear.
- They have a noticeably different posture, either more closed off or more intrusive.
- They change their gestures to be atypically more emphatic, excessive, or reserved.
- They change from being moderate or highly expressive with their face to using little or no facial expressions.
- They change from a typically relaxed facial expression to a more tense, clenched facial expression.

With more people in distributed, remote, and hybrid workplaces, you might not have access to all the cues you'd have in person. For example, if someone has their camera off, that could give you less to assess visually. If you're interacting over the phone, you'll also have fewer cues to guide you. And while written communication, including text and email, involves reading and not listening, you might also look for cues in those situations to identify how someone is currently feeling. For example, are messages coming in rapid succession, when the person usually types at a more measured pace? Whatever the case, do your best to confirm their emotional state based on the cues available to you.

Imagine the same peer from the previous example reached out and said, "Hey, can I get your advice on this project?" Only this time when you arrive ready to Listen to Advance and give your advice, it's clear that your peer is not calm. They're sitting with their head in their hands; their face is scrunched up like they're trying hard to concentrate; their body posture is tense, almost rigid. As they go over the reason they need your advice, you notice their speaking rate is quicker than usual. These behaviors are unusual for your peer, and these cues help you determine that your peer is nervous or anxious, which means they're uncomfortable.

Once you confirm their uncomfortable state, you'll **validate their emotions** with the techniques covered at the beginning of this chapter. Your exchange with your peer might unfold like this:

> **Peer**: (increased speaking rate, darting eye contact) So...uh...yeah...I need this pitch to go over well. And I'm worried about the way the pieces are coming together. I don't have time to start all over, but I could use your eyes on this.
>
> **You**: (match the increased speaking rate) Ugh! It's such a pain knowing you have all the info, but it's just not clicking!
>
> **Peer**: Exactly! (sigh of relief) I know it's all here...but something just isn't right...
>
> **You**: (mirroring the sigh of relief) Hey. You've already done the hard work of getting everything down and in one place. Now, let's dive in together and figure this out.

You watch as your peer slowly transitions to a more comfortable state. Their body posture goes from rigid to more relaxed. Their speaking rate slows down. Even though they're not smiling, their face is no longer in their hands, and their brow isn't furrowed. Your words of validation didn't get them to a happy or confident place, but it did get them to a more comfortable place.

With that, you're ready to **adapt to their primary goal.** For the rest of this interaction, you Listen to Advance as you help your peer rework their pitch. As the meeting ends, you send your peer off feeling empowered by adding, "Yeah, I think once you do the things we talked about, it'll be ready to submit. But hey, it was strong already! I think they'll like it."

Adaptive Listeners in training have asked, "What if I *don't* know this person well? How will I spot a change in someone when I'm unfamiliar with their typical voice or body movements?" Maybe they're new to your organization, they're a new customer, they're a new vendor, or they're a guest speaker. Although it's less likely that a stranger would come to you in a moment of emotional distress, it could happen. In that case, you can look for more general signs associated with uncomfortable emotions, like watery eyes that lead to/follow from crying, increasing volume that's trending toward yelling, or heavy sighs as a cue for agitation or aggravation. You can also look for micro expressions associated with anger, sadness, fear, or disgust.

When you're with someone experiencing an uncomfortable emotion, but they still have a job to do, you'll work to strike a delicate balance as you Listen to Support while helping them meet their primary goal. If you choose to only Listen to Support in these situations, your peer could fall into a negative spiral and feel even worse. They might believe they lack control and are stuck, making it even harder for them to get to a more comfortable emotional state.[45] Over time, you'll improve your ability to know how much you should Listen to Support in these complex situations.

**Table 9.6. Adapt in Complex Support Situations**

| When Support Is a Nice-to-Add | When Support Is a Need-to-Add |
|---|---|
| • Confirm their comfortable state | • Confirm their uncomfortable state |
| • Validate their emotion | • Validate their emotion |
| • Meet their primary goal | • Adapt to their primary goal |
| • Briefly add Support Listening | |

## Be Brave and Bring the Warmth

If Support Listening is hard for you in common or complex situations, try using this mantra to get into the right mindset: *"I'm here for this person or group."* Whenever you need to adapt to Support Listening, you'll focus on prioritizing the speaker's feelings.

If you're an Advance Listener, you won't fix their problem. If you're an Immerse Listener, you won't only focus on the content. If you're a Discern Listener, you won't dissect their problem. Instead, you'll listen for the emotion within and behind their words. Then, your responses will feel like a high five if you're celebrating with them or a warm hug if you're commiserating with them. If the speaker already feels comfortable, you'll focus less on Support Listening. If they're uncomfortable, you'll focus on more Support Listening.

Over time, you might even develop a Support Listening shorthand with the people you work with closely. If either Maegan or Nicole types the other person's name in all caps over our internal chat (e.g., "MAEGAN!" Or "NICOLE!"), that's a cue: one of us needs Support Listening.

Bringing warmth and emotion into professional interactions might be challenging, especially if you aren't a Support Listener by default. If you're worried about being too soft or mushy, remember there are organizational and professional benefits to prioritizing emotions in the workplace. Whether celebrating or commiserating, you'll be taking an active role in building stronger workplace relationships. You might even find that as you practice Support Listening for others, they start giving it back to you, too.

## Chapter 10

# Adapt to Advance

What do a green traffic light, a *bang* at the start of a race, and a full bladder have in common? They're all unmistakable cues that it's time to act! Just as these cues in everyday life tell us to move, similar cues exist in the workplace. They let us know when it's time for action, which means it's time for Advance Listening. When someone needs you to Listen to Advance, you'll process and respond in a way that helps move projects, people, and processes forward.

Sometimes it's obvious that you need to Listen to Advance because it's the type of listening that helps you succeed in your role, whether you're an Advance Listener by default or not. For instance, a project manager might inherently use Advance Listening to translate information into action plans. Customer service representatives likely use Advance Listening to efficiently resolve customer issues. Maybe you're the person who takes something from point A to point B. You write the code, manage the social media, or pay the invoices. You already listen to your leaders, peers, or customers for what needs to be done. Then, you confirm and say, "Yep! I will do that."

Other times it's obvious you need to Listen to Advance, whether it's part of your job or someone asks you directly. A peer might say, "I need your help finishing this project." A direct report might say, "I need your advice on what to do next." A customer might say, "I need you to fix this problem." A vendor might say, "I need to tell you about updates to the invoice." There's not much ambiguity in these situations. The speaker has made it clear that they want you to help them move forward.

Even when you know you need to listen and respond in a way that helps move people, projects, and processes forward, it doesn't mean you always know *how* to do it. Plus, Advance Listening situations aren't always obvious. Sometimes you need to hunt for cues that your leader, direct report, coworker, or customer needs you to Listen to Advance.

This chapter offers Advance Listening techniques across common and complex situations. It will help you become an Adaptive Listener who can fluidly move between different listening styles, using each one as the situation demands and the speaker needs. If you're already an Advance Listener, you'll likely find new techniques that sharpen your skills. If you default to one of the other listening styles, the techniques in this chapter give you a way to start building your Advance Listening skills so you can continue to grow as an Adaptive Listener.

## Adapt in Common Advance Situations

You've probably listened in one or all the following common Advance Listening situations before: at the end of a presentation or meeting, when you need to relay information from one person to another person or group, and when you need to generate new ideas. If you aren't an Advance Listener, you might struggle in these common situations.

Take, for instance, Mark, a software developer who's an Immerse Listener. During team brainstorms, he prefers to make sure he thoroughly understands the ideas others are sharing before jumping in with his own contribution. Sometimes, he doesn't contribute at all because he's so consumed and intrigued by what others say. But Mark was invited to the brainstorm for a reason! The group wants and needs his ideas, too.

Similarly, you might find it uncomfortable to listen with a focus on moving people, projects, and processes forward, especially if you aren't used to doing it. You might think it's overstepping or even being aggressive to interject, offer advice, or initiate next steps, especially if no one directly asked you to do it. The following sections will give you the confidence to know when and how to use Advance Listening in common situations.

## Advance as Interactions Conclude

You've probably been there. You get to the end of a meeting and think, "What was the point of that? We didn't get anything done!" But don't think about those poorly run meetings right now. Think about the meetings when you *do* accomplish a goal. When you reach the end of a planning meeting, and a timeline gets finalized. When you reach the end of a budget meeting, and the funding gets allocated. When you reach the end of a meeting with a prospective customer, and the sales process moves forward. You might have some tedious or unproductive meetings, but you also have meetings where you know the goal is to finish a task or move things along.

Just as your role can dictate the need for Advance Listening, so can the situation. Consider the presentations you attend at work. The speaker often wants you to do something once they're done presenting. Maybe they want you to decide on their proposal, enact a new workflow, or sign up for a task force. If you're at a sales kickoff presentation, the speaker likely wants you to implement the updated tools to increase your sales. If you're in a benefits presentation, the speaker might want you to pick your healthcare provider.

Here's where it gets complicated: unless the person speaking says, "This is your call to action," or "I need you to do this," you might not recognize when it's time to move something forward. Even though many business interactions are about getting things done, speakers aren't always great at clarifying they need you to Listen to Advance. An Adaptive Listener knows they can help the person or group by pausing at the end of all interactions as they **check for next steps** and **confirm any actions.**

Imagine you're attending a company meeting where a leader shares the company's overall financial results from the last year. Given that these types of meetings often have routine updates, you decide you'll show up ready for Immerse Listening (and if you don't know that yet, you will after you read Chapter 11: Adapt to Immerse). Once everyone settles in, your leader begins:

> **Leader:** Good morning, everyone! Let's dive in. This year, we've had a steady increase in revenue, surpassing our targets. We've also been great at managing our costs during this growth. We're ending the year with an 18 percent profit margin, which exceeds our goal! Our collective efforts have paid off.
>
> We're investing these profits in our greatest asset—our people. We've implemented several initiatives to support your professional development, including training programs, mentorship opportunities, and cross-departmental collaboration initiatives. We want to empower you to reach your full potential and grow alongside the company.
>
> As we move forward, it's essential to remember our core mission and values because they serve as our guiding principles, shaping every decision we make. Together, we can continue to create an inclusive, innovative, and sustainable future. Thanks, everyone, and congratulations to us all! I'm happy to answer any questions.
>
> *The group applauds*

Once your leader is done, you realize you're not just proud of your company's efforts, but you're proud of your listening skills. You were focused on the details, tracking along with what your leader said (Immerse Listening). You even maintained eye contact with the leader, nodded and smiled along as they spoke, and quickly joined in the applause at the end (offering nice-to-add Support Listening like you read in Chapter 9). As the applause dies down, though, you realize that this is the end of the interaction. You decide that, as an Adaptive Listener, you should also determine whether Advance Listening is warranted.

First, you **check for next steps.** You ask yourself the following questions:

- Did the speaker mention me, my team, or my department? If so, were any action items referenced?
- Was there a due date or deadline mentioned? If so, am I responsible for it, or can I contribute?
- Was there a call for volunteers? If so, can I help?
- Was there a reference to a future activity or vision? If so, is there a role for me to play in contributing to that future?

You think back on what your leader said. They never mentioned your name, your team, or your department. There was no talk of specific deadlines or due dates. There were no calls for volunteers. But now that you think about it, your leader referenced the future. They talked about new professional development initiatives that would help the organization grow. You don't think there's anything for you to do right now, but you decide the best way to know for sure is to **confirm any actions.** You take your leader up on the offer and ask a question.

> **You:** These new professional development initiatives sound exciting. Is there anything we should be doing now to set ourselves up to be ready for them?
>
> **Leader:** Thanks for that question. There's nothing anyone needs to do right now. We'll let you all know more soon.

It's not uncommon for there to be no action items or next steps at the end of an interaction, particularly during routine meetings and presentations. But you lost nothing by using Advance Listening techniques at the end of the interaction to make sure that was the case. In fact, you might have even gained something—the reputation as someone who is future-focused and ready to act when it's needed.

Plus, there's always the possibility that your leader *did* want people to prepare for the new professional development opportunities but didn't clearly state the call to action. One power of Advance Listening lies not just in facilitating progress, but also in revealing the unspoken needs that can truly drive an organization forward. When you take the initiative to **check for next steps** and **confirm any actions**, you're seizing the opportunity to make an impact.

## Advance to Relay Information

You don't only want to be primed for Advance Listening at the end of interactions. From emails to chats to back-to-back meetings, information is constantly moving throughout your organization. Sometimes you'll take action based on the information, like when your manager shares details about an upcoming project you'll complete, or your colleague asks for advice about a problem you'll help them solve. But sometimes that information is meant to be passed *through you*. You'll need to listen to what a leader, customer, or colleague says and then relay that information to another person or group.

Relaying information might sound simple. You might think, "Okay, I'll Listen to Immerse, take notes, remember the details, and pass this information along. No problem." But relaying information requires you to listen differently than if you were the final link in the listening chain. You'll see why soon when you read about Luke, a customer success manager who felt the strain of his colleagues not using Advance Listening when he needed it.

You can use the following Advance Listening techniques when you know other people need to receive the information after you: **prepare to pass the baton, frame your follow-up questions, and show your note-taking**.

If your future #CareerGoals include leading people or initiatives, relaying information will be a routine part of your job. If you're already leading people or initiatives, you know this is true. One sales manager at a Fortune 100 company counted the number of times senior leaders asked him to pass on messages from them to his team. In just seventy-eight days, he was tasked with relaying fifty messages to his direct reports. All in a day's work for a role like that.

Accurately relaying information to others is important because strategies only get executed if everyone in the organization is up-to-date and on board with current plans. In larger organizations, there's not always enough time for senior leaders to talk to each person or department directly. Even if they did have the time, some news might be better received when delivered by team leaders and mid-level managers in a timely fashion because those people often have established trust and rapport with their teams.

When you're expected to relay information, you'll listen as you **prepare to pass the baton.** In a relay race, a team of runners work together to get to the finish line. Each runner is assigned a specific part of the race. Once the first runner gets to the end of their assigned part, they pass the baton to the next runner, who then takes off and runs their assigned distance before passing the baton to the next runner, and so on until the last runner crosses the finish line. But each runner isn't only thinking, "I need to get to the end of my assigned distance." They also think, "I need to successfully pass the baton to the next runner." If the runners lose focus, they risk dropping the baton, which could cost them extra time and hurt their chance of crossing the finish line first.

The same is true when you're listening in these relay situations. If you only focus on what you need to get out of the interaction, and you don't think about what your direct reports or absent team members might need to know, you could cost everyone time or keep them from getting to the finish line. Instead, you can prepare to pass the baton by listening with their context in mind. You'll consider what you know about their current skills, goals, priorities, motivations, and worries. When you do, you'll be more active in contributing to a successful outcome.

Asha is a mid-level manager at a large corporation, and Kiara is a team lead at a small start-up. Asha has a larger team and a more hierarchical structure to navigate. She attends quarterly meetings with her organization's senior leadership team where leaders share updates about the company's goals and progress. Kiara juggles multiple roles as a team lead, and she routinely passes information from one group to another. Regardless of the organization's size or structure, when acting as the information conduit, you need to Listen to Advance.

Both leaders have trained themselves to prepare to pass the baton by asking themselves the following questions while they're listening:

- Will my team/another stakeholder have a positive, neutral, or adverse reaction to this information, and how will this impact us moving forward?

- If my team/another stakeholder agrees with the information, what details do they need to move forward?
- If my team/another stakeholder disagrees with the information, what evidence do they need to be convinced they should move forward?
- If my team/another stakeholder is confused about the information, what clarity do they need to be ready to move forward?
- If my team/another stakeholder is unsure about the information, what reassurances do they need to move forward?

If one of these questions warrants more attention, Asha and Kiara use that information along with the second technique: **frame the follow-up** to the person who initially passed them the information. For Asha, that follow-up is usually directed at her senior leaders. For Kiara, that follow-up could be directed at anyone in the start-up who needs her to pass along information.

Instead of asking a point-blank question like, "Why are we doing this?" or making a declarative statement like, "People will be excited about this," these listeners frame their follow-up with context about their team's potential reaction or additional questions they expect other stakeholders to ask. The follow-up helps Asha's senior leaders and Kiara's colleagues know that neither is speaking on behalf of themselves *only*—they're rising leaders who consider broader organizational context and impact.

Potential ways to frame the follow-up include:

- "My team is probably going to have questions about..."
- "I can see the more senior people on my team asking me..."
- "The information my team will need to move forward on this is..."
- "What you said is similar to something that came up in a meeting, and people will be curious how..."
- "My team will be eager to get on board because..."

But managers and team leaders aren't the only people who need to relay messages. Cross-functional teams often pass information from one group to another. For example, a product team might share updates about features and benefits to the marketing team, who then goes on to relay those features and benefits to potential customers. Or a department head might tell a recruiter the skills and qualities ideal for a new hire, and the recruiter relays that information to job candidates. When done right, everyone benefits from the information relayed. When done poorly, you end up in a situation like Luke, the customer success manager mentioned at the start of this section.

As a customer success manager, Luke wasn't responsible for closing the sale or onboarding the new customer. His job was to partner with a customer once the sale and onboarding was complete. Luke spent years collaborating with customers so they could get the most out of the product they purchased and proactively working to ensure the customers would want to keep using the product for years to come.

After a sale was won, Luke would seek out customer information from the salesperson so he could be prepared to manage the relationship moving forward. He'd go into the system where the salesperson would put notes about the customer, but the notes would be sparse or nonexistent. He'd schedule a hand-off meeting so the salesperson could tell Luke more about the customer's pain points and why they decided to buy the product, but the salesperson would come to the meetings unprepared. The salesperson would often say, "Sorry. I don't have much to share."

Luke was frustrated. He said, "I don't need them to do my job for me, but we are all in this together! If they don't set *me* up for success, I can't keep the customer happy. Why go through all the effort of making the sale if we can't retain the customer?!"

Luke didn't know it at the time, but he needed the salesperson to prepare to pass the baton. He needed the salesperson to do more than just listen to close the sale. He needed the salesperson to consider that every team member had a role in setting up and maintaining a successful relationship.

If you're in a situation where you know another team or stakeholder will need to move forward after your part of the project or process is over, you can ask yourself these questions while you're listening:

- What might the next person in this chain need to know to make this successful?
- What question might the next person ask that I can easily get an answer to now?
- What information might help the next person move forward?

A final technique you can use when you're responsible for relaying information is to **show your note-taking**. Although you'll also review note-taking techniques in Chapter 11: Adapt to Immerse and Chapter 12: Adapt to Discern, the emphasis in this chapter is more on *showing* your note-taking and less on the note-taking itself.

When Listening to Advance, you can also satisfy your leaders, colleagues, and customers' need to feel confident by using your note-taking as a nice-to-add Support Listening technique. They'll be more likely to feel assured that you can accurately relay information and that you value what they're telling you when they see you taking notes.

Even if you don't need the notes yourself or are already confident you'll remember the information you need to relay, you can still select key moments to write or type what they're saying. You might even say, "Let me grab a pen/open a document to write this down." What goes in your notes is up to you. The key here is *showing* someone else that what they're saying is important enough for you to write it down. Plus, the notes will probably make it easier for you to accurately relay the information, too.

Adopting these Advance Listening techniques in common situations brings clarity and efficiency to your workday and paves the way for career growth. Over time, your ability to **prepare to pass the baton, frame your follow-up questions,** and **show your note-taking** can influence others to recognize you as a valuable team player and a potential leader, thus enhancing your professional prospects.

## Advance to Generate Ideas

The third common Advance Listening situation is when a group comes together to generate new ideas. You might be asked to dream up potential products and services, create or refresh a mission and vision, plan an event or offsite, build a new training, or find a creative solution to a problem. Some people struggle to process and respond the right way when they're asked to generate ideas as part of a group, but two techniques can help: **pull back** and **push ahead**. These techniques can work in different ways depending on your S.A.I.D. Listening Style.

If you're an Advance Listener by default, don't assume you have idea generation in the bag. You may tend to latch onto an idea shared early in the discussion and be eager to offer steps that could put that idea into action. Once you hear something that sounds great or even just good enough, you might think or respond, "Let's move forward with that one!" Or you might be the Advance Listener who is always ready to share a new idea. If someone let you, you'd take up the entire meeting adding one idea after the other to the list. Neither of these approaches is quite right for this situation, though.

If you're a Support Listener by default, you may already excel at creating space for your colleagues to share their new ideas. The trouble is that you might be so concerned with *their* needs that you don't contribute as much (or at all). That means the group is missing out on your great ideas—those that could inspire even more great ideas from your colleagues.

If you're an Immerse Listener, you may approach these situations how Mark did, the software engineer mentioned at the beginning of this chapter. You may prefer to think deeply about each idea your colleagues share and then ask follow-up questions to gather more details or confirm what they said to ensure you fully understand their ideas. Before you offer your ideas, you may stall your contributions until you're sure your ideas are fully formed in your head. These behaviors could halt the group's momentum and prevent you from contributing as much as others.

If you're a Discern Listener, you might want to evaluate each idea as it's shared. While the group generates ideas, you might naturally decide which ones are good and which should be eliminated from the list. You might also critique and evaluate your ideas, deciding which ones are worthy to share with the group. These critical thoughts and commentary can also be a momentum breaker.

To be a better contributor to these situations, keep in mind that someone asked the group to generate ideas because of the power that comes from everyone listening, sharing, and building on ideas *together*. Sometimes you'll need to **push ahead** and force yourself to process and respond differently than you'd prefer. Other times, you'll want to **pull back** on the type of thinking and contributing that's most comfortable to you. Use the techniques in Table 10.1 to improve your Advance Listening based on your S.A.I.D. Listening Style.

**Table 10.1. Push Ahead and Pull Back Techniques for Generating Ideas**

| If your S.A.I.D. Listening Style is... | And you find yourself... | Try this instead: |
|---|---|---|
| Support | Holding back your ideas to give space for others to contribute | **Push ahead:** Force yourself to contribute a minimum number of ideas to this interaction, aiming for one more idea than you're comfortable. |
| | Excessively cheerleading others | **Pull back:** Write a note to yourself of people you want to applaud for their ideas (instead of responding to everyone with your praise). |
| Advance | Sharing so many ideas you're not giving space for everyone else in the group to contribute | **Pull back:** Set a maximum number of ideas you're allowed to share in this interaction, aiming for one idea fewer than you're comfortable. |
| | Excited about an idea and you want to move forward on it now | **Pull back:** Write a note to yourself when you're eager to move forward with an idea (instead of pushing the group to jump to next steps). *you read that correctly—two pull-back techniques for Advance Listeners who often struggle to pull back. |

| | | |
|---|---|---|
| **Immerse** | Holding back on sharing your idea because you haven't thought it through yet | **Push ahead:** Let yourself off the hook with an opening clause like, "Here's the seed of an idea," and then share your idea anyway. |
| | Wanting to go into depth on an idea someone shared | **Pull back:** Write a note to yourself to follow up with that person if you want to know more (instead of going into deep discussion during the interaction). |
| **Discern** | Holding back on sharing your idea because you don't think it's good enough | **Push ahead:** Let yourself off the hook with an opening clause like, "Maybe someone can strengthen this," and then share your idea anyway. |
| | Critiquing each idea as it's shared | **Pull back:** Write the critiques down in your notes (instead of sharing them aloud or being mentally distracted by them during the interaction). |

New ideas help you and your organization keep up with trends, delight customers, own existing markets, enter new markets, and discover better ways of working. Interesting and innovative ideas often come from the seeds of individual contributions that grow when they're watered by the rest of the group's contributions. When you **push ahead** and **pull back** at the right times, you become an Adaptive Listener who moves the group toward a unique and unexpected future.

**Table 10.2. Adapt in Common Advance Situations**

| Advance as Interactions Conclude | Advance to Relay Information | Advance to Generate Ideas |
|---|---|---|
| • Check for next steps<br>• Confirm any actions | • Prepare to pass the baton<br>• Frame the follow-up<br>• Show your note-taking | • Push ahead<br>• Pull back |

## Adapt in Complex Advance Situations

Of course, your workday might be a lot easier if you could stick to Advance Listening in common situations, but that's not always the case. Some complex Advance Listening situations require forward momentum, too. Your peer might not directly ask for your help on a project, but you might recognize cues that they're out of time and have lost steam. Your customer might not blatantly ask for your advice, but their body language might tell you they're at an impasse about which product or service they should choose for their business-critical issue. Your direct report might claim they're on top of their busy workload, but you've been in their shoes, and you recognize the barrier even though they don't see it.

Two types of complex situations warrant Advance Listening:

- When the situation is urgent *and* the person speaking is overwhelmed
- When the stakes are high *and* you have expertise to share

You've likely had to listen in these situations before, but you might have missed cues that Advance Listening was needed. Cut yourself some slack because these Advance Listening situations aren't always easy to spot. You must hunt, gut-check, and consider the context before you can listen the way others need, whether they're aware of those needs or not.

### Advance When It's Urgent and They're Overwhelmed

When you know the situation is urgent *and* the person speaking is overwhelmed, it's time to Listen to Advance. Note, it's the existence of *both* conditions that make Advance Listening the best option in these situations. Urgency alone isn't enough. Many people are skilled at working under time pressure, so an urgency cue by itself doesn't necessarily signal the need for advice or action. These people can tackle urgent situations without needing help.

Similarly, if the person speaking feels overwhelmed but there's no urgency to the situation, that isn't enough to warrant Advance Listening. Instead, that situation might warrant a type of Discern Listening that helps the speaker find the right answer themselves (as you'll read in Chapter 12: Adapt to Discern). Or maybe the overwhelmed speaker needs the space to vent, so you'll give them Support Listening (as covered in Chapter 9). But when the situation is urgent *and* the speaker is overwhelmed, you'll want to Listen to Advance.

To confirm both conditions are present, you can look for cues. First, check if there are *urgency cues* based on the context the speaker is operating within. Urgency looks different across departments and organizations, but Table 10.3 offers potential urgent cues to consider.

**Table 10.3. Urgent Cues based on the Context**

| Urgent Cues | Urgent Examples |
|---|---|
| Fast-approaching deadline | A leader suddenly needs a deliverable by the end of the day. |
| | A client or customer meeting is happening in the next hour. |
| | The budget deadline is fast approaching. You'll have to "use it or lose it." |
| Major mistake or complication | A crucial application or webpage is down. |
| | A key customer is upset. |
| | An inappropriate social media post, email, or other communication went out. |
| Physical or psychological safety concern | A team member was mistreated. |
| | The product was delivered damaged or malfunctioned. |
| | An unregistered/unattended guest is in the building. |

Next, check if there are *overwhelmed cues* in the speaker's mannerisms. As with urgency cues, being overwhelmed looks different on different people. If you notice a departure from how the speaker normally behaves, and it aligns with the cues in Table 10.4, then it's reasonable to assume they're overwhelmed.

**Table 10.4. Overwhelmed Cues based on Speaker's Mannerisms**

| Overwhelmed Cues | Overwhelmed Examples |
|---|---|
| Unusual indecision | Excessive verbal fillers |
| | Long, unintentional pauses |
| | Uncharacteristically withdrawing during interactions |
| Noticeable fatigue | New dark circles under their eyes |
| | Drooping facial expressions |
| | More slouching than is typical |
| Excessive hurriedness | Speaking at a faster rate |
| | Flustered while looking for items or files |
| | More nodding than is typical |

Not all cues in both categories need to be present to justify Advance Listening. If you observe at least one urgent cue *and* at least one overwhelmed cue, Advance Listening is an empathetic move, even if the person doesn't verbally request it. Once you identify the presence of both cues, the best way to give the speaker what they need is to **consider ways to help them**, **make a specific offer**, and **reiterate the offer *once*** as needed.

You can practice looking for cues as you picture yourself in this situation:

You and a colleague are working together on a project. You both have the same roles and similar levels of experience. You've agreed to divide and conquer the workload. You'll do individual work throughout the week and come together for working sessions on Mondays, Wednesdays, and Fridays. So far, the work is going as planned. At this pace, the project will wrap up by its upcoming Friday deadline.

You join your colleague for a working session the Monday before the deadline. Now, all these working sessions include some Advance Listening because you're trying to move this project forward to get to the finish line. Sometimes you need Immerse Listening and Discern Listening, but your working sessions often skew toward Advance Listening.

At the same time, since you know all interactions require some level of Support Listening, you also need to consider how much support your colleague needs today. You enter the interaction prepared to observe your colleague's emotional state to determine whether they feel comfortable or uncomfortable. As you read in Chapter 9, their emotional state will let you know if Support Listening will be a nice-to-add or a need-to-add situation.

The session starts with the following exchange:

> **You:** (smiling and eager) Hi! I'm still working on my section from last week. What are you working on right now?
>
> **Colleague:** (slightly frowning, slouched posture) Hey. So, I *was* working on my section—the competitive analysis. But I haven't even looked at it today (heavy sigh). Sorry. Yesterday, a leader asked for my help with another project that's due on Thursday. I'm trying to juggle both, and I'm behind on our work. There's a lot going on right now.

As you listen to your colleague, you notice they seem withdrawn and never smile. They didn't even hint at a smile when they said, "Hey," and they usually smile throughout meetings with you. Then, instead of their normal, upright posture, they're slouched. As they tell you about their new project, you see them subtly shrug their shoulders a few times and shake their head from left to right. They even sigh in the middle of their sentences. Based on these observations, you determine your colleague is feeling uncomfortable. That means Support Listening is a need-to-add in this interaction so you can help your colleague get to a more comfortable place.

But you also notice that this situation calls for a different kind of Advance Listening than is common in these working sessions. There's now a sense of urgency to this situation (there's not one but two approaching deadlines this week), and your colleague is overwhelmed (they're displaying cues that show fatigue), so you need to Listen to Advance in a specific way.

First, you use Support Listening and validate your colleague's feelings:

> **You:** (mirroring your colleague's slouched posture, shrugged shoulders, and flat facial expression) Ugh, I'm sorry. That sounds stressful.

Then you **consider ways to help them**. You:

- Consider the *skills* required to help and whether you're capable of taking over.
- Consider whether you have *time* to help and if so, how much.

You recall that your colleague said they're working on a competitive analysis—you have the skills to take on that task because you've done it before. You also do a quick mental scan of your work calendar for the rest of the week and realize you easily have time to take over your colleague's portion of the project and manage your workload.

Since you have both the skills and the time, you can **make a specific offer.**

Note, making a specific offer does *not* mean asking the speaker, "Do you need help?" or, "What can I do to help you?" Here's why: Imagine you're about to host a dinner party after a long workday. Your partner enters the room and asks, "What can I do to help you?" A nice offer, right? But you know what would be even nicer? If they looked around the room, noticed what needed to be done, and made some suggestions for how they could help. "How about I set the table?" or, "Would you like me to set up a beverage station?" Now that's a specific offer that moves things forward and removes the burden of someone who's overwhelmed and in a time crunch.

Although you might have the best intention for asking others, "How can I help?" or something similar, this question might create more work for that person. By asking them to think about how you can help, you're burdening them with an additional task. Instead, notice what needs to be done, tell the other person specifically what you can do to help them, and then do it if they accept your offer.

> **You:** You know what? I have time this week. Let's cancel our Wednesday working session. You focus on the ask for Thursday, and I'll keep going on this project, including that competitive analysis. Once you're done, we'll use our Friday working session to take this project to the finish line.

You've clearly outlined what needs to be done and made a specific offer to your colleague about what you can do for them. You watch as your colleague takes a deep inhale and lets it out slowly, a sign they're starting to feel more comfortable.

They remain silent for a few seconds, processing what you just said. You have a pretty good guess what they're thinking because you've thought the same thing when someone else offered you help on a project: "Can I let them take this project over for me?" You decide to **reiterate the offer *once*.**

> **You:** It's no trouble, and I can take it on this week. You'd help me out if you could.

You want to respect your colleague's boundaries if they don't want to accept your offer. They could be declining for reasons you don't know about. Reiterating the offer *once* lets your colleague know that you mean it. Pressing them more than once could be seen as intrusive and aggressive.

In this situation, though, your colleague agrees. The two of you align on next steps. They leave the working session to tackle their other project while you keep this project moving forward.

Some Adaptive Listeners in training have asked, "What if I consider ways to help and discover I don't have the skills or time? What do I do then?" Here's how the exchange with your colleague could go if your quick mental scan of your work calendar revealed you are booked back-to-back for the rest of the week:

> **You:** You know what? Let's cancel this working session. You focus on whichever project makes the most sense for you. I'll keep working on my part, and we can see where we're at after you submit the other project on Thursday.
>
> **Colleague:** I'm just worried there won't be enough time.
>
> **You:** I know. But we won't know if you have enough time until you dive into that other project. Send me a note on Thursday after you submit it. We'll figure it out.
>
> **Colleague:** All right. Thanks. I'll get back to you soon.

If you don't have the time and/or skills to take on the burden yourself, consider other ways you can help them:

- Can you cancel this meeting to give the speaker time to focus?
- Do you know of another team member with the time and skills who can step in?
- Do you have the authority to change one of the deadlines or ask one of the leaders to change it?

If those options aren't available, the best way to be an Adaptive Listener is to offer Support Listening. Will that meet the speaker's needs? Maybe not. But at least you'll be empathetic to this person in this situation.

Of course, colleagues aren't the only people who might need Advance Listening when there's urgency and they're overwhelmed. Look for moments when you can Listen to Advance for your managers, direct reports, or customers to help them in complex situations. You can help them meet their needs if you **consider ways to help them**, **make a specific offer**, and **reiterate the offer *once*.**

## Advance When You Have Expertise and the Stakes are High

Not only will you Listen to Advance when the situation is urgent *and* the speaker is overwhelmed, but you'll also Listen to Advance when you have expertise *and* the stakes are high. Just like the previous complex situation, both cues must exist to warrant Advance Listening.

You likely have some expertise in your industry, company, or role. If you're early in your career, you'll develop that expertise over time. But just because you are (or will become) a smarty pants, it doesn't necessarily mean you should always offer advice or provide insights. If you try to move people, projects, and processes forward in every interaction, you may get a reputation as someone who doesn't trust others to make decisions. You might even come across as a micromanager or a know-it-all, especially if you frequently offer advice when no one asks.

But when the stakes are high, that's the time to use your expertise to engage in Advance Listening. You'll know the stakes are high if you determine that the speaker would likely lose something critical or fail if you withhold your expertise. High stakes include outcomes like reputational damage for the speaker or organization, potential harm to employees or customers, and a significant decline in business performance. High stakes can also mean losing out on a big win or stellar outcome if your expertise isn't considered. If these outcomes sound scary, that's the point. Something significant needs to be on the line for you to determine that the stakes are high.

Do an honest check-in with yourself and ask, "*If I withhold my expertise, will it lead to failure?*" If your answer is no, then maybe you just want to share your expertise to suit your own needs instead of the speaker's needs.

If you have expertise to share *and* the stakes are high, then you can meet the speaker's needs by **tactfully offering advice.** But you'll also want to make sure that you **invite them to decline** your offer. Even if the stakes are high, speakers can turn down your expertise.

Kelvin, a senior and tenured manager, experienced this kind of complex situation when interacting with his direct report, Jordan, during a routine weekly one-on-one meeting. The two have a healthy working relationship and their one-on-ones generally cover the same topics: Jordan updates Kelvin on his current projects, the two discuss any questions or concerns surrounding

Jordan's tasks, and they work on Jordan's career development goals. These are relatively casual and conversational meetings. But during a particular one-on-one, after Kelvin and Jordan exchange pleasantries, the following conversation happens:

> **Kelvin:** So, how's that latest project coming along?
>
> **Jordan:** I was going to bring that one up today!
>
> **Kelvin:** Oh yeah? What's going on?
>
> **Jordan**: To be honest, I'm a bit lost right now. When I read the brief I thought, "Okay, no problem," but then I started researching, and I realized there's a lot more information on this topic than I initially thought. So now I feel like I'm all over the place, and I don't really know where to start.

Now, as a manager, Kelvin has a lot of expertise to share. He's completed many projects like this while he was in Jordan's role. He knows all the steps to complete the project, how to read briefs, how to conduct research, how to start, and how to conclude. But having that expertise alone doesn't necessarily warrant Advance Listening. The stakes must also be high. To determine if that's the case, Kelvin does a quick check-in and asks himself, "*If I withhold my expertise, will Jordan or his project fail?*"

To answer this question, Kelvin considers the following: Jordan said, "I don't really know where to start." That concerns Kelvin because the project is being presented to senior leadership next week. While Kelvin isn't necessarily concerned that Jordan won't complete his assignment, he knows that this is the first time Jordan is presenting to senior leaders. If Jordan hasn't started it yet, the final project is unlikely to meet the leadership's standards.

In addition, Kelvin knows that Jordan wants to be a leader someday. Turning in a subpar project could damage his confidence and leave the leadership team with an unfavorable impression. Kelvin knows that once leadership forms a negative opinion about someone, they typically stick with it. Based on these conditions, Kelvin determines that the stakes are indeed high and his expertise will prevent Jordan from making a critical mistake. So, he decides to **tactfully offer advice.**

Giving advice tactfully means balancing warmth and strength in your words and delivery. Your goal is to avoid making the other person feel inadequate for being unable to move forward on their own.[46] Plus, it's possible that they don't realize how dire their situation might be—you don't want to make them feel more uncomfortable by alarming them. Bringing warmth to your words, facial expressions, tone, and body language will create a sense of collaboration. You're not giving them valuable insights because they're incompetent. Your offer to help them has nothing to do with your ego and everything to do with your desire to watch them succeed. A balance of warmth and strength lets the speaker know you're in this situation *with* them.

Using warmth is also a way of adding some nice-to-add Support Listening. You'll recall from Chapter 9 that all speakers require some support in every interaction. By tactfully offering advice, you're not only meeting the speaker's need for Advance Listening, you're also meeting their emotional need.

But being tactful doesn't mean you'll be *so* warm that you diminish the importance of your expertise. After all, this is a high-stakes situation. You want the other person to know that it's important they have a successful outcome. To make that clear, you need to convey your authority and confidence in the subject matter. The speaker must believe you're a trusted source. That means your words, facial expressions, tone, and body language must reflect that, too. The goal is to balance warmth with strength, as Kelvin did when he tactfully offered his advice to Jordan.

> **Kelvin:** (soft smile and measured volume and speaking rate) Jordan, how about this: given that the project is due soon, I can share my expertise if you're interested. I know how to read this brief, and I can help you get started if you'd like.

Notice that Kelvin incorporated two important phrases when he tactfully offered his advice: "If you're interested" and "If you'd like." By doing so, Kelvin let Jordan know that it's okay if he doesn't want his expertise. Some people might be afraid to admit they need your help to move something forward. Others might prefer to complete the work, fix problems, and complete tasks without guidance from others, and that's okay. To avoid putting people in an awkward or defensive position, you can do what Kelvin did in this situation and **invite them to decline** your offer.

Before you give them your expertise, allow them to bow out by saying, "It's okay to say no to my advice" or "You won't offend me if you prefer to go it alone." Let them know that you'll be there for them with your expertise if they change their minds.

Remember, while it's not always appropriate to offer your thoughts and opinions, if the stakes are high and you've got expertise to share, you can Listen to Advance and help the speaker move things forward. If you believe your expertise can help your leader, direct report, colleague, customer, or group avoid failure, you can **tactfully offer advice**. Just make sure you also offer the speaker an out with an **invite to decline**. By doing so, you'll build a reputation as a sort of superhero who offers expert thoughts and opinions—but only when someone's ready to be rescued from potential disaster.

**Table 10.5. Adapt in Complex Advance Situations**

| Advance When it's Urgent and They're Overwhelmed | Advance When it's High Stakes and You Have Expertise |
|---|---|
| • Consider ways you can help<br>• Make a specific offer to help<br>• Reiterate the offer *once* | • Tactfully offer advice<br>• Invite them to decline |

## Be Brave and Take the Leap

If Advance Listening is challenging for you in either common or complex situations, you can get into the right mindset with this mantra: "*I'm here to help this person or group move forward.*" Repeating the mantra can be particularly helpful if you default to a Support, Immerse, or Discern S.A.I.D. Listening Style. The mantra can prime you to listen and respond in a way that keeps the momentum going.

If you're anxious or apprehensive to try these techniques, trust that you've done the work to identify that this person will benefit from Advance Listening. Be brave and take the leap. Then, you'll be an Adaptive Listener working to listen the way your leaders, direct reports, peers, and customers need.

## Chapter 11

# Adapt to Immerse

Of all the S.A.I.D. Listening Goals, you might have thought, "Listen to Immerse just sounds like plain old listening to me." That's a reasonable reaction based on some people's definition of listening as paying attention. It even makes sense that one Adaptive Listener in training initially said, "Immerse Listening is the *only* goal that's actually listening." But that listener eventually learned, as you now know, that being skilled at Immerse Listening is only one part of being an Adaptive Listener.

When someone needs you to understand and remember the information they're sharing, you need to Listen to Immerse. In these situations, the speaker doesn't need you to move something forward (like with Advance Listening), they don't need you to evaluate or critique the information (like with Discern Listening), and they don't *only* need you to validate their emotions (like with Support Listening).

Of course, the prerequisite for Immerse Listening is paying attention, but that's true for all the listening goals. Still, if you only equate Immerse Listening with paying attention, you risk brushing it off as a type of listening that's easy or doesn't take much effort to get right.

But the truth is, many people struggle with Immerse Listening because it doesn't seem like there's much to *do* as a listener compared to the other styles. Even when listeners concede that understanding and remembering information is crucial for workplace success, Immerse Listening can feel passive, especially if the content is meant to entertain, like when you're listening to a guest speaker tell a personal story. It's why some listeners get distracted and tune out while Immerse Listening. Although distractions happen to everyone, if they occur repeatedly over time, you might become known as someone who doesn't listen.

Luckily, the techniques in this chapter will help you approach Immerse Listening as a goal-oriented activity across common and complex situations. Not only will building these skills help you become an Adaptive Listener who helps other people meet their goals, but it can also set you up for short- and long-term career success.

## Adapt in Common Immerse Situations

Common Immerse Listening situations at work can happen in group and one-on-one settings. You're often expected to listen when a speaker sets the context with information you don't need to put into action yet, when you're listening as part of a culture-building activity, and even when the information seems irrelevant to you.

When listening in a group, you probably know that multitasking or getting distracted while your colleagues and leaders talk isn't empathetic. But because you're human, you probably do it anyway. You know...just a quick scan of your email or wrapping up that task you almost finished before this meeting. It can be hard to stay focused on the content when you know you aren't expected to act on it or immediately respond to the person speaking to you. You're probably less likely to multitask when interacting with someone one-on-one, but you might still have trouble remembering the information the speaker shared with you.

The techniques in this section can help you stay present, remember the information, and potentially build stronger connections with your colleagues and customers during common Immerse Listening situations.

## Immerse During Context-Setting

Think about the last time you went through onboarding at a new organization or when you were joining a new department. You probably did a lot of listening. Sometimes you needed Advance Listening, like when you were given explicit instructions on how to set up your email or were told which forms required immediate signatures.

But other parts of your orientation didn't have immediate action, like when you listened to an overview of the employee resources or were told about the company's vision and mission. The goal was to give you context now so it wouldn't be new information when it came up later.

This type of context-setting is common at work, perhaps even more than you realize. Think of context-setting as gathering the information you need to fully understand a topic. You might not need to use or act on that information immediately, but you might need to do so later.

For example, your organization's Learning and Development department (L&D) might alert you to a training they'll eventually want you to take, but they want you to have the context now, so you're not surprised later. The IT department might alert you about a systems update that they don't expect to interrupt your workday, but giving context means you won't panic if you get the spinning wheel of death when that update occurs (if you know, you know). A new customer might share details about their current problem and ways they've already tried to fix it. That way, you have the context to fully understand what they've been going through.

Even when there's no task to complete (yet), you can use one or all four Immerse Listening techniques: **take keyword notes, paraphrase the information, attach an emotion,** and **visualize the information.** These techniques can increase the likelihood you'll remember the information. If you don't make the extra effort while listening, it could cost you, as you'll see in this example with Pam and her L&D leader:

Pam is listening to a presentation by her company's L&D department. As the presentation concludes, the L&D leader makes one final announcement.

> **L&D leader:** Oh! I don't want to leave this out! I wanted to let you know that we'll ask everyone to complete an Unconscious Bias Training next quarter that we think will help. We're still putting it all together, so you have nothing to do just yet. You'll get a notification when the training is ready for you, and we'll be sure to give you enough time to complete the training within your normal workflow. That's all for now!

Once Pam's L&D leader said, "There's nothing for you to do yet," Pam decided, "Okay. I'll just keep my eyes on the presenter, smile, and nod to give them nice-to-add Support Listening." But by only Support Listening, Pam made no real effort to retain the information. She heard it. She even smiled and nodded. But it basically went in one ear and out the other.

Next quarter, when Pam receives a notification that says, "You have one outstanding training to complete," she thinks, "What's this?" She decides to reach out to her manager to figure it out.

> **Pam:** I wanted to check in about this training notification from L&D. Do you know what this is about?
>
> **Manager:** Yeah, this was the training L&D mentioned last quarter. We all need to complete it. Let me or L&D know if you have any questions.
>
> **Pam:** Got it! Thanks.

Now, it was easy enough for Pam to ask her manager for clarification. It didn't seem like a big deal, and Pam immediately added the training to her to-do list. But whether she meant to or not, she revealed that she wasn't listening in the right way during last month's meeting.

Pam and her manager were in the same company meeting, yet Pam didn't recall the information the L&D leader shared. Now, it's not that Pam can't *ever* ask others for a reminder. In fact, an organization that discourages people from reaching out to others might inspire an unhealthy culture of fear.[47] But Pam will want to make sure this doesn't become a pattern of behavior. If it does, her manager might be left with the impression that Pam's the type of person who doesn't listen. Her manager might wonder, "If Pam can't pay attention or remember in these situations, what other situations might she struggle with?" Long term, that could have more serious consequences for Pam. Her repeated lack of attention could lead to the perception that she's uncommitted or unprofessional.

To ensure she remembered that training, Pam could have tried to **take keyword notes.** In context-setting situations, you can jot down a few keywords to help you remember the information. Keyword note-taking means listening for and then writing down proper nouns like people, places, departments, products/services, and events. You can also tune into any references to time like new/old, now/later, quick/slow, and dates/deadlines.

Writing keywords can trigger memory recall. For example, if a friend tells you a lengthy story about their trip to Hawaii, and you want to remember some of the highlights for *your* upcoming Hawaiian vacation (lucky you), you might write the name of the specific hotel they stayed in and highly recommended. You might also write a few restaurants, including the shaved ice spot they loved and the fish taco truck they discovered on a side street. You might not, however, write all the details about their surf lesson mishap or the fact that it rained half the time. Taking keyword notes means writing only the things you want to or need to remember later.

Then, get into the habit of reviewing your notes the same day or at the start of the next day. When you review your notes soon after you take them, you increase the odds you'll remember the information.[48]

If you're thinking, "Even if I write keywords and review them after, I'd probably forget," then this keyword note-taking technique will allow you to check your notes before asking someone else to remind you. If Pam had written

"Unconscious Bias Training" in her notes, she might have saved herself the trouble of asking her manager about the training.

A second technique that can help you remember context-setting information is to **paraphrase the information**. To paraphrase, you restate what the speaker said but put it in your own words. Paraphrasing doesn't only mean verbalizing the rephrased information aloud, which could be intrusive or inappropriate in some situations. Instead, you can mentally paraphrase. Try reframing the information, or you could even jot down paraphrased notes for your reference.

In Pam's case, she could have paraphrased to herself with a mental note like, "The Unconscious Bias Training is coming in two months. Got it!" Paraphrasing requires more cognitive effort than merely repeating the same information. The act of rephrasing gives your brain a chance to encode the information differently. That extra work can pay off. The more cognitive effort you put into a task, the more likely you are to remember the information.[49]

A third technique to remember context-setting information is to **attach an emotion** to it.[50] Studies in psychology and neuroscience suggest emotion and memory are closely tied. We remember emotional events more vividly and accurately, and we even remember them longer than non-emotional events. Think about a moment in your career that stands out to you. There's a good chance a strong emotional reaction accompanied that experience. You felt overjoyed when you got a promotion. You felt immense pride when you successfully finished a project. You felt rage when someone else's carelessness undid your progress. You felt intense guilt about the way you handled a complicated situation. You might not remember all the details or nuances of the experience, but because it was connected to an emotion, you're more likely to remember it happened.[51]

To increase the likelihood you'll retain what's being shared with you, start by asking yourself, "How do I *feel* about this information?" Put a label on your emotion. It doesn't have to be an emotion with a positive association, either. For example, you might feel annoyed or irritated when your senior leader tells you about an external networking event that they'd like you to attend two months from now, requiring some weekend travel. Simply attaching those emotions of annoyed or irritated might help you recall the details of that event.

Although Pam might not have felt an intense emotional reaction to the L&D leader's announcement about an upcoming training, if she dug deeper, she might have attached an emotion to the information. She could have thought about these emotions to herself, written her reactions in her notes, or even commented to a colleague after the presentation was over:

- "Unconscious Bias Training sounds different. I'm *excited* to learn more about it."
- "Don't *freak out* when that Unconscious Bias Training hits my inbox next quarter. The L&D leader said I'd be given enough time to complete it."
- "I'm *proud* of the steps the L&D team is taking with this training to make sure our biases aren't getting in our way of doing great work."

When you attach an emotion to the information, you don't have to go overboard. You don't have to pretend what you're listening to is thrilling or devastating if you don't genuinely feel that way. But by trying to find an emotional connection to the information, it's more likely you'll remember it.

A final technique that may help you remember context-setting information is visualization. **Visualizing the information** involves creating mental images related to the content, which can significantly enhance recall. Words can go in one ear and out the other, but studies have found that people are more likely to remember information when they use visual thinking.[52]

An effective way to visualize information is to close your eyes and picture the scene with as much detail as possible. For example, Pam could have thought visually about the information in the following ways:

- Envisioned herself completing the training next quarter
- Imagined the training notification hitting her inbox
- Pictured the certificate she'd be awarded after she finished the training

In context-setting situations, visualizations like these might not help you remember all the details, but they can give you a baseline. That way, you can avoid relearning the same context all over again or relying on someone else to get you up to speed.

Given that it's common for managers, leaders, colleagues, and customers to give you context-setting information long before you need to act on it, it's worth trying these techniques: **take keyword notes, paraphrase the information, attach an emotion,** and **visualize the information.**

When you find the ones that work best for you, you'll remember the appropriate context and show up as a reliable and efficient contributor.

## Immerse During Culture-Building

It might surprise you, but culture-building is another common Immerse Listening situation. Culture-building refers to activities and practices reinforcing a shared set of values, goals, and behaviors among team members. When you hear "culture-building," you might think of connection, collaboration, and team events, all of which can give you warm and fuzzy feelings. You might therefore assume that Support Listening is the best option during culture-building situations. Of course, all situations require some level of Support Listening, but the primary goal in these culture-building situations is usually Immerse Listening. To illustrate why, here's a glimpse of what Maegan and Nicole's team does during their weekly team syncs:

If you were in the Monday gathering for Duarte's Communication Services department, you'd find a fully remote team of writers, strategists, and coaches who span three time zones and are often onsite with clients around the world. You'd listen to twenty-five minutes of reviews about the shows or podcasts they just binged, rundowns of what's currently in their virtual shopping carts, retellings of the precarious comments from their family members, replays of adorable kid videos, and recaps of how they made fools of themselves over the weekend.

If you're worried about the productivity in this team sync, don't be. Other meetings are scheduled throughout the week with agendas and action items. But this gathering is about culture-building (notice how it's called a "sync" and not a "meeting"). Given the importance of culture-building for remote teams,[53] Duarte's Monday sync is curated so everyone knows what to expect when they join; everyone knows to show up and Listen to Immerse (and include Support Listening as needed).

Culture-building can happen in formally curated moments, like in Duarte's team sync. It can also happen while listening to a guest speaker or participating in a group activity at an event, a kickoff, a conference, or an offsite.[54] But culture-building can also happen in spontaneous moments, like having lunch with your team in the break room or bumping into your colleague at a coffee shop on the way into the office. (Yes, culture-building can happen one-on-one, not only in groups.)

Some people struggle in these culture-building situations. Focusing on understanding and remembering for the sake of entertainment might feel like a waste of time. Maybe you show up to listen to a guest speaker, and instead of trying to enjoy the information they're presenting, you keep judging and critiquing it (like a Discern Listener). Or you get in a breakout group for a team activity, and you're preoccupied with getting the group to the finish line (like an Advance Listener). Or you're so focused on how a speaker or team member feels, you can't absorb the information (like a Support Listener). If you struggle with culture-building situations, you can **lean into curiosity**, **ask probing questions**, and **land a callback**.

Consider this example of Riley, a project manager at a tech firm. Riley has a meeting with three colleagues to review potential options for a project they're collaborating on and then select which option the group will take forward. Riley is the first person to join the meeting, quickly followed by another colleague. Then, they wait. Thirty seconds. Sixty seconds. The minutes keep ticking.

They can't start reviewing potential options until the other two colleagues arrive, so Riley has a choice: they can sit in awkward silence and stare at the colleague who arrived on time, agree to tackle other items on their respective to-do lists while they wait, or maybe, Riley can **lean into curiosity** and take advantage of this spontaneous culture-building situation.

Leaning into curiosity means taking an active interest in the other person's world. It's often easier to be curious about topics you already have an interest in, like when you're listening to a guest speaker giving insights about your favorite hobby. But research has also found that you're more likely to be curious if you perceive the information you're listening to as valuable.[55]

Think of "leaning into curiosity" as nurturing a genuine interest in understanding and learning from others. By doing this while you Listen to Immerse, you're contributing to a culture that values inclusivity, fosters empathy, and drives engagement. Companies with these cultures are more likely to meet their goals and have happier employees. When employees are happy, they stay at their organizations, preventing high turnover costs and avoiding negative perceptions that can deter potential hires.[56]

You can lean into curiosity about your colleague's day, a project you know they're working on, a timely world event, or even something you notice on their desk or in their virtual background. Riley opts for a simple topic choice—this colleague's workload—while waiting for other colleagues to join the meeting:

> **Riley:** How's the rest of your day looking?
>
> **Colleague:** Oh, ya know, same old.

No one said Riley's colleague was a stellar conversationalist. That's why Riley adds the second technique: **ask probing questions**. You can look for moments where you might probe with follow-up questions to invite the speaker to say more, instead of engaging in forced small talk. If you're listening in an audience, you might think about potential probing questions you *could* ask once the speaker is done or in a follow-up email or chat.

During this exchange, Riley mixes probing questions with nice-to-add Support Listening to mirror the emotional reaction their colleague is sharing (a technique covered in Chapter 9).

> **Riley:** So, are we talking slow, manageable, or out of control?
>
> **Colleague:** (calmly) It's pretty manageable right now.
>
> **Riley:** What else is on your plate besides this project?

> **Colleague:** (smiling) I'm working on another project with the two people we're waiting for.
>
> **Riley:** Ah, so you probably know them better than I do.
>
> **Colleague:** (nodding emphatically and smiling) Oh yeah. Between this project and the other one, we see each other more than we see our spouses.
>
> **Riley:** (chuckling) I know how that goes! What's your spouse up to when you're stuck with us all day?
>
> **Colleague:** (raising eyebrows and vocal pitch) They're at home with the kids.
>
> **Riley:** (playfully) I'm guessing your spouse's days fall closer to the "out of control" side of the spectrum.
>
> **Colleague:** (chuckling) Sounds like you've met my kids. There's some serious wrangling that goes on.
>
> **Riley:** (smiling) How many and what ages?
>
> **Colleague:** We have—

Just then, the two other colleagues join the meeting. It's time to get down to business. But first, Riley invites the new arrivals into the conversation:

> **Riley:** (smiling) Hi there, you two! I just learned that the three of you are working on another project and are basically each other's surrogate spouses.
>
> **New arrival:** You've got that right!
>
> **Riley:** We haven't started reviewing the options for the project yet, but I'm ready to dive in when you are.

The group spends the rest of the meeting reviewing the options and finalizing their decisions. Before the end of the meeting, Riley decides to use the final technique for culture-building situations: **land a callback.**

In comedy, a callback is a humorous reference to something that happened earlier, delivered in a clever way. Television shows like *Seinfeld* ("Believe it or not, George isn't at home"),[57] *Arrested Development* ("I've made a huge mistake"),[58] *Martin* ("Damn, Gina"),[59] and *How I Met Your Mother* ("Slap bet")[60] successfully used callbacks to build comedic continuity for the audience.

In Immerse Listening, a callback refers to something that was said earlier, but it may or may not be humorous (in fact, if you're not a funny person, don't force it). The point of a callback in this situation is to show the other person that you understand and remember something about them. You're using the callback to reinforce that culture-building is a good use of everyone's time. But hey! If your callback happens to be funny...kudos!

Riley offers a kind-hearted callback as the meeting ends:

> **Colleague:** All right, everyone, decision made. I'll type up these notes and send them out later today.
>
> **Riley:** Sounds good! (smiling) And I'll send positive, kid-wrangling vibes to you this weekend.

Even though the group didn't have an in-depth conversation about their kids, it was still a valuable moment. Plus, Riley learned something new, which could be a building block for future conversations. If they hadn't used these techniques, Riley would have missed out on a key relationship-building opportunity. If they were a listener who avoided these opportunities over time, they might even get a reputation for being an unfriendly or disinterested colleague.

Whether it's a micro-moment with a colleague or customer, or a special occasion where the goal is obvious, you can actively participate in culture-building through Immerse Listening. Not only will it bring value to your organization when you **lean into curiosity**, **ask probing questions**, and **land a callback**, but it could also help you build strong connections that foster your long-term career goals.

## Immerse When the Information Seems Irrelevant

Perhaps the hardest common Immerse Listening situation is when you're listening to information that doesn't seem relevant to you or your role. Do a quick scan: How many meetings or presentations do you attend each week where leaders or colleagues share information that doesn't impact your day-to-day activities or priorities? Two a week? Five a week? More than you want to count?

In Chapter 7, you read how your listening L.E.N.S. could become unfocused if the news isn't relevant to you. If you're still wondering, "Do I really need to listen if the information isn't relevant to me?" you're not alone. The Discern and Advance Listeners who wrote this book initially had the same struggle. But the answer is a resounding "Yes!" When you Listen to Immerse, you show leaders and colleagues that you respect them and the work they put into their goals, initiatives, or projects. Not only do you make them feel good, but you set the foundation for a more trusting workplace relationship.[61]

Unfortunately, professionals aren't always trained to deliver relevant messages across all settings. That means you're left with three choices as a listener: You can 1) get up and leave the interaction, which will likely be seen as rude and inappropriate. You can 2) pretend like you're listening and start multitasking, which is also rude and could get you into trouble if you miss a relevant piece of information that pops up. Or you can 3) **take verbatim notes** and **lean into curiosity,** which will help you build a reputation for being a strong listener and trusted partner.

Consider this example of Edwin, a marketing associate, to better illustrate these points:

Edwin attends a quarterly virtual meeting where various division leaders give updates on progress and new goals. When the VP of marketing comes off mute and starts her presentation, Edwin is alert. He's primed for Advance Listening because his VP often shares updates that directly impact Edwin's job. He's got his camera on and a document open on his computer to show his note-taking (a technique covered in Chapter 10).

Sure enough, the VP of marketing mentions potential changes to the company's social media campaign, which is the project Edwin is working on. He makes a note to ask his manager how these changes might impact his current workflow.

Once the VP of marketing is done speaking, it's time for the VP of engineering to present. Edwin is not an engineer. In fact, he doesn't know the ins and outs of what the engineering division does. He's tempted to turn off his camera and peek at his unread email backlog—but he stops himself. Instead, he keeps his document open to **take verbatim notes** while this leader is speaking.

These notes look different than the notes Edwin just took while the VP of marketing was talking because this time, he's taking notes for a different reason. Just a few moments ago, Edwin kept track of potential actions or next steps that might become his responsibility. Therefore, he only wrote down key actions and potential questions about how to move forward with this information.

However, now that the VP of engineering is talking, Edwin is taking notes as a technique to help him stay focused on the content. It's unlikely that Edwin will personally need this information in the future, and it's not crucial that he knows what to do with the information next (like he would with Advance Listening). He probably doesn't even need to remember this information. If he did, he might decide to take hand-written notes that included summaries, paraphrasing, or key takeaways to increase his retention.[62]

But in this situation, Edwin is typing nearly every word the VP of engineering says simply to help him stay alert.[63] These notes, which almost look like an AI-generated transcript, help him avoid distractions and Listen to Immerse. Plus, he's keeping his camera on while the VP of engineering is talking so he can include nice-to-add Support Listening via a relaxed facial expression and nodding to help this leader feel valuable.

The second technique that can improve your Immerse Listening when the information seems irrelevant is to **lean into curiosity.** Although this technique is also helpful during culture-building opportunities, you'll approach it differently in this situation. Instead of listening with the certainty that the information is irrelevant, you can remain curious about the *potential* for the information to be relevant.

- *What if* you used Immerse Listening to learn more about how other groups or departments approached their work? You might gain a perspective you could apply to your work.
- *What if* you used Immerse Listening to learn why another group or department fell short of their goal? You might gain insights as to how you could avoid a similar misstep in the future.
- *What if* you used Immerse Listening to learn why another group or department exceeded their goal? You might gain a tactic you could deploy to achieve your goals.
- *What if* you used Immerse Listening to learn more about how other groups or departments are working cross-functionally? You might gain a broader picture of how your organization works as a system, which could benefit you no matter where your career takes you.

If you would never dream of tuning out or multitasking while someone was sharing seemingly irrelevant information with you, then you are a unicorn who can bask in these authors' praise and admiration. But for the rest of us who struggle to stay connected in these situations, **taking verbatim notes** and **leaning into curiosity** can improve your Immerse Listening skills.

**Table 11.1. Adapt in Common Immerse Situations**

| Immerse During Context-setting | Immerse During Culture-building | Immerse When Info Seems Irrelevant |
|---|---|---|
| • Take keyword notes<br>• Paraphrase the information<br>• Attach an emotion<br>• Visualize the information | • Lean into curiosity<br>• Ask probing questions<br>• Land a callback | • Take verbatim notes<br>• Lean into curiosity |

## Adapt in Complex Immerse Situations

Outside of situations where Immerse Listening is common, there are complex situations where it can be harder to figure out that you need to Listen to Immerse. These situations are further complicated because even when people realize that Immerse Listening is warranted, many haven't been trained to listen and respond correctly. There are two complex Immerse Listening situations where you can use techniques to help the speaker and yourself: when someone needs to talk out an idea and when someone needs to tell you bad news.

### Immerse When They Need to Talk It Out

The first complex Immerse Listening situation is when the person speaking needs to talk out an idea because the thoughts swimming in their brain aren't fully formed yet. Some people believe that talking out loud isn't productive. You may have heard these famous quotes, or something similar:

> "Listen more than you talk. Nobody learned anything by hearing themselves speak."
>
> —***Richard Branson***

> "I never learned anything while I was talking."
>
> —***Larry King***

Although these quotes offer a well-meaning attempt at telling people to listen more, it's simply untrue to say no one learns by speaking. Sometimes, people need space to think and talk aloud. They need to take a stab at making sense of the jumbled thoughts in their head, and they want to do that in front of someone else, so they have an accountability partner. That's where Immerse Listening comes in.

Sometimes a colleague or customer will tell you they need the floor to verbally sift through their ideas. They might say, "I need to talk this out for a moment," or "Let me think about this out loud." But of course, speakers aren't always that direct. It's possible that they won't explicitly tell you they need to verbalize their thoughts so they can land on an idea. They might not even know that's what they need.

Instead, you can look for cues in their voice and body language that let you know they need your Immerse Listening. Then, to help them get to their idea, you'll **take verbatim notes**, **read your notes back to them** to help them get clarification on what they said, and **ask clarifying questions**, not only to ensure *you* understand and retain the information, but more importantly, to help the speaker land on their idea faster.

Now, Adaptive Listeners in training sometimes ask, "How do I know this rambling person doesn't need Advance Listening?" In Chapter 10 you read that Advance Listening is only warranted in complex situations when there's urgency *and* the speaker is overwhelmed or when the stakes are high *and* you have expertise to share. But Immerse Listening is the right choice when you know the speaker isn't in a rush to find the idea and doesn't appear excessively overwhelmed.

Sunil, an instructional designer, is meeting with Maria, a training facilitator. Sunil creates professional development and learning content for their organization internally, while Maria is responsible for delivering those trainings to various teams.

The two are tasked with developing and delivering a new training course. They have plenty of time to complete it—these two are pros, and the training isn't due for another six months. Sunil and Maria are in a working session where the conversation flows evenly between them. When it's Sunil's turn to respond, his long pause abruptly halts the conversation.

This pause gives Maria a moment to look for cues that tell her how to adapt to the right kind of listening so Sunil gets what he needs in this moment. Does he need Support Listening to encourage him to continue speaking? Does he need Advance Listening to generate new ideas? Does he need Discern Listening to help him evaluate his existing ideas? Maria silently observes Sunil's mannerisms while he begins to speak again:

> **Sunil:** (looking down at the floor while he paces) What if we...no, that won't work. Okay, what about if we did this: switch module 1 with module 2? But maybe this part of the course could go—(gets quiet) where could it go—toward the beginning?... But then (starts looking around the room) maybe swi—Okay, maybe a switch to this middle part. Hmm, okay, if we did that, I guess this exerci—we could go here instead of here...

Sunil is giving several cues with his voice and body that let Maria know he needs to talk out an idea. When it's time to Listen to Immerse in these situations, you can look for similar verbal and nonverbal cues like the ones listed in Table 11.2. Of course, this list isn't exhaustive, and these cues might look different from person to person.

### Table 11.2. Cues a Speaker Needs to Talk It Out

| Verbal Cues | Nonverbal Cues |
|---|---|
| Uses fragmented words and phrases | Paces the floor[64] |
| Starts framing statements as questions under their breath | Looks around their space as if searching for ideas |
| Trails off at the end of sentences | Shakes their head and shrugs shoulders in indecision |

After Marie notices these cues, she grabs her pen and notepad to **take verbatim notes**, capturing everything Sunil is saying, not just what she *perceives* to be important. After all, neither of them knows which thoughts will be worth keeping.

Unlike the detailed notes you'd jot down when the information is for your own memory and recall, when someone needs to talk out an idea, these exhaustive records aren't for you—they're for the speaker. Sometimes when speakers are talking through an idea out loud, they land on the solution but then quickly forget that smart thing they just said (sort of like they blacked out even though they were the one talking).

Now, taking verbatim notes might not be as easy in these complex situations as it is in the more common Immerse Listening situations. When speakers are rambling, it can be difficult to keep up with their train of thoughts. But you never know what useful insights might surface amongst the sentence fragments you document, so do your best to capture as much as you can.

As Maria starts to document Sunil's thoughts, he continues...

> **Sunil:** (still pacing around the room) Soooo, if we couple this module with this new exercise, it will give us space to put this other activity in the third modu—Oh (gets quiet) but do we have to move this breakout session? Would the flow even make sense...

Sunil finally stops talking out his idea and reestablishes eye contact with Maria. It's time for Maria to help Sunil process what he just said by **reading her notes back to him.** She knows that doing so will help Sunil get clarification on what he said.

> **Maria:** Okay, Sunil. I'm gonna read my notes back to you so you know exactly what you said. Then we can unpack it together. You said, "What if we switched module 1 with module 2. And maybe this part of the course could go toward the beginning...and then perhaps the beginning could be switched to this middle part." Then you said, "I guess this exercise could go here instead of here," and then you said you wanted to "couple this module with this new exercise, so it gives us space to put this other activity in the third module." If we did that you questioned if we'd have to move the breakout session for the flow to make sense. That's everything I captured.
>
> **Sunil:** Thanks for writing all of that down! I didn't even realize what I was saying while I was rambling. Ha!

Now that Maria has read her notes to Sunil, she's ready to **ask clarifying questions,** not only to ensure *she* understands and retains the information, but more importantly to guide Sunil toward his idea faster.

Clarifying questions are different from probing questions. Whereas probing questions are meant to gather more information, clarifying questions are meant to ensure the listener understood the information. When a speaker needs to talk out an idea, they don't usually leave the listener wanting more information—they've given them *plenty* of info! What the speaker needs in that moment are questions that will help them uncover their idea amidst the sea of words. Clarifying questions are the best way to do that.

> **Maria:** (smiles and adds a nice-to-add Support Listening comment) No worries! I ramble all the time and it's perfectly understandable while you're trying to think out your ideas. But I do have some clarifying questions about that rambling!
>
> **Sunil:** I bet you have questions after all that mess! Go for it...
>
> **Maria:** So, if we put module 2 first, instead of module 1, then the planned exercises are scaffolded better for the learners. Is that right?
>
> **Sunil:** Yes! That's precisely what I'm thinking.
>
> **Maria:** (checks her verbatim notes) Okay, and then if we take the introduction and move it after module 2, that will help the flow, too?
>
> **Sunil:** I think so, yes.
>
> **Maria:** Okay, and then, I'm not sure I know what you meant when you said you wanted to move that final exercise? Can you talk a little more about what you were thinking there...

**Taking verbatim notes, reading those notes back to the speaker**, and **asking clarifying questions** are valuable strategies when your colleague, direct report, leader, or customer needs to talk out an idea. You can give them the space to think aloud without interruption, judgment, or excessive encouragement, and then be their accountability partner by helping them uncover the smart thoughts amongst the fragments.

## Immerse During Bad News

There's a second complex Immerse Situation you should be aware of, and, well, it's not fun. But it's going to happen. Someone will give you bad news at work—news that might have negative consequences for you and your role. Your organization might not hit their goals, or they might need to cut back on perks and benefits you've come to expect, or they might need to lay off employees in another department, creating more work for you. Someone on your team might be under-delivering, or a high performer might decide to leave your organization. You might not get the promotion you expected. A marquee customer might decide to end their relationship with you. Or perhaps worst of all, you might be part of furloughs or layoffs.

When you receive bad news, there's a good chance you'll experience an uncomfortable emotion. If the news is about the organization, you might worry about its position in the market. You might be concerned about the company's long-term potential and wonder if you should continue investing your time and talent there. If the news involves a colleague or a team you work with closely, you might feel sad for them or uncertain about how the news will impact your working relationship. If the bad news directly affects you, you might experience sadness or anger.

You'll recall in Chapter 9 that people bring their emotions to work. That chapter focused on the emotions of the person speaking to you and how you can validate them to make them feel more comfortable. But your emotions matter, too! You can feel nervous, anxious, sad, or angry, especially when you receive bad news at work. But if these emotions are strong enough, they can impact your ability to Listen to Immerse.[65] And Immerse Listening is exactly what you need to do when receiving bad news. Remember, Immerse Listening is about focusing on understanding and absorbing the information presented to you. In these situations, you still need to understand and absorb bad news, despite how you feel about it.

In these complex situations, Immerse Listening techniques are less about *how* to listen and more about attaining a comfortable emotional state. This adjustment will allow you to concentrate and truly absorb the information. Only then will you be able to Listen to Immerse and receive the bad news.

You'll know your emotions are too high for Immerse Listening if you do a self-scan and uncover one or more of the following:

- Clenched fists, a tight jaw, or other muscle tension
- A fast heart rate
- Feeling flushed in your face, neck, or chest
- Holding back tears
- Shortness of breath
- A quivering or shaky voice
- Your mind is racing

If your emotional reaction is manifesting in one of these ways, you can use the following techniques to emotionally prepare yourself for Immerse Listening: **use emotional self-talk, find your calm,** and **ask for a moment to process** the information.

**Using emotional self-talk** means acknowledging and labeling your emotions, rather than ignoring them. Say, "I'm feeling upset about this news," or "This information feels disappointing." Then pair that acknowledgment with a pep talk. Tell yourself you're perfectly capable of putting your feelings aside...for now. Remind yourself, "It's okay to feel these emotions, but I need to postpone my reaction for a later time, so I can be present with the information being shared with me."

Now, self-talk doesn't work for everyone. Instead, you may be able to **find your calm** by making changes to your body. Try deep breaths. Even in a one-on-one meeting, breathing deeply can happen slowly and steadily without drawing attention to yourself. Inhaling slowly through your nose and exhaling slowly out of your mouth can decrease your heart rate and blood pressure.[66] After a few rounds, you're more likely to calm down and be better prepared for Immerse Listening.

You could also try tapping into the brain-body connection. In her popular TED talk and book, Amy Cuddy unpacks how body postures can trigger psychological changes.[67] Her work popularized "power poses," which are body poses that convey power, confidence, and openness. She found that if you held a power pose for two minutes, such as standing with your legs apart and your hands on your hips like Wonder Woman, you could feel more confident. As executive communication coaches, the authors of this book have recommended power poses to thousands of nervous speakers.

If a full-on power pose sounds like an awkward choice to make in the middle of receiving bad news, try one of these other options:

- **Upward-facing hands:** If your body scan uncovered muscle tension in your hands, try unclenching your fists and facing your palms upward. In yoga, a palms-up hand posture signals openness and willingness.[68] When you place your palms on your lap facing upward, you're signaling to your brain that you're ready to receive the information being presented.

  Dr. Marsha Linehan calls this technique "willing hands" because it can help you do something your brain might not be willing to do—like be willing to receive bad news. Lineman is the creator of Dialectical Behavior Therapy (DBT), a type of talk therapy for people who experience emotions intensely.[69] Linehan says the willing hands technique is particularly helpful in reducing anger or frustration.[70] If you're standing, drop your hands to your sides with your palms facing frontward for the same effect.

- **A half-smile:** Another DBT technique, the half-smile, is a subtle way to calm uncomfortable emotions. This doesn't mean using a big fake smile. In fact, smiling while receiving bad news would be strange, and might come across as inappropriate, even diabolical. Instead, upturn your lips slightly and relax your jaw. When you frown or scowl while receiving bad news, it encourages your brain to feel uncomfortable emotions.[71] But if you use a half-smile, you tell your brain, "It's okay. You're in a neutral, safe space."

By changing your body, you can change your mindset, too. One or all of these activities is bound to help you get back to a more manageable emotional state, better preparing you to Listen to Immerse. The best part about these techniques is that they can be done subtly when you're receiving bad news in front of others.

If you're experiencing high emotions, even after trying techniques like emotional self-talk or attempting to find your calm, remember that it's okay to **ask for a moment to process** the information. When you recognize that your emotions are inhibiting you from receiving bad news, despite trying mental and physical techniques, let the speaker know that you need time before you can fully absorb and respond to what they've said. In person, you might leave the room for a moment. If you're in a virtual meeting, you might choose to tell the speaker you need to turn your camera off for a minute. During that private time, you might try some of the calming techniques previously mentioned. Or you might give yourself permission to cry, talk to yourself aloud, let out a muffled scream, or throw a couple of jabs into a pillow (things you might not feel comfortable doing in front of others).

Be honest with the person delivering this bad news. Admitting that you're having trouble processing everything they're telling you right now can help both of you navigate the conversation more effectively. Ask them to reschedule the rest of the meeting for a later day or time when you've had a chance to think about what they've said. After you've processed on your own, you'll likely be more emotionally prepared to ask follow-up questions or gather more information.

But your emotions aren't the only ones that matter when receiving bad news. The person delivering the bad news still has emotional needs. In these complex situations, Adaptive Listeners know they must also consider the speaker's feelings. That's not easy to do when someone is delivering bad news to you. But, while it might be challenging to offer Support Listening in these situations, doing so can also serve as a form of emotional regulation for you, the listener. Research shows when you offer empathy to others, you feel better yourself.[72]

Maegan had to check her emotional response when a complex situation arose with a product logistics manager at Duarte. Maegan spent years developing a product and was eager for its upcoming launch. Finally, she'd share the product with the world and celebrate. The logistics manager pinged Maegan via internal chat and asked if they could meet virtually. They had the following exchange over video:

> **Logistics manager**: (slumping shoulders, drooping face, quiet and slow voice) Maegan, I've got some bad news to share.
>
> **Maegan**: Uh-oh (takes a deep inhale and exhales). Okay, lay it on me.
>
> **Logistics manager**: I'm afraid we have to push back the date of your product release. I know how hard you've been working on this, and I'm sure this news is hard to hear. We want to make sure we get this launch right, and we can't do that while juggling so many other priorities. I'm sorry.
>
> **Maegan**: It must have been hard for you to tell me about this. If I were you, I wouldn't have wanted to give me that news.
>
> **Logistics manager**: (posture straightens, facial expression changes to relief, louder voice) Oh my gosh! I *did not* want to tell you!
>
> **Maegan:** (silently nodding while looking away from the screen) Okay (pause). Of course I don't like this (pause). But tell me the details anyway.

Before co-creating *Adaptive Listening*, Maegan admits that she might have let her emotions take over in this situation. She might have felt anger or rage, and that could have shown up in her facial expressions, volume, or even an unkind word or two about the circumstances that led to this decision.

Lucky for Maegan (and the logistics manager), this interaction happened while Maegan and Nicole were *immersed* in developing the Immerse Listening concepts and techniques. So, this time Maegan knew how powerful it could be if she offered nice-to-add Support Listening first while she worked to find her calm. Most people don't like delivering bad news. Not only did Support

Listening help the logistics manager, but it also helped Maegan listen to this bad news and retain the necessary details.

When it comes to receiving bad news, remember that preparing yourself emotionally is key, especially because Listening to Immerse involves focusing on understanding and absorbing the information presented. That can be hard to do if you're not emotionally ready. You can prepare yourself by using **emotional self-talk**, **finding your calm**, and/or by **asking for a moment to process** the information. Since emotional regulation techniques may produce varied results depending on the individual, circumstances, and context,[73] it's worth trying each of them in various workplace situations to see how they work for you.

**Table 11.3. Adapt in Complex Immerse Situations**

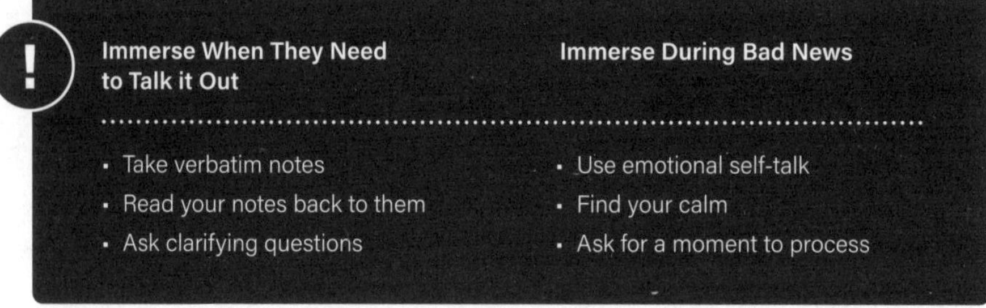

| Immerse When They Need to Talk it Out | Immerse During Bad News |
|---|---|
| • Take verbatim notes | • Use emotional self-talk |
| • Read your notes back to them | • Find your calm |
| • Ask clarifying questions | • Ask for a moment to process |

## Be Brave and Stay Present

If Immerse Listening is challenging for you in either common or complex situations, get into the right mindset with this mantra: "*I'm here to be present with the information.*" Repeating the mantra can be particularly helpful if you default to a Support, Advance, or Discern Listening Style. Then you'll be ready to process and respond to ensure you'll retain and recall the information the speaker is sharing.

Immerse Listening might take extra effort if you're a listener who prefers to be more participatory in workplace interactions. But remember, Listening to Immerse doesn't mean you'll shut your brain *off*. You still need to be present and engage with the information. You might not know how or why yet, but the knowledge you absorb during Immerse Listening situations could benefit your organization and career. So be brave and stay present. Even if the information doesn't seem relevant. Even if there's nothing for you to do with that information. Even when your emotions are high. Doing so will help you develop a reputation as an Adaptive Listener who gives the speaker what they need.

## Chapter 12

# Adapt to Discern

Some listening models claim that judgment has no place in listening and that you're always supposed to listen free of critique. But imagine if everyone listened that way in the workplace. If all listeners entered a judgment-free zone in every interaction, would the workplace also be void of critical thinking? Would presentations, projects, processes, or people ever improve? Would dangerous mistakes go unnoticed or unchecked?

Discern Listening can play a crucial role in workplace communication when you need to evaluate information. Your peers, leaders, customers, and partners need you to critique ideas and identify potential risks. While some may argue that you should always practice judgment-free listening, there are situations where a lack of Discern Listening could lead to missed opportunities or avoidable mistakes.

If the thought of calling out potential problems or concerns has you nervous or worried, you're not alone. Not everyone feels comfortable putting Discern Listening into practice. But because there are common situations where the speaker or group will be primed for your evaluation, it's important for you to develop these skills. People might directly ask for your critique if it's the evaluation step of the project or process, or if it's part of your role. Still, even when people anticipate criticism, receiving it can be hard, so you'll want to respond strategically.

Then there are more complex situations where you'll recognize that the person or group needs Discern Listening, maybe even before they do. These situations often require extra care as you balance the need for critical feedback with the uncomfortable emotional reaction that might follow. If you're a Discern Listener by default, you might not naturally know how to blend your critique with kindness. Fear not. You're about to learn how.

Discern Listening intends to analyze the information critically, evaluating its strengths and weaknesses. This chapter covers techniques across common and complex situations so you can build the skills to be an Adaptive Listener who offers evaluation at the right time and in the right way.

## Adapt in Common Discern Situations

Common Discern Listening situations are often expected in the workplace, like when someone asks you to critique their presentation, proposal, project, or process. Or they ask you to help them prepare for potential objections they might encounter in an upcoming interaction; they need you to find hypothetical red flags, poke holes in their argument, or imagine worst-case scenarios so they can prepare for tough questions or comments.

But there's one common Discern Listening situation when the person speaking might not ask for your evaluation, and that's when it's time to mentor that person. In these situations, it will likely be up to you to determine that Discern Listening is warranted based on cues from the person speaking and the situation.

Just because these three situations are common and expected doesn't mean you always know how to do your best Discern Listening. Even if you're already a Discern Listener, the following techniques might help you give the speaker more of what they need.

## Discern to Critique

At Duarte, several coaches help clients improve their communication skills. Whether for an internal sales kickoff presentation or an external customer keynote, the world's top brands come to Duarte for big moments (yes, that is a not-so-humble brag). These coaches critique the client's strategy, content, delivery, and design. Why? Because the client asked for that critique.

That's the thing about critiquing. It's wise to give your critique when people ask for it, and it can be tricky to critique when they don't. Except in specific Discern Listening situations (stay tuned), critiquing should be avoided unless the person speaking asks for it directly. If you critique someone who is unprepared, it might erode their confidence in their performance. They might wonder if they have the skills to complete the job. They might question whether they can spot areas of strength and weakness on their own.[74] The best way to know that the person is ready for your critique is for them to make that request.

Now, the word "critique" has a bad reputation. When some people hear "critique," they associate it with negative feedback. This assumption, however, is not necessarily true. Critiquing uncovers both what's *not* working and what *is* working—it's a combination of positive and negative feedback. Will the positives and negatives be an even, 50/50 split every time you critique? Maybe. Maybe not. Sometimes you'll have more to say in the "what's not working" column than in the "what is working" column or vice versa. The important thing is giving the person speaking what they need at that moment: an honest and clear evaluation of the information they're sharing with you.

Once the person speaking requests your critique, you can give that to them in four steps: First, **align on feedback criteria** to make sure you're on the same page about what you're critiquing and how. Then **create criteria notes** to document your critique in an organized way. When you deliver your feedback, make sure you **offer rationale** for each piece of the critique, briefly explaining the why behind your feedback. Finally, wrap up by **summarizing your findings,** providing the speaker with a holistic view of your critique.

Reggie, an operations lead, is preparing to ask his leadership team for a budget increase. He's created a proposal with specifics around his ask, including justification for why he needs more money and what he and his team plan to do with it if the leadership team says yes. Reggie emails his peer, Sara, with a direct request:

> **Reggie:** I'm delivering that budget proposal I told you about on Friday. I'd like to run it by you if you have a half hour today or tomorrow. Thanks for your help!
>
> **Sara:** I'd be happy to! I'm free this afternoon around three o'clock if that works for you.

Reggie and Sara agree on the time and decide on a conference room location. When Sara arrives, Reggie is already in the conference room, setting up his proposal on the screen and reviewing his notes. Sara knows she needs to uncover whether Support Listening will be a nice-to-add vs. a need-to-add in this interaction (Chapter 9). To gage Reggie's emotional state, she asks him this question:

> **Sara:** So, how are you feeling about the proposal?
>
> **Reggie:** (smiles, has a relaxed posture, uses a steady voice with moderate volume) I feel pretty good, actually.

Based on these cues, Sara determines that Reggie is feeling comfortable. She'll offer him a nice-to-add Support Listening response and then move right on to Discern Listening so she can give him the critique he requested.

> **Sara:** That's great! Well, I can't wait to hear your proposal. I know how hard you worked on it.

Sara understands the importance of **aligning on feedback criteria** before Reggie begins to ensure their perspectives match on what needs to be critiqued. She knows these kinds of common Discern Listening situations can go awry when both parties think they're on the same page about the criteria but they're not. Sara doesn't want to give Reggie feedback on something he isn't expecting, and she doesn't want to overdo her critique by delivering too much feedback if Reggie only needs her to critique one section of his proposal. At best, that kind of misalignment might waste both of their time. At worst, it could push Reggie into an uncomfortable emotional state and damage their relationship.

Aligning on feedback criteria is also a great way to prevent your biases from taking over. If you're aligned on criteria, you and the speaker have a more concrete, focused plan.

To ensure she and Reggie are on the same page, Sara asks:

> **Sara:** Hey, before we begin, what specifically would you like me to critique?
>
> **Reggie:** Great question. I'm looking for feedback on whether this proposal will persuade the leadership team to increase my team's budget. I'd like to know which parts of the proposal are persuasive, and which aren't convincing.

It's great that Reggie could clearly articulate what kind of critique he needed, but that's not always going to happen. Sometimes a speaker's response will be generic like, "I just want to know if it's good or not." Or they might not have a clue what they need from your critique, and they'll say, "I'm not sure." If this happens, you can help them define the criteria by:

- Asking a clarifying question like, "What does 'good' mean to you?"
- Offering suggestions for criteria like structure, clarity, engagement, uniqueness, effectiveness, or other criteria that makes sense for your industry and the topic.

Once Sara and Reggie align on feedback criteria (Reggie wants to know which parts of his pitch are persuasive and which aren't), Sara grabs a pen and paper to **create criteria notes** for her critique. Think of criteria notes as scoring guides that can organize your feedback and keep you accountable for adhering to the agreed-upon criteria. Although it's certainly possible to create criteria notes in your head, you'll have to deliver your critique verbally later in the interaction, so you might find it easier to keep track of your points if you write them down.

When creating criteria notes, there are three components to include: The feedback criteria in the form of a yes/no question, examples of "what's working" and "what's not working," and rationale for why you think something is working or not working (see Table 12.1). You want to **offer rationale** to ensure you're giving the speaker the type of evaluative, Discern Listening they need. Responding only with a judgment like, "That was good," or "It wasn't my favorite," doesn't give the speaker enough context to decide whether they should agree with your critique.

**Table 12.1. Feedback Criteria Notes**

| What's working? | | What's NOT working? | |
|---|---|---|---|
| Examples of content that aligns with the feedback criteria | Rationale | Examples of content that aligns with the feedback criteria | Rationale |
| | | | |
| | | | |
| | | | |
| | | | |
| | | | |

Since Reggie asked Sara to determine if the proposal would persuade the leadership team to increase his team's budget, Sara writes, "*Is this proposal persuasive?*" at the top of her page. That yes/no question will keep her focused on the feedback criteria.

Below her question, Sara forms two columns: "persuasive examples" for what's working, and "not-so-persuasive examples" for what's not working. When Reggie delivers a persuasive message, Sara puts it under the first column. When he delivers a message that doesn't, Sara puts it under the second column (see Table 12.2).

**Table 12.2. Example of Feedback Criteria Notes**

## Is this proposal persuasive?

**What's working?**

| Persuasive points | Rationale |
|---|---|
| The data point in the introduction | This is convincing. It's proof your team's current budget isn't sufficient. |
| How you've been using your current budget | This clearly shows the leadership team how little you can accomplish with these current funds. |
| The quote you have from your team member about their frustrations | Tells the leadership team that this low budget is taking a toll on your team! That matters to them. |
| The amount of money you're asking for | It's clear and direct, and it tells the leadership team exactly what you need. |

**What's NOT working?**

| No-so-persuasive points | Rationale |
|---|---|
| How you'll allocate the funds | This isn't very specific. The leadership team will want to know exactly how you'll use the additional funds. |
| The closing | There's no direct ask for the leadership team. |

When Reggie is done speaking, Sara takes a moment to finish writing down her last point on her criteria notes. Then she verbally explains all her written points to Reggie, rationale included.

Finally, she wraps up her critique by **summarizing her findings**. Summarizing gives the speaker a clearer, more concise picture of how they did. A great way to offer a summary to the person speaking is to start with the word "overall" and then fill in the blank with how they met (or didn't meet) the feedback criteria. This is especially helpful if your critique is lengthy and/or detailed, which might make the speaker feel overwhelmed.

> **Sara:** Overall, this was a persuasive pitch. Based on what I know, I think you've made it easy for the leadership team to say yes. Nice job (a nice-to-add Support Listening response to help Reggie go from feeling "pretty good" to "confident")!

Sara's Discern Listening was strong in this situation. She didn't Listen to Advance. In this case, Reggie asked Sara to critique whether his proposal would persuade the leadership team to agree to his budget request. She didn't tell Reggie *how* he could improve the parts that weren't working because he didn't ask her to do that. If Reggie had said, "I need to know *how* I can make this better," that would have been an Advance Listening opportunity. In that case, Sara would have included advice after her rationale.

Similarly, if Reggie asked Sara if she had any ideas about how he could improve on her "what's not working" observations, it would be appropriate for her to Listen to Advance. But when a speaker asks for your critique, it's safer to assume that's all they need, unless they make an additional request for guidance (or you are in the complex Advance Listening situations covered in Chapter 10).

Even though critiquing can feel uncomfortable to both the non-Discern Listener delivering the critique and the person receiving it, if you **align on feedback criteria**, **create criteria notes**, **offer rationale**, and **summarize your findings**, you'll be more likely to give the speaker what they need in a way that feels comfortable for both of you. Just remember to keep an eye on their emotional state. If you notice they're experiencing uncomfortable emotions, especially if you're providing more "what's not working" comments than "what's working" comments, it might be time to include some need-to-add Support Listening to help them feel more comfortable.

## Discern for Potential Objections

Helping a speaker handle potential objections is another common Discern Listening situation, but it's different from critiquing in one way. When you're asked to critique, you're evaluating something that already exists. The product or prototype has already been built, the presentation or outline has already been created, or the new process has already been drafted.

When you're asked to Listen to Discern for potential objections, however, you're dealing with hypotheticals. A sales trainer needs the sales team to play devil's advocate and prepare for all the reasons a potential customer *might not* move forward with a sale. An executive needs their internal team to prepare responses for tough questions that *might* come up during the earnings call, investor day, board meeting, or media interview. A social media manager needs their leader to pressure test a new campaign and spot reasons it *might not* lead to clicks and conversions.

Who knows if any of these outcomes *will* happen? But waiting to find out until the salesperson is already talking to a customer, a leader is already in front of analysts, or the campaign is already deployed might not be a risk worth taking. If finding red flags, poking holes in arguments, or imagining a worst-case scenario is challenging for you, there are techniques you can use to help you Listen to Discern.

To uncover potential objections, you can **act as a proxy** and **get skeptical**. These two techniques are meant to help you get in the mindset of the speaker's intended audience. They'll prime you for Discern Listening so you can implement the final technique, **challenge assumptions**, which will help the speaker prepare for objections.

**Acting as a proxy** means thinking and acting like the speaker's intended audience. By putting yourself in their shoes, you'll create a more realistic mock scenario for the speaker to practice handling objections. If the speaker is a salesperson, you'll imagine you're the customer listening to their pitch. If the speaker is an executive, you'll imagine you're the analyst listening to the latest annual report. If the speaker is a social media manager, you'll imagine you're the marketing leader listening to their new campaign ideas.

Of course, you can only act as a proxy if you clearly understand the intended audience. It's likely that the speaker came to you because you know this audience. Perhaps you're also a salesperson who deals with this customer or this kind of customer. Perhaps you're also an executive who's presented to analysts in the past. Perhaps you're a marketing leader, so you know how another marketing leader might think in this situation.

To help you get into the audience's mindset, ask yourself the following questions:

- What are their goals?
- What are their hopes and ambitions?
- What are their fears and concerns?
- What do they like?
- What do they dislike?

If you don't know the answers to these questions, ask the speaker to help you better understand the audience before you start listening. Quickly reviewing these questions could be enough for you to think like the intended audience. You might even find that writing them down helps keep them top of mind as you're listening.

But if that's not enough, picturing yourself in the exact setting of the intended audience might also help you act as a proxy. You can visualize where the intended audience will be when they receive the information. Are you a customer on a noisy showroom floor or on the other side of a computer screen? Are you an analyst on a virtual call, sitting in your office or home? Are you in the room with the executive? Are you a marketing manager on the phone while riding a bus or on your tablet cuddled up on your couch?

If you can physically put yourself in that location, great. Doing so might help you embody the characteristics and mindset of the intended audience. Being in the space can also help the speaker feel more confident when it's time to handle those objections for real. When speakers practice in the same setting where they'll deliver the information, they're more likely to feel prepared. But if it's not possible to physically be in the same location, visualization techniques are a great option.[75]

Acting as a proxy can help the speaker prepare for handling objections, generally speaking. But if you've ever delivered information to a tough audience, you know that sometimes those objections can be challenging, if not downright aggressive. Sometimes, simply acting as a proxy is not enough. To fully prepare the speaker for the toughest circumstances, you'll need to embody a more challenging role—you'll have to **get skeptical.**

Think of all the objections the audience might have when the speaker delivers this pitch, annual report, or campaign. Think of what the audience might object to, what they might push back on, and what they'll be concerned about.

To help yourself get skeptical, think about the following before you Listen to Discern:

- How might this go wrong?
- What are the risks associated with this?
- What will this cost?
- How much time and/or resources will this occupy?
- How will this impact ROI?
- How will this affect employee morale?
- How might our stakeholders react?

Getting skeptical can be challenging for some people because it can feel like you're being negative or even aggressive. If this technique feels uncomfortable for you, remember that you're there to help the speaker handle potential objections. You're not offering incessant and unsolicited responses that will surely grate on the speaker's nerves. Rather, you're helping someone uncover potential problems so they can properly address them. They've asked for your help, so you've been given a free pass to be a skeptic.

You might also consider getting your body involved. Displaying facial expressions and body language that appear skeptical might help you get in the mindset of the intended audience. Recall the brain-body feedback loop from Chapter 11. Your brain often believes what your body conveys.[76] As a bonus, appearing skeptical might also help the speaker picture how the intended audience might come across when posing tough objections.

Here are some *skeptical facial expressions* you could show to help you Listen to Discern as the intended audience:

**Anger**

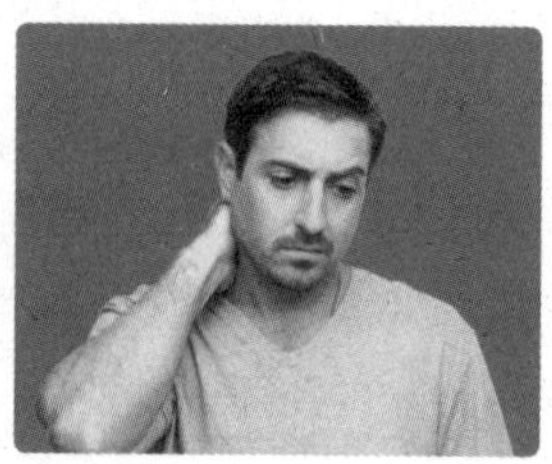

**Anxiety**

**Confusion**

**Disagreement**

**Disgust**

**Disinterest**

**Distrust**

**Fear**

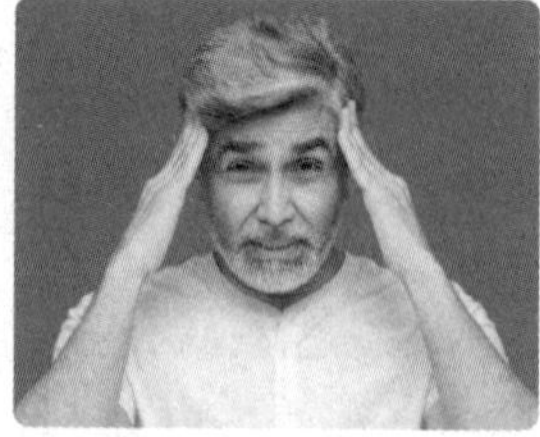

**Frustration**

Table 12.3 includes sample *skeptical body positions* you could show to help you Listen to Discern as the intended audience:

**Table 12.3. Example Skeptical Body Positions**

| Body Position | Why | Note |
|---|---|---|
| **Angle your body away from the speaker** | Tells your brain you are disinterested or you disagree | You don't have to face the wall or turn your back to the camera. |
| **Clench your fists** | Tells your brain you're angry or frustrated | You can make this visible to the person asking for you to Listen to Discern or you can keep it under your table/ desk or at your side. |
| **Bounce your leg or tap your fingers** | Tells your brain you're anxious | You're not doing this technique to cause distraction to the person speaking to you, so don't overdo it. |
| **Lean far back and subtly nod your head from left to right** | Tells your brain you disagree or are disgusted | You don't have to do this the entire time you're listening. Instead, use this technique at the start, a few times throughout, and at the close. |
| **Cross your arms in front of your chest** | Tells your brain you disagree or are fearfully protecting yourself | Feel free to uncross your arms if you need to take notes. |
| **Lean in almost too close to the speaker or screen** | Tells your brain you are trying to focus intently | This position might be distracting to the speaker. Strike the right balance so it's not counterproductive. |

Once your brain and body are primed to act as a proxy and be a skeptic, you're ready for Discern Listening. To help the speaker handle potential objections, you'll need to listen for the claims they make and **challenge their assumptions**.

An assumption is something the speaker believes to be true. They might even make decisions based on the assumption that something is true, even though there's no proof or confirmation that it is. For example, after a harrowing meeting, a peer might say, "I can't wait for retirement." They're assuming retirement will be better than the work they're dealing with now—but they don't know that to be true. They're assuming it will be.

Now, it's unlikely you'd challenge that assumption! Most people believe retirement will be more enjoyable than working over forty hours every week. This person likely needs only your Support Listening and a response like, "Ugh! I know, right?"

But Support Listening might not be enough if the speaker is preparing to handle potential objections. In these situations, you can use Discern Listening to uncover their assumptions and challenge them with "what if" questions. In response to your peer dreaming about retirement, you could get hyper-discerning and ask, "*What if* you haven't saved enough money for retirement? *What if* you get bored in retirement? *What if* the people you thought you'd spend time with aren't available or around when you retire?" If any of these "what if" questions spark their concern or dread, then you've uncovered a potential objection to their claim.

Across workplace situations, possible assumptions and "what if" questions might look like this:

- If you're acting as a customer proxy for a salesperson and they say, "This product will absolutely meet your needs," there are some underlying assumptions you can challenge. In response, you could ask, "*What if* our needs change next quarter?" or "*What if* the company changes the product?"
- If you're acting as an analyst proxy for an executive and they say, "We're going to take over this market segment in the next twenty-four months,"

there are some underlying assumptions you can challenge, even if the executive has data to support the claim. You could ask, "*What if* the newest player to enter the market continues to grab more market share?" or "*What if* there's another economic slowdown?"

- If you're acting as a marketing leader for a social media manager and they say, "Users will like this type of post," there are some underlying assumptions you can challenge. In response, you could ask, "*What if* the latest trend fizzles out after we initiate our campaign?" or "*What if* our competitors use the same approach?"

When you challenge a speaker's assumptions, you're trying to trip them up or see where their idea will fall apart. You're not listening to make them feel good about the information (Support Listening), move forward with the information (Advance Listening), or remember the information (Immerse Listening). The speaker is likely coming to you because they struggle to uncover potential objections or are too close to the work and can't see them. By **acting as a proxy**, **getting skeptical**, and **challenging assumptions,** you'll play a valuable role in ensuring the speaker successfully handles potential objections.

## Discern to Mentor

The final common Discern Listening situation is when it's time to mentor someone. Although mentoring others at work is common, it can be confusing to know whether it's time to offer direct advice (Advance Listening) or gently guide the mentee toward their own decisions. Should you *tell* them what to do because you know better or best? Or should you encourage them to uncover the answers themselves with your mentorship?

Many of the team, people, and organizational leaders the authors interviewed shared that they approach their roles from a problem-solving perspective. They see it as their job to solve problems for others. But as you read in Chapter 10, it's important to remember that just because you have expertise to share, it doesn't mean you should always take the reins. You want to reserve your advice for situations when the stakes are high. If the stakes aren't high, you might want to use Discern Listening to mentor the speaker.

When it's time to mentor, you'll guide the mentee to determine the way forward themselves. This can be done through several strategies:

- **Ask them to start at the beginning** so they can review their process and potentially identify where they can improve.
- **Invite them to explore options** so they can consider different possibilities and expand their problem-solving skills.
- **Entice them to uncover why** so they can learn to critically evaluate their choices.

Regardless of your current role, the principles of mentoring can be valuable to you. These skills are useful in various scenarios—whether it's helping a colleague navigate a challenge or stepping into a mentorship role in the future. Embracing these techniques can equip you for success in many aspects of your professional life.

In Chapter 10, you read about a complex Advance Listening situation between Kelvin, a senior and tenured manager, and his direct report, Jordan. A slight adjustment to this situation demonstrates when to use Advance versus Discern Listening.

As a reminder, Kelvin and Jordan have a healthy working relationship and their weekly one-on-ones generally cover the same topics: Jordan updates Kelvin on his current projects, the two discuss any questions or concerns surrounding Jordan's tasks, and they work on Jordan's career development goals. These are relatively casual and conversational meetings. But during this one-on-one, after Kelvin and Jordan exchange pleasantries, the following conversation happens:

> **Kelvin:** So, how's that latest project coming along?
>
> **Jordan:** I was going to bring that one up today!
>
> **Kelvin:** Oh yeah? What's going on?
>
> **Jordan:** To be honest, I'm a bit lost right now. When I read the brief I thought, "Okay, no problem," but then I started researching, and I realized there's a lot more information on this topic than I initially thought. So now I feel like I'm all over the place, and I don't really know where to start.

Kelvin has a choice to make: Which S.A.I.D. Listening Goal will help Jordan succeed? It would make sense for Kelvin to pick up on Jordan's short-term goal to move the project forward and assume that Advance Listening is the best option. But Kelvin has some knowledge about Jordan that's making him think twice about Listening to Advance in this situation.

Kelvin knows Jordan's long-term career goals include taking on more complicated projects. He wants to become an influential member of the organization. Before he can reach those goals, Jordan will need to strengthen his problem-solving and self-reliance skills. That includes researching projects like this one. Giving Jordan the answer is unlikely to help him learn and grow.

Plus, the stakes aren't high in this situation. Jordan isn't presenting this project to senior leadership like he was in Chapter 10. This project is for a peer-to-peer lunch-and-learn. Plus, he isn't presenting this project next week like he did in Chapter 10. This presentation isn't due until next month. In the absence of high stakes and urgency, Kelvin knows sharing his expertise is probably not the best option. There's plenty of time to mentor Jordan, rather than give him the answers directly, so Kelvin decides to Listen to Discern so Jordan can problem-solve his way through this project—with Kelvin's guidance.

> **Kelvin:** (beginning with nice-to-add Support Listening) I remember how overwhelming these projects can be in the beginning. Let's figure this out together—we have some time until you present at the next lunch-and-learn. Why don't you **start at the beginning** and tell me what you've tried so far?

The purpose of asking your mentee to start at the beginning is so they can review the details of their problem again and potentially solve it themselves. Simply by stating aloud the who, what, where, why, and how, they might catch a detail they missed previously. Their retelling of the context with fresh eyes and ears might make them understand things differently. Sometimes when people review their problem or situation out loud, they uncover the strengths and weaknesses they didn't notice before.[77] They may find errors in their initial approach or uncover a new strategy.

> **Jordan:** Well, I went down a rabbit hole on our website. I tried to gather information through our published whitepapers and articles. There's a lot of good stuff on there—almost *too* much. I also conducted a web search and interviewed several cross-functional team leaders to get their take on the topic. I ended up getting conflicting information and opinions.

It's clear that Jordan feels comfortable sharing his trials and tribulations with Kelvin, but that might not always be the case. There's a power differential in the mentee-mentor relationship that you don't want to overlook. Even if they don't show it, your mentee might worry they're wasting your time or giving you too many details. Plus, they might feel particularly vulnerable sharing their mistakes and losses with someone more senior. Make sure to hold space for your direct report or mentee. You can reassure them, with your words and a calm and inviting demeanor, that this mentoring moment is exactly where you're both supposed to be and what you're supposed to be doing.

Starting at the beginning might give your mentee some insights into what they might have done wrong or where they got stuck. But that might not be enough for them to find their way out of that position. If that's the case, your mentoring responsibilities aren't over. The next thing you can do is **invite them to explore options** by asking open-ended follow-up questions. These questions will help them consider potentials, hypotheticals, or scenario plans that could get them unstuck. Potential questions include:

- What could the possible first steps be?
- What do you think will happen if you do it that way?
- Let's play that out—how would it unfold?

Be cautious that you don't offer advice disguised as a question like, "Have you tried XYZ?" When you invite your mentee to explore options, you want to encourage them to uncover their path, not tell them what you think the right answer is. Notice how Kelvin handles his conversation with Jordan. He's careful to ask open-ended questions that encourage Jordan to find solutions, avoiding the pitfall of disguising his suggestion as a question:

> **Kelvin:** Information overload can be confusing. I get why you feel lost right now (including more nice-to-add Support Listening). Where do you think you went wrong?
>
> **Jordan:** I think it's possible I gathered too much information from too many sources. I know there's value in getting information from various places, but what I uncovered wasn't consistent across sources, so I wasn't sure how to proceed.
>
> **Kelvin:** Ahh, I see. So, given that you have all of this research completed, but it's disorganized and inconsistent, what do you think your options are at this point?

At this stage of the mentoring moment, you can **entice them to uncover why** for themselves. In other words, help them find the reasons and justifications for choosing each option. Help your mentee explore why they've added each new potential or hypothetical to their list by asking them, "Why do you think that is?" or "That's interesting! Why did you land on that option?" Helping them go deeper and think through their options and why they may or may not work will help them evaluate their ideas and grow their problem-solving skills. It might even inspire them to refine an existing idea or add another solution.

> **Jordan:** Well, I guess I could choose three sources that share a consistent point of view and dig deeper into that segment of the topic.
>
> **Kelvin:** Okay, that's option one. Tell me why you think that might be a good option.
>
> **Jordan:** It would eliminate some conflicting points of view, making things easier for me! It might also give my peers a clear and concise message. Too many angles might be confusing.
>
> **Kelvin:** That's a smart analysis. What do you think might be the drawbacks of this option?
>
> **Jordan:** Sharing only one point of view wouldn't give them the full picture of the topic. And it wouldn't be a balanced presentation. It may be the

easier option, but it's certainly not complete and maybe even biased. So, Option 2 might be to admit that there are a lot of conflicting opinions and thoughts on the topic and share them all briefly.

**Kelvin:** And what might the benefits and drawbacks be with that option?

**Jordan:** Well, it would be less biased and more comprehensive. But if all that conflicting information is difficult for me to process and organize, it's probably going to be difficult for my peers to process and organize. They might walk away without remembering anything because I gave them too much. So, I wonder if a happy medium would be to uncover the three most common angles to this topic and share those.

**Kelvin:** All right, and how might that option work for your peers?

**Jordan:** It would show that there are numerous views and thoughts out there, but they'd get the high-level gist about what most people think and believe. Plus, with only three angles to cover, they're more likely to remember what I share.

**Kelvin:** That sounds like a smart plan. You've considered what you can handle *and* what you think your peers want to get out of this lunch-and-learn. Let me know if you need any additional guidance, but it sounds like you've got it covered.

When your direct report or mentee is on a professional development path, has a skills gap, and comes to you with a low-stakes problem without urgency, Discern Listening might be the best way to mentor them.

Keep in mind that your direct report or mentee could get frustrated if you don't give them advice right away. If you sense their frustration, try reminding them of their professional goals. Highlight how this is a great opportunity for them to practice with you in a low-risk space. You can offer them something like, "If we can't land on an answer together, then I'll happily tell you what I would do. But let's try this out first." Then, **ask them to start at the beginning, invite them to explore options,** and **entice them to uncover why.**

By doing so, you'll gently guide them to uncover their answer instead of giving it to them. If they want to grow in their career, they'll thank you for your Discern Listening. Maybe not today. Maybe not tomorrow. But soon, and for the rest of their professional lives.

**Table 12.4. Adapt in Common Discern Situations**

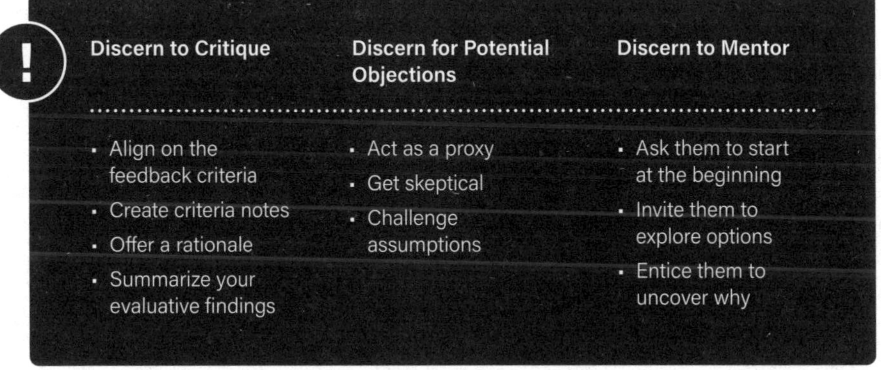

| Discern to Critique | Discern for Potential Objections | Discern to Mentor |
|---|---|---|
| • Align on the feedback criteria<br>• Create criteria notes<br>• Offer a rationale<br>• Summarize your evaluative findings | • Act as a proxy<br>• Get skeptical<br>• Challenge assumptions | • Ask them to start at the beginning<br>• Invite them to explore options<br>• Entice them to uncover why |

## Adapt in Complex Discern Situations

While it's often expected you'll use Discern Listening in common situations, the complex situations are usually unexpected. In other words, you'll have to put in more effort to determine if it's time for Discern Listening. The two complex Discern Listening situations are 1) when the stakes are too high for you to *avoid* Discern Listening, and 2) when it's time to adapt to another S.A.I.D. Listening Goal to meet the speaker's needs.

The first situation—when the stakes are high—can be complicated because it requires you to evaluate even if the person or group isn't ready or expecting evaluation. If you aren't a Discern Listener by default, taking the leap to evaluate could be nerve-racking. If you are a Discern Listener, you might evaluate when the time isn't right.

The second situation—when it's time to adapt your listening—may surprise you because it's a bit meta: you use Discern Listening to determine how to adapt when you're unsure what the speaker needs from you. For both situations, the techniques in this section will help you know when and how to listen in the right way.

## Discern When the Stakes Are High

There's a danger in Listening to Discern when no one is expecting it. If you point out all the typos you see in your peer's report when they didn't ask you to do that, you might come across as negative, especially if you do it repeatedly. If you call out the one minor flaw in a direct report's project when the rest is stellar, you might make that person feel inadequate. If you identify a timeline error when the product manager was trying to give you information about the budget, you might get a reputation for being nit-picky. Sometimes, the evaluation you want to make is your opinion or preference, and the person or group would be better served if you listened in a different way.

That is, unless the stakes are too high for you to do anything other than Listen to Discern. Assessing high stakes in these situations is similar to assessing high stakes when you need to Listen to Advance (Chapter 10). If the speaker or group would likely lose something critical or fail in some way if you didn't speak up, then the stakes are high. When you spot a potential damage or danger to employees, customers, business performance, or the organization's reputation, you'll want to use Discern Listening. Unlike the complex Advance Listening situation, though, you don't necessarily need expertise to offer advice that moves the person or group forward.

When you've identified that the stakes are high, even if no one asked you to evaluate, it's time to Listen to Discern. You can **prime with support** and **offer a rationale** before you **sound the alarm**. You'll also want to **invite them to disagree** as you **prepare for defensiveness** from the speaker. In some cases, you might even need to **retreat or get reinforcements**.

An early-stage tech start-up is getting ready to launch their new app. The following group gets together for a meeting tomake sure everything is on schedule: Jansi, the project manager; Sandy, the developer; Mason, the designer; Peter, the marketing analyst; and Casey, the customer service representative.

> **Jansi**: All right, team, we're almost there. Just a few more tweaks, and we'll be ready to launch! Let's have everyone give a quick update and then we'll dive in. First, let me introduce you to Casey, our new part-time customer service representative! Casey's blend of thoughtfulness and thoroughness is just what we need in this pre-launch phase. Casey is just finishing up their degree, so they'll be with us three days a week. Welcome, Casey!
>
> **Casey**: Thanks everyone! So excited to be here.
>
> **Jansi**: Great. Now, let's get to the updates. Sandy, let's start with you.
>
> **Sandy**: Everything seems to be in order on my end. The coding is tight, and the features are working smoothly. We've done tests with potential users, and there are no major complaints.
>
> **Mason**: Agree! The designs have come together perfectly. It's looking good.
>
> **Peter**: From a marketing perspective, I think we have a compelling launch plan. I reviewed it with you last time, so nothing new to add. I'm excited!
>
> **Jansi**: Great updates all around. Let's move on.

While listening to the updates, Casey had a concern they didn't know how to bring up to the group. For the last two days, Casey had been testing out the app. Casey agreed with Sandy that there weren't any major bugs or errors. What concerned Casey, though, was a potential problem with some of the design elements. They knew that user experience was crucial to the success of any app. If a significant portion of the population struggled with the interface, it could spell trouble for the launch. In fact, Casey is colorblind, and it was hard for them to navigate the interface. Casey didn't know much about the users who had already tested the app, but what if people who are colorblind weren't included?

It was obvious the group was energized and ready to keep moving forward, and Casey didn't want to overstep their boundaries as the newest and least experienced team member. Still, the stakes were high enough that Casey decided to speak up.

> **Casey**: Hey, Jansi. Before we move on, I was wondering if it would be okay if I said something.
>
> **Jansi**: Of course!
>
> **Casey**: I've been in the app the last few days, and what you've all done is impressive! I can see so many people getting value out of this. I did notice something, and I don't want to slow us down so please do whatever you think is best with this feedback. I'm colorblind, and I'm having a hard time seeing a few of the screens. I don't know if other people would have the same issues I did, but I thought it was important to bring it up.

Given that the group was experiencing a comfortable emotion, and there was a potential for Casey's response to shift them into an uncomfortable emotion, Casey decided to **prime with support** first. This nice-to-add Support Listening validated the current emotions of the group. Remember from Chapter 9 that you can validate a person or group's emotions even if you don't completely agree with their reaction. When you prime with support, you soften the blow and prime them to hear the unexpected evaluation you're about to make.

Next, Casey **offered a rationale** about their experience with the app before **sounding the alarm** that something might not be working right. This technique helps you slowly build a case that the person or group can follow as you respond. You may be able to guide them to the same conclusion you've made before you need to say the potentially unsettling news.

Casey also decided to **invite them to disagree** with the evaluation by saying, "I don't know if other people would have the same issues I had." By offering an invitation to disagree, you put some power back in the person or group's hands. It's a more collaborative approach than forcing the group to see the situation the way you see it or demanding they do something about it.

Some readers might argue that a response like Casey's was too passive or that they used too much hedging language (e.g., "I just wanted to bring it up"). This critique is often brought up in discussions about effective communication. After all, if Casey found a problem, then why not just be direct about it? Oh, what a different working world it would be if offering an unexpected evaluation was easy for everyone!

Workplace norms influence what people can say without the potential for negative consequences. If the person is new to the company or team, if they're young, if they're a minority, if there's a power difference, if there are office or personality politics—these might impact how someone feels about their psychological safety at work. With tactics like **prime with support**, **offer rationale**, and **invite them to disagree**, you might create a safe(r) foundation for **when you sound the alarm**.

However, it's worth noting that even though these techniques can generate a more productive conversation, people can get defensive when your Discern Listening is unexpected. That's why you want to **prepare for defensiveness**. When someone gets defensive, it's often because they have a fear that you, and other people, might think their ideas, plans, or contributions aren't good enough. You can better prepare yourself by remembering that if they do get defensive, it's likely because they feel threatened by your feedback.[78] People aren't always at their most thoughtful or rational when they feel a threat. So instead of matching their defensiveness with defensiveness, you can be ready for it and validate their emotions with need-to-add Support Listening.

If tensions arise, you can reiterate your invitation for them to disagree. That technique can help take some heat off an interaction. You're letting the other person know you aren't forcing them to make any changes or include additional considerations. If they continue to show intense uncomfortable emotions like rage or disgust, you have a choice to make: **retreat or get reinforcements**.

After you've offered an unexpected evaluation, if tensions keep rising, sometimes the safest and most productive choice is to retreat. Concede their point. Walk away. You can take comfort in knowing you said your piece. But if the stakes are so high that you don't think the person or group should be allowed to move forward, you need reinforcements. Seek out a manager, a leader, or a subject matter expert for help. You don't want the guilt or blowback of potential danger or damage happening when you knew about it all along.

Lucky for Casey, their colleagues didn't get defensive. Instead, the group realized there was a gap in their user testing pool. In fact, they decided it was time to reconsider the accessibility of their design altogether.

If people aren't expecting your Discern Listening, but you see a red flag or concern that is too important to ignore, you can **prime with support**, **offer rationale**, **sound the alarm**, **invite them to disagree**, **prepare for defensiveness**, and potentially **retreat or get reinforcements**. These techniques will make it easier (and hopefully safer) for you to speak up and will help the person or group receive your response in the spirit of your good intentions.

## Discern to Adapt Your Listening

Get ready: Adaptive Listening is about to get meta. Throughout the last four chapters, you've read various common situations that could be more successful if you use listening techniques that correspond to the right S.A.I.D. Listening Goal. You've also read about complex situations where you'd first need to identify cues that tell you it's time to listen a certain way before you start processing and responding. At its core, Adaptive Listening requires you to *evaluate* what type of listening the person speaking needs from you. As you now know, when you need to evaluate, it's time to Listen to Discern.

"What?!" you might be thinking, "You mean I can use Discern Listening techniques to determine what type of S.A.I.D. Listening Goal I should help them meet?!" The authors are just as excited as you are, dear reader. When you **avoid autopilot**, **notice shifts**, and **ask yourself, "What does the speaker need from me now?"** you'll be using Discern Listening to become an Adaptive Listener.

Here's the same *morning update* you read throughout Part I:

> *It's nine o'clock on a typical workday. You sit down at your desk and open your laptop. You've got your go-to beverage and are ready for your first*

*meeting. It's a regular morning update where the project leader, someone you work with closely, provides information on revised goals, adjusted timelines, and progress reports. These updates are standard in your work, and the project leader usually shares information that's not particularly exciting or troubling. You're in this meeting with five other people.*

This time, imagine that the project leader is *your* project leader. The updates on revised goals, adjusted timelines, and progress reports are specific to the project you and your team are working on. Everyone in this meeting has a project they are working on with this leader, but you are the only member of your specific team in the meeting.

Given this additional context, you decide to show up ready for Advance Listening. You'll be focused on what you can do to move things forward and what details you need to relay to your team (Chapter 10). Ten minutes into the meeting, you realize that Advance Listening was the right decision. The project leader has outlined clear action steps for you and specified the appropriate messages for you to pass along to your direct reports.

As you become more familiar with the common and complex situations, you'll make a probable, educated guess on how you'll need to listen before you enter the room, join the virtual meeting, or peek your head over the cubicle at your colleague. But once that interaction begins, **avoid autopilot**. You never know when you might need to adapt your listening for this speaker or someone else in the group.

Throughout the interaction, you can use Discern Listening to **notice shifts**. Is there a shift in topic? A shift in the speaker? A shift in the emotions of the speaker or the emotional energy in the room? When a shift occurs, that's the time to **ask yourself, "What does the speaker need from me *now*?"** The listening goal you've been helping the speaker or group meet may remain the same after a shift. But it's also possible you may need to adapt your listening.

During the *morning update*, imagine your project leader, mid-sentence, abruptly shifts from discussing your project to sharing updates about a different team's project. You think, "Okay, that's a shift in topic. What does the speaker need from me now?" You evaluate the situation: the updates aren't about you, but you recognize the value in listening to seemingly irrelevant information, so you decide it's time for Immerse Listening (Chapter 11).

Suddenly, a person from one of the other teams interjects, "This timeline update will make things difficult. I don't know how we'll make it all work." You notice a shift in who's speaking, but you also notice that their emotions are different than the rest of the group. You see that this person is avoiding eye contact as they share this news. Their voice is quieter than usual, and their facial expression shows concern or worry.

What does *this* speaker need from you now? You decide it's time for Support Listening because this new speaker is experiencing an uncomfortable emotion (Chapter 9). You respond by saying, "These timeline changes can be hard and stressful." Your colleague nods in agreement, but you notice them exhale deeply and slowly, a sign they're calming down.

The project leader jumps in and asks your colleague to share more about their concerns. Together, they come up with three possible ways to move forward, but they seem stuck on which one to choose. Your project leader says to the group, "Well, what are the pros and cons of these options?" This one is almost too easy. You've just been asked to critique the options, which means it's time for Discern Listening. You help the group align on feedback criteria. Then, you use that feedback as a roadmap for how to critique which option is best.

As the meeting closes, you include a nice-to-add Support Listening response. You say to your colleague, "Thanks for being so open with us today. I'm here if you need to talk through any of those options again." Off to the next meeting you go, ready to **avoid autopilot**, **notice shifts**, and **ask yourself, "What does the speaker need from me now?"** so you can adapt your listening again.

**Table 12.5. Adapt in Complex Discern Situations**

| ! Discern When the Stakes Are High | Discern to Adapt Your Listening |
|---|---|
| • Prime with support<br>• Offer rationale<br>• Sound the alarm<br>• Invite them to disagree<br>• Prepare for defensiveness<br>• Retreat or get reinforcements | • Avoid autopilot<br>• Notice shifts<br>• Ask yourself, "What does the speaker need from me *now*?" |

## Be Brave and Shine the Light

If Discern Listening is difficult for you, remember this mantra: *"I'm here to uncover what's working and what's not."* This mantra works when you're listening to others and when you're listening to yourself as you decide the right way to listen next.

If you're an Advance Listener by default, you might have to stop yourself from jumping to the next steps or an immediate resolution. The speaker might need you to evaluate and explain the rationale for your decisions before moving ahead. If you're an Immerse Listener, you might need to push yourself to do more than understand the information so you're ready to evaluate it. If you're a Support Listener, your style will likely help you bring warmth and care to Discern Listening situations where you're delivering unexpected evaluations. Still, you'll need to be ready to use the techniques in this chapter to avoid getting stuck in Support Listening.

Some people find it daunting to deliver critical or candid evaluations, especially in a professional setting where the stakes are high. As long as you aren't operating from a place of malice or ill will, and you've done the work to identify that you're in a common or complex Discern Listening situation, then be brave. Shine the light on the strengths and weaknesses or guide them as they find their path.

## Chapter 13

# Embrace an Adaptive Listening Culture

Adaptive Listening can help you improve your workday, build relationships, and reach your goals. But even if you're fully committed to becoming an Adaptive Listener—and the authors hope you are—you won't become a world-class listener overnight. Your journey started when you picked up this book, and it won't stop after you put it down.

Maybe when you started reading, you were completely unaware of your S.A.I.D. Listening Style, and now you recognize the characteristics and benefits of how you process and respond to information. You might also recognize the S.A.I.D. Listening Styles of others you interact with at work.

Maybe you were unaware of the barriers preventing you from listening, and now you know how your Listening L.E.N.S. impacts your ability to focus on the speaker with empathy. You also know how to pull your listening into focus.

Maybe you never realized the person speaking to you has a S.A.I.D. Listening Goal every time they interact with you. Now, not only do you know speakers have goals, you also know how to help them get what they need across a variety of workplace situations.

Maybe you were unaware of how to process and respond differently to your colleagues, leaders, direct reports, and customers, and now you have the tools to give each speaker exactly what they need.

But you can still do more to learn and grow as an Adaptive Listener. Not only will it help you, but it will be powerful for the people around you. With your new skills, you can help build an Adaptive Listening culture—one with improved communication, increased connection, and greater overall productivity. This journey of cultivating trust and traction starts with you but can extend to your entire organization and even your network, growing the benefits exponentially.

## Adapt, Reflect, Adapt Again

Remember, Adaptive Listening is a skill; the more you work on it, the better you'll become. Be prepared to experience periods of wild success and complete misses. Patience is key. Becoming an Adaptive Listener requires self-compassion and continuous improvement. Be kind to yourself when you make mistakes, and think of each interaction as an opportunity for growth. You can reflect on your listening during and after your interactions—just make sure you reflect with empathy for others and yourself.

To continue your growth, you can build more awareness about your S.A.I.D. Listening Style. The S.A.I.D. Listening Style Finder is a great place to start, but you might want to collect more data points. Reflect on your listening skills in the wild. Notice when you default to your style and ask yourself why. Make notes to yourself like, "Whoa, I'm leaning into my S.A.I.D. Listening Style right now. Is that the right choice here? Or is it just my listening habits kicking in?" or, "I can feel myself getting agitated that the group isn't listening like I am, but I think they're listening in the right way. I still need to work on that."

Next, when you adapt to other listening styles, think about how easy or difficult it is for you. Praise yourself when you get it right. You might reflect by saying, "I used Immerse Listening in that interaction well! I've never done that before." When you get it wrong, recognize that you're still learning. Reward your effort with an internal response like, "Support Listening is still hard for me. But I'm getting better at it in one-on-one meetings."

Of course, as you've learned, a big part of your success as an Adaptive Listener comes from your ability to read cues from the speaker. Unfortunately, sometimes you'll try your best to identify the speaker's S.A.I.D. Listening Goal so you can listen with empathy, but you'll still be at a loss for what the speaker needs from you. If you're struggling to read the cues that guide you on how to adapt, here's what you can do:

If the person speaking to you is familiar with Adaptive Listening, you can use Adaptive Listening language to communicate with them. Start by telling the person that you've tried to figure out their goal on your own, then narrow the focus of the S.A.I.D. Listening Goal for them. Tell them the cues you've observed and suggest how they need you to listen. You might say something like, "I want to give you what you need, and I think you want me to Listen to Advance, but I'm not sure." Avoid saying, "Do you want me to Listen to Support, Advance, Immerse, or Discern?" This way, you're taking some of the burden off the speaker and demonstrating that you've worked hard to uncover their goal and meet it.

If the person speaking to you *isn't* familiar with Adaptive Listening (and you don't have time to teach them yourself, recommend this book, or send them to Duarte's Adaptive Listening workshop), then you'll let them know you're trying to give them what they need without using Adaptive Listening language. Once you think you know what they need, use the corresponding sentence from the list below. Then, pause and observe their reaction to see if you got it right:

- If you think the person needs Support Listening, you can say, "I'm here if you want someone to talk to," or "I appreciate you sharing this with me."
- If you think the person needs Advance Listening, you can say, "I've got some ideas for what you can do next, but only if you want them right

now," or "I know how I would move this forward, but I'm not sure if you're looking for my help on this."

- If you think the person needs Immerse Listening, you can say, "I'm ready to soak in all the details," or "I can't wait for you to tell me more."
- If you think the person needs Discern Listening, you can say, "I can see what's working and what's not working, if you want me to share more," or "I'm here to help you evaluate this if you want me to."

If they express relief or gratitude in their response to you, then you've probably guessed right.

Of course, even though you'll do your best to identify what the person speaking needs, you'll inevitably get it wrong sometimes. You might identify the wrong goal. You might get the goal right but linger too long and miss the cue to adapt to a different goal. You might make well-intentioned mistakes. If you do, you might receive the following cues from the person speaking:

- They'll suddenly go silent and disengage.
- They'll use vocal cues like a heavy, exasperated sigh to express frustration.
- They'll display shocked, annoyed, or hurt facial expressions and body language.

These are obvious cues you missed the mark, and you'll need to adapt to another style. But sometimes you won't get those obvious cues from the person speaking. You might walk away, unsure whether you helped them meet their goal. When you're not sure how well you adapted, it's time to reflect. Ask yourself the following questions after your listening interactions:

- Did I identify the right S.A.I.D. Listening Goal?
- Did I implement the proper techniques to give the speaker what they needed in this interaction?
- Was my Listening L.E.N.S. focused during this interaction? If not, did I accept, voice, or change it to get back on track?

- Did I adapt to another style when I got cues from the speaker that I didn't get it right?
- What can I do better next time?

In addition to individual reflection, involving others in your Adaptive Listening journey can be incredibly beneficial. Find a listening accountability partner—someone you interact with often like a peer or supervisor—and tell them what you're working on as a listener. Ask them to give you feedback based on a specific aspect of your listening. For example, if you're working on avoiding the cautions associated with your S.A.I.D. Listening Style, you can ask your accountability partner to help with the following:

- If you're a Support Listener, you might say: "I'm trying to avoid excessively cheerleading in meetings. If you hear me do it, can you call me out on it after we're done?"
- If you're an Advance Listener, you might say: "I'm trying to do a better job acknowledging how others feel, instead of just focusing on the tasks we need to complete. I'd appreciate it if you could monitor my behavior and responses in this next meeting and tell me how I'm doing after."
- If you're an Immerse Listener, you might say: "I've realized I tend to take so many notes while I'm listening that I forget to connect with the person speaking. Is that something you've noticed from me in our interactions?"
- If you're a Discern Listener, you might say, "I want to build on others' ideas during brainstorms instead of critiquing them. Can you give me feedback on how I do in the next meeting?"

If you offer to be an accountability partner for the other person in exchange, voila! You've just created an opportunity for mutual support and feedback on your listening skills and contributed to a strong Adaptive Listening culture.

Remember, if you're getting even *some* of the Adaptive Listening techniques right, you're doing great! But if you missed the mark, consider following up with an apology or requesting feedback from the speaker on why your listening wasn't quite right during the interaction. Even when you get it wrong, your next chance to improve is only one meeting, conversation, presentation, or recording away.

## Influence the Way Others Listen

After reading this book, you'll likely find it difficult to ignore how you listen. But you might also find it hard to ignore how others listen to you. You might be thinking, "Now, how do I get my leaders, direct reports, colleagues, customers, or suppliers to listen to *me* like I plan to listen to *them*?" or, "How can I introduce Adaptive Listening to my team and organization so everyone I work with can reap the benefits?" After all, you're doing the work, and it's reasonable to want the same empathy and effort from others.

In an ideal world, you'd have the time to share the principles of Adaptive Listening with your colleagues, and they'd eagerly embrace these concepts, striving to enhance their listening skills just like you. But until that happens, it's still possible for you to get the benefits of their Adaptive Listening, even if they don't know they're doing it. You can use a simplified shortcut to increase the likelihood that you'll get what you need when others are listening to you.

Getting others to adapt their listening requires you to explicitly state what you *don't* need the listener to do as much as what you *do* need from them. If you're interacting with a familiar listener and you know (or can reasonably assume) their S.A.I.D. Listening Style, you can guide them away from their default behaviors and explicitly state what you *don't* and *do* need from them. Try using the following formula:

*"You might want to do* **X** *right now, and I appreciate that, but what I need from you as a listener is* **Y**."

What you say for **X** depends on their listening style. What you say for **Y** depends on how you want them to listen. Table 13.1 offers suggestions for how to cue others to listen the way you need.

## Table 13.1. Cueing Others to Meet Your S.A.I.D. Listening Goal

**1 Determine Their S.A.I.D. Listening Style**

| Support Listeners | Advance Listeners | Immerse Listeners | Discern Listeners |
|---|---|---|---|

**2 Sentence Starter**

You might want to...

**3 Reference a Characteristic of their Listening Style**

| Support Listeners | Advance Listeners | Immerse Listeners | Discern Listeners |
|---|---|---|---|
| ...cheer me on right now,<br>...commiserate with me right now,<br>...make me feel better right now, | ...give me advice right now,<br>...fix my problem right now,<br>...take over this task right now, | ...soak in what i'm saying right now,<br>...dig for more information right now,<br>...ask me some clarifying questions right now, | ...evaluate this information right now,<br>...offer feedback on this idea right now,<br>...help me spot the red flags right now, |

**4 Transition**

And I appreciate that, but what I really need from you as a listener is...

**5 Reference Your S.A.I.D. Listening Goal**

| Support Listeners | Advance Listeners | Immerse Listeners | Discern Listeners |
|---|---|---|---|
| ...for you to give me a moment to vent.<br>...to celebrate with me!<br>...to tell me it makes sense that I'm feeling this way.<br>...give me a (boost, kudos, high-five, hug, etc.) | ...your help landing on the right next step.<br>...your advice.<br>...for you to help me move this forward.<br>...for you to think about how the rest of the team will respond to this information when you pass it on. | ...for you to let me talk this out for a moment.<br>...for you to write down the details so you can remember them later.<br>...to hold your questions until the end so I can explain all these details.<br>...to sit back and enjoy! | ...for you to give me your feedback on this.<br>...for you to help me uncover the strengths and weaknesses.<br>...to let me try to figure it out, but help me think through it.<br>...think of any alternatives I've missed. |

Juan, an Adaptive Listener in training, used this formula when he interacted with his team co-lead, May. After attending the Adaptive Listening workshop, Juan began observing the way May listened during their team meetings. She gave him advice most of the time. Juan decided that May was probably an Advance Listener.

"A lot of the time, that advice is exactly what I need," Juan said. "May is helping me fix a problem, unblock a process, or move things onto the next phase. Advance Listening usually serves both of us well, so it makes sense that she continues to default to that style with me."

But when Juan interacted with May and he *didn't* want her advice, he started using the formula. He'd say, "You might want to give me advice when I tell you this, May, and I appreciate how you always help me. But right now, I need to update you on where the team is with this project. I can handle it from here, but I want to keep you in the loop in case anything comes up later."

Juan guided May away from her Advance Listening Style and cued her to Listen to Immerse, even though May didn't attend the workshop. He asked her to remember the information. He also asked her to avoid the urge to move things forward, give him advice, or fix a problem.

If the listener is not familiar to you, and you don't know or can't reasonably assume their S.A.I.D. Listening Style, then you can still use the suggestions in step 5 of Table 13.1 to cue them to meet your listening goal. It's still reasonable, and ultimately kinder, to tell people what you need instead of making them guess. When you use specific and clear language about what you need (and what you don't need), you're helping others become Adaptive Listeners like you. You're also setting the stage to receive the same empathy you're giving to others. Everyone wins.

## Appreciating Diverse Listening Styles

Embracing an Adaptive Listening culture isn't only about improving your listening or getting others to improve theirs. It's also about accepting and appreciating listening differences.

By now, you know that people listen differently from one another. That might have been an entirely new concept to you, or you might have thought, "Well, yeah, of course they do!" But even if you recognized listening differences from one person to another, it's possible that you labeled them as poor listening, ineffective listening, or even a lack of listening altogether.

Before learning the S.A.I.D. Listening Styles, you might have been annoyed when a Support Listener focused on emotions more than the task at hand. You might have been agitated and rushed when an Advance Listener urgently nodded their head and added several "mm-hmms" between your words. You might have felt ignored by an Immerse Listener who gazed out the window while you were talking to them. You might have felt embarrassed when a Discern Listener made a skeptical facial expression while you were presenting your idea.

Now that you understand listening differences, you might have a different perspective. When a Support Listener focuses on emotions, you might think, "Oh look, that person is a Support Listener. I matter so much to them that they're focused on my feelings more than the message I'm sharing."

When an Advance Listener urgently nods and interjects with "mm-hmm," you might think, "Oh look, that person is an Advance Listener. They have an innate desire to move this forward, which could be good for all of us in the long run."

When an Immerse Listener looks out the window while you're speaking, you might think, "Oh look, that person is an Immerse Listener. They're looking out the window so they can better absorb and retain the information I'm giving them."

When a Discern Listener is being skeptical while you're speaking, you might think, "Oh, look, that person is a Discern Listener. They're evaluating what I'm saying to make sure it hits the mark."

As you begin noticing listening differences in others, try to accept them as just that—differences. Instead of criticizing listening styles different from yours, appreciate the differences for the value they bring to the workplace. By having a more tolerant and accepting mindset, you'll not only help build an Adaptive Listening culture, but you'll also create a more inclusive workplace.

## Duarte, Inc.: An Adaptive Listening Case Study

As mentioned in Chapter 1, Nicole and Maegan are communication consultants at Duarte, Inc. As an organization, Duarte is on a mission to improve how millions of people communicate, and we believe transformation must start from within. That's why every Duarte employee (or "Duartian," as we call ourselves) attends every workshop offered in the Duarte Academy and reads every book Duarte publishes. Adaptive Listening is no exception.

Before Duartians were trained in Adaptive Listening, they were great at telling and visualizing stories, delivering presentations, and strategizing the best way to enact change efforts. But their mindset was largely speaker-to-audience-focused, and not listener-focused. This lack of attention to listening often led to misunderstandings, missed information, and mismatched expectations. Sometimes people neglected to uncover crucial mistakes in a deliverable, and more time and resources were required to fix those mistakes. Sometimes people overlooked emotional cues and missed an opportunity to care for someone else. Sometimes leaders rushed to fix problems for their direct reports, limiting growth opportunities for everyone.

For a group of people that considered themselves communication experts, Duartians weren't always getting listening right. As it turns out, Duarte was just as desperate for a memorable listening model and actionable techniques as the rest of the working world.

To implement Adaptive Listening at Duarte, all Duartians completed the S.A.I.D. Listening Style Finder and were encouraged to share their results with others. Today, intact and cross-functional teams have an awareness of each other's listening styles. Not only does that help everyone appreciate listening differences, but it also helps people know who to seek out when they have a particular listening goal.

Every Duartian has also attended a version of the Adaptive Listening workshop, whether an alpha, a beta, the full-day course, or a company-wide virtual retreat where Adaptive Listening was included as a community-building activity. Training in Adaptive Listening is also part of internal onboarding and leadership development programs.

Duarte now has a shared language for effective listening. That shared language helps listeners adapt, encourages speakers to ask for what they need, and creates accountability and coaching opportunities between leaders, direct reports, and peers.

One of the most exciting outcomes of Adaptive Listening is how fully the Duarte executive leadership team embraced it. Duarte's CEO, Nancy Duarte, and the other executives have expressed how much Adaptive Listening has helped them communicate better with one another, mid-level managers, and all Duartians. They use the language and techniques to hold one another accountable for listening the right way at the right time when they're in executive leadership meetings and offsites.

Even in heated conversations, they can take a step back, analyze how Adaptive Listening might create better results, adjust, and improve. On a team with a lot of Advance Listeners, one leader said, "Sometimes, the conversations will speed up, and there will be more and more interrupting and advice-giving because there are so many Advance Listeners in the group."

When there is no lead facilitator, and the discussion is going off the rails, this leader uses Adaptive Listening techniques to contribute to the meeting's success. "I need to consider what kind of role I want to play as a listener at that moment," she said. "I can Listen to Discern to help the group slow down and evaluate our options more. I can Listen to Support and acknowledge everyone's emotions and validate them. I can Listen to Immerse and soak it all in."

Does this leader always get it right? Of course not. Leaders try their best and don't always succeed, just like everyone else. But the point is, this leader has changed the way she thinks about listening. All Duarte leaders have made the change, and it's transformed the way they lead. What's more, their belief in Adaptive Listening has had a trickle-down effect. With their buy-in, all Duartians are motivated to buy in, too. Although no person or organization listens perfectly all the time, Duarte's progress shows the power of investing in better listening skills.

Of course, you don't have to be a senior leader in your organization to embrace Adaptive Listening and influence others to use it. You're already well on your way by accepting these truths:

1. Listening is *not* synonymous with paying attention.
2. People don't all listen the same way.
3. You (and the people around you) have a S.A.I.D. Listening Style, which is how you prefer to process and respond to information.
4. You can accept, voice, or change your Listening L.E.N.S. to be fully focused on the person speaking to you.
5. Whenever a person interacts with you at work, they have a S.A.I.D. Listening Goal.
6. You have the power to identify and meet that goal using your Adaptive Listening skills.
7. Every speaker needs some Support Listening in every interaction.
8. You'll still listen the wrong sometimes, and that's okay—your intentions and willingness to improve will pay off over time.
9. You can cue others to be Adaptive Listeners for you by clearly stating your goals for the interaction.
10. There's no one right way to listen. Being a "good listener" means being an Adaptive Listener: someone who adapts the way they process and respond to meet the speaker's goals during the interaction.

Listening is hard. If you're thinking, "Gee, thanks, Nicole and Maegan. Being a great listener is going to take *even more work* than I thought," we're sorry and you're welcome. A skill as important and powerful as listening *should* take effort. But the authors hope that amidst your hectic workday, the Adaptive Listening techniques can make listening easier and more effective.

One day, your listening skills could be your differentiator. You'll be seen as a better colleague, direct report, leader, and partner. Maybe even a better person. People might seek you out or become drawn to you, without even knowing why. But you'll know why. You'll know that Adaptive Listening is helping you build trust and traction at work (and maybe even in your personal life, too).

# Acknowledgments

Writing this book was not the hardest thing we've ever had to do, but it was close. The following people made it remarkably easier than it could have been, and we thank you:

To Jeff Davenport and Patti Sanchez, who were the first people we told about our wild idea to change the way the world listens. Not only did you tell us the idea was worth pursuing, but you encouraged us to think bigger and, thus, this book was born. And Patti, your attention to detail on our early book proposal and drafts kept us focused on our intended reader. Thank you for being persona-fierce!

There are (too) many logistics that go into writing and publishing a book, and Julie Leong was our savior who had a handle on all of them. Thank you for the timelines, status updates, and the sanity checks along the way. And cheers to Melissa Adams for caring for our mental and physical well-being during this process.

Diandra Macias lead the design charge for this book. Oscar Chacon, Ash Oat, Ira Pietojo, and Fabian Espinoza collaborated with and built on the visual inspiration of nearly forty Duartians to create and finalize our cover art. And an additional special thanks to Diandra for also helping us with visuals inside the book. Together, you all brought our ideas to life like only Duarte designers can. We can't wait for you to design our forthcoming Adaptive Listening tattoos.

The entire Duarte Strategy, Content, and Coaching team gave feedback on drafts (and drafts, and more drafts), helped us collect client stories, and graciously went hunting for additional research when we suspected that someone probably already said the smart thing we wanted to say. We are forever grateful to our teammates: Dave DeFranco, Kristin Eskind, Sarah Vartabedian, Anne Marie Rhoades, Josh Storie, and Phoebe Perelman. We love you awesome nerds.

Speaking of research, Hayley Hawthorne was a tremendous help. She identified gaps in current listening research and trainings so we could work to fill them. We were lucky to have her collaboration and thoroughness in the early days of Adaptive Listening. And a special shout out to Robin Gay and Melissa Chen for helping us double check that ever-growing reference list.

To our colleagues, clients, customers, friends, and family who participated in interviews, focus groups, alpha and beta tests of exercises and techniques, and were early readers, we thank you. Your experiences and insights are all over this book. Maegan would especially like to thank/apologize to her husband, Kevin Lao, for feeding her when she could not remember to feed herself. Nicole would like to thank/apologize to her friends and family for saying "no" a *lot* during this writing process. A special shoutout goes to her nephews who, for three years, heard "Auntie Nicki can't play right now. She's writing."

To the entire Mango team: we let out the biggest sigh of relief after our kickoff meeting with you. Your expertise inspired us and your eagerness to help us bring Adaptive Listening to the world energized us. We especially want to thank our editor, M.J. Fievre. Whenever we were in a writing crisis or moment of despair, one of us would say, "It's ok. M.J. will help us fix it." And then she always did. Without M.J., this book wouldn't be nearly as informative or engaging as it is today.

Of course, this book wouldn't have even been possible without Nancy Duarte. Nancy knows better than most how intense and arduous book-writing can be, and we're lucky that we had her in our corner. It is a true honor to have her and Duarte, Inc. invest in us, this body of work, and this book. From the bottom of our hearts, we thank you for believing in us, Nancy.

Finally, we'd like to thank each other. No one in the world will ever know what this exact process was like or how it changed us. We're forever indebted to each other and grateful that we didn't have to go it alone. In true elder millennial form, LYLAS.

# About the Authors

**Nicole Lowenbraun, MS, CCC-SLP**

Nicole offers a unique perspective on why what you say and how you say it matters, because she's equal parts speech-language pathologist and business communication expert. Nicole has coached and written for thousands of clients, most of whom top the Fortune 100, with a focus on helping clients find their most authentic and powerful voice.

After decades of helping others master their expressive communication skills, Nicole realized the business community (herself, included) was widely neglecting the receptive side of communication—listening. She's now committed to teaching the world the value of improving both sides of the communication equation and continues to nurture her own skills as a writer, speaker, and listener.

With a Master's in Communication Disorders, Nicole is passionate about fostering more inclusive communication in the workplace, especially with neurodiverse populations. Nicole believes that acceptance of communication differences and a commitment to constant progress is the key to a happier future of work, regardless of industry, role, or experience.

Nicole lives in Brooklyn with her plants and is a proud "pizza bagel": half Italian-Catholic, half Polish-Jewish. She puts the Star of David on top of her Christmas tree.

### Maegan Stephens, PhD

Maegan became a communication nerd back when she was a competitive public-speaker in high school and college (yes, that's a thing). She knew at sixteen years old she wanted to help people become better communicators.

She earned her "10,000+ hours" as a communication expert with a combination of book smarts and street smarts. After sharpening her research skills with a PhD in Communication Studies from The University of Texas at Austin, Maegan transitioned from academia to industry and is now a communication consultant for individuals and teams at the world's top brands. She's written for and coached Fortune 50 executives, TED speakers, start-up founders, and aspiring leaders.

She continues to combine theory and practice as the co-creator of the Adaptive Listening methodology. When she's not researching, writing, or consulting, she's leading a team of writers, strategists, and coaches at Duarte, Inc. to transform the way people communicate.

After work, she's cheering on her beloved Detroit sports teams atop her Peloton from San Jose, California, where she lives with her fellow Detroit-ish native husband, Kevin Lao.

# Endnotes


1 Daniel Ames, Lily B. Maissen, and Joel Brockner, "The Role of Listening in Interpersonal Influence," *Journal of Research in Personality* 46, no. 3 (2012): 345–349, doi: 10.1016/j.jrp.2012.01.010.

2 Mary Stine, Teresa Thompson, and Louis Cusella, "The Impact of Organizational Structure and Supervisory Listening Indicators on Subordinate Support, Trust, Intrinsic Motivation, and Performance." *International Journal of Listening* 9, no. 1 (1995), doi: 10.1080/10904018.1995.10499143.

Dotan R. Castro, Frederik Anseel, Avraham N. Kluger, Karina J. Lloyd, and Yaara Turjeman-Levi, "Mere Listening Effect on Creativity and the Mediating Role of Psychological Safety," *Psychology of Aesthetics, Creativity, and the Arts* 12, no. 4 (2018): 489–502, doi: 10.1037/aca0000177.

3 Stephen Hansen, Tejas Ramdas, Raffaella Sadun, and Joe Fuller, "The Demand for Executive Skills," *NBER Working Paper Series* 28959, no. J23, J24, M12 (June 2021).

4 Omar S. Itani, Emily A. Goad, and Fernando Jaramillo, "Building Customer Relationships While Achieving Sales Performance Results: Is Listening the Holy Grail of Sales?" *Journal of Business Research* 102 (2019): 120–130, doi: 10.1016/j.jbusres.2019.04.048.

5 "The Heard and Heard-Nots," UKG.com, UKG: Workforce Institute (2021), workforceinstitute.org/wp-content/uploads/The-Heard-and-the-Heard-Nots.pdf.

6 Darlene Marcroft. "Press Release: A Silenced Workforce: Four in Five Employees Feel Colleagues Aren't Heard Equally, Says Research from the Workforce Institute at UKG," 2021, www.ukg.com/about-us/newsroom/silenced-workforce-four-five-employees-feel-colleagues-arent-heard-equally-says.

7 Avraham N. Kluger and Guy Itzchakov, "The Power of Listening at Work," *Annual Review of Organizational Psychology and Organizational Behavior* 9, (2022): 121–146, doi: 10.1146/annurev-orgpsych-012420-091013.

Michelle K. Johnston and Kendra Reed, "Listening Environment and the Bottom Line: How a Positive Environment Can Improve Financial Outcomes," *International Journal of Listening* 31, no. 2 (2014), doi: 10.1080/10904018.2014.965391.

Jasmine Bergeron and Michel Laroche, "The Effects of Perceived Salesperson Listening Effectiveness in the Financial Industry," *Journal of Financial Services Marketing* 14, (2009): 6–25.

8 Bill Trott, "Ram Dass, Psychedelic Drug Pioneer, Dies at Home Aged 88," last modified December 22, 2019, www.reuters.com/article/us-people-ram-dass/ram-dass-psychedelic-drug-pioneer-dies-at-home-aged-88-idUSKBN1YR0KY.

9 Stephen R. Covey, *The 7 Habits of Highly Effective People: Powerful Lessons in Personal Change* (New York: Simon & Schuster, 2013).

10 Carl R. Rogers, *Active Listening* (Chicago: The Industrial Relations Center of the University of Chicago, 1955).

11 Kittie W. Watson, Larry L. Barker, and James B. Weaver III, "The Listening Styles Profile (LSP-16): Development and Validation of an Instrument to Assess Four Listening Styles," *International Journal of Listening* 9, no. 1 (1995): 1–13, doi: 10.1080/10904018.1995.10499138.

12 [12] "Empathy," Greater Good Magazine, University of California–Berkeley. Accessed August 14, 2023. greatergood.berkeley.edu/topic/empathy/definition.

13 Alan Alda, *If I Understood You, Would I Have This Look on My Face: My Adventures in the Art and Science of Relating and Communication* (New York: Random House, 2017).

14 "The Heard and Heard-Nots," UKG.com, UKG: Workforce Institute (2021), workforceinstitute.org/wp-content/uploads/The-Heard-and-the-Heard-Nots.pdf.

15 Emily Killham, "2023 Special Report: The State of Employee Listening," 2023, go.perceptyx.com/research-the-state-of-employee-listening-2023.

16 Fernando Flores, "Innovation by Listening Carefully to Customers," *Long Range Planning* 26, no. 3 (June 1993): 95–102, doi: 10.1016/0024-6301(93)90011-4.

17 Martin Storme, Orit Suleyman, Michel Gotlib, and Todd Lubart, "Who is Agile? An Investigation of the Psychological Antecedence of Workforce Agility," *Global Business and Organizational Exc*ellence 49, no.6 (July 2020): 28–38, doi: 10.1002/joe.22055.

18 Steven Rappaport, "Cutting Edges: Listening-Led Marketing Science, Media Strategies, and Organizations," *Journal of Advertising Research* 50, no.3 (September 2010): 30–41, doi: 10.2501/S0021849910091154.

19 "Emotions in the Workplace," Quantum Workplace, accessed August 14, 2023, marketing.quantumworkplace.com/hubfs/Marketing/Website/Resources/PDFs/Emotions%20in%20the%20Workplace.pdf.

20 N., Sam, "MIRRORING," in *PsychologyDictionary.org*, last modified April 7, 2013, psychologydictionary.org/mirroring.

21 Carol Kinsey Goman, "The Art and Science of Mirroring," *Forbes* (May 31, 2011), www.forbes.com/sites/carolkinseygoman/2011/05/31/the-art-and-science-of-mirroring/?sh=5c143a1c1318.

22 Robin T. Peterson and Yam Limbu, "The Convergence of Mirroring and Empathy: Communications Training in Business-to-Business Personal Selling Persuasion Efforts," *Journal of Business-to-Business Marketing* 16, no. 3 (2009): 193–219, doi: 10.1080/10517120802484551.

23 Jeremy Sutton, "How to Read Nonverbal Communication Cues: 5 Techniques," last modified February 4, 2022. positivepsychology.com/nonverbal-communication-cues.

24 Brett Q. Ford, Phoebe Lam, Oliver P. John, and Iris B. Mauss, "The Psychological Health Benefits of Accepting Negative Emotions and Thoughts: Laboratory, Diary, and Longitudinal Evidence," *Journal of Personality and Social Psychology* 115, no. 6 (2018): 1075–1092, doi: 10.1037/pspp0000157. www.ncbi.nlm.nih.gov/pmc/articles/PMC5767148.

25 Alison Levine, *On the Edge: The Art of High Impact Leadership* (New York: Business Plus, 2014).

26 Alejandra Alonso, Jacqueline van der Meij, Dorothy Tse, and Lisa Genzel, "Naïve to Expert: Considering the Role of Previous Knowledge in Memory," *Sage Journals* (2020), doi: 10.1177/2398212820948. www.ncbi.nlm.nih.gov/pmc/articles/PMC7479862/.

27 E.L. Thorndike, "A Constant Error in Psychological Ratings," *Journal of Applied Psychology* 4 (March 1920): 25–29.

28 Brad Mayer, Kathleen Dale, and Marilyn L. Fox, "The Effects of Goal Clarity and Goal Commitment on Performance in a Business Strategy Game," *Business Education Innovation Journal* 12, no. 2 (December 2020): 62–69.

29 Katarina L. Stetler and Mats Magnusson, "Exploring the Tension between Clarity and Ambiguity in Goal Setting for Innovation," *Creativity and Innovation Management* 24 (2014): 231–246, doi: 10.1111/caim.12102.

30 Owen Hargie, *Skilled Interpersonal Interaction: Research, Theory, and Practice* (London: Routledge, 2011), 177.

31 C. Daryl Cameron, Cendri A. Hutcherson, Amanda M. Ferguson, Julian A. Scheffer, Eliana Hadjiandreou, and Michael Inzlicht, "Empathy Is Hard Work: People Choose to Avoid Empathy Because of Its Cognitive Costs," *Journal of Experimental Psychology: General* 148, no. 6 (2019): 962, doi: 10.1037/xge0000595.

32 Sieun An, Li-Jun Ji, Michael Marks, and Zhiyong Zhang, "Two Sides of Emotion: Exploring Positivity and Negativity in Six Basic Emotions across Cultures," *Frontiers in Psychology* 8 (April 20, 2017): 610. doi: 10.3389/fpsyg.2017.00610.

Paul Ekman, "Are there basic emotions?" *Psychological Review* 99, (July 1992): 550–553. doi: 10.1037/0033-295X.99.3.550.

33 Chun Liu, "Chinese, Why Don't You Show Your Anger?—A Comparative Study between Chinese and Americans in Expressing Anger." *International Journal of Social Science and Humanity* 4, no. 3 (May 2014): 206–209, doi: 10.7763/ijssh.2014.v4.347.

34 Flemming Hansen, "Distinguishing between Feelings and Emotions in Understanding Communication Effects," *Journal of Business Research* 58, no. 10 (October 2005): 1426–1436, doi: 10.1016/j.jbusres.2003.10.012.

35 Kaitlin Woolley and Ayelet Fishbach, "Motivating Personal Growth by Seeking Discomfort," *Psychological Science* 33, no. 4 (April 1, 2022): 510–523, doi: 10.1177/09567976211044685.

36 Alicia Grandey, Su Chuen Foo, Markus Groth, Robyn E. Goodwin, "Free to Be You and Me: A Climate of Authenticity Alleviates Burnout from Emotional Labor," *Journal of Occupational Health Psychology* 17 no. 1 (2012): 1–14, doi: 10.1037/a0025102.

37 Erkan Yakut, and Ergün Kara, "Determining Role of Employee Empowerment and Perceived Organizational Support in the Effect of SHRM on Job Satisfaction and Turnover Intention," *Ege Academic Review* 22, no. 1 (January 2022): 17–31, doi: 10.21121/eab.902277.

38 Alisa Yu, Justin M. Berg, and Julian J. Zlatev, "Emotional Acknowledgment: How Verbalizing Others' Emotions Fosters Interpersonal Trust," *Organizational Behavior and Human Decision Processes* 164, (2021): 116–135, doi: 10.1016/j.obhdp.2021.02.002.

39 Paul Ekman and Erika L. Rosenberg, *What the Face Reveals: Basic and Applied Studies of Spontaneous Expression Using the Facial Action Coding System (FACS) (2 ed.)* (Oxford University Press, 2005).

40 "Micro Expressions," Paul Ekman Group, accessed August 14, 2023, www.paulekman.com/resources/micro-expressions.

41 Chin Ming Hui, Jane Mang Yan Fung, Yiu Yuen Hui, Jacky C. K. Ng, "Why Goal Pursuers Prefer to Seek Support from Close Friends: The Roles of Concerns for Accessibility," *Asian Journal of Social Psychology* 23, no. 4 (December 2020): 435–46, doi: 10.1111/ajsp.12416.

42 Jennifer Stoops, Marriage and Family Therapist, personal interview, March 27, 2023.

43 Katheryn Ostermeier, Danielle Cooper, and Miguel Caldas, "Can I Be Who I am? Psychological Authenticity Client and Employee Outcomes," *Human Performance* 35, No. 1. (2022), doi: 10.1080/08959285.2021.1998060.

44 Susan Torres, and Mehmet A. Orhan, "How It Started, How It's Going: Why Past Research Does Not Encompass Pandemic-Induced Remote Work Realities and What Leaders Can Do for More Inclusive Remote Work Practices," *Psychology of Leaders and Leadership* 26, no. 1 (February 2023): 1–21, doi: 10.1037/mgr0000135.

45 Kristin Knipfer and Barbara Kump, "Collective Rumination: When 'Problem Talk' Impairs Organizational Resilience," *Applied Psychology: An International Review* 71, no. 1 (January 2022): 154–73, doi: 10.1111/apps.12315.

46 Manuel London, *Job Feedback: Giving, Seeking, and Using Feedback for Performance Improvement,* 2nd ed. (Mahwah, NJ: Psychology Press, 2003).

47 Jennifer J. Kish-Gephart, James R. Detert, Linda Klebe Treviño, Amy C. Edmondson, "Silenced by Fear: The Nature, Sources, and Consequences of Fear at Work," *Research in Organizational Behavior* 29 (2009): 163–193, doi: 10.1016/j.riob.2009.07.002.

48 John Whittman, "The Forgetting Curve," California State University, Stanislaus, 2018, www.csustan.edu/sites/default/files/groups/Writing%20Program/forgetting_curve.pdf.

49 Jacquelyn F. Gamino, Sandra B. Chapman, Elizabeth L. Hull, G. Reid Lyon, "Effects of Higher-order Cognitive Strategy Training on Gist-reasoning and Fact-learning in Adolescents," *Frontiers in psychology* 1 (2010): 188, doi: 10.3389/fpsyg.2010.00188.

50 Chai M. Tyng, Hafeez U. Amin, Mohamad N. M. Saad, and Aamir S. Malik, "The Influences of Emotion on Learning and Memory," *Frontiers in Psychology* 8 (2017), doi: 10.3389/fpsyg.2017.01454.

51 Deborah Talmi, "Enhanced Emotional Memory: Cognitive and Neural Mechanisms," *Current Directions in Psychological Science* 22, no. 6 (2013): 430–436, doi: 10.1177/0963721413498893.

52 Alessandra S. Souza, Laura Rerko, Klaus Oberauer, "Refreshing Memory Traces: Thinking of an Item Improves Retrieval from Visual Working Memory," *Annals of the New York Academy of Sciences* 1339, no. 1 (March 20, 2015): 20–31, doi: 10.1111/nyas.12603.

James M. Honeycutt, "Imagined Interaction Theory: Mental Representations of Interpersonal Communication." In L. A. Baxter & D. Braithwaite (Eds.). *Engaging Theories in Interpersonal Communication* (pp. 77–87). Thousand Oaks, CA: Sage.

53 Aleksandre Asatiani, Julia Hämäläinen, Esko Penttinen, and Matti Rossi, "Constructing Continuity across the Organisational Culture Boundary in a Highly Virtual Work Environment." *Information Systems Journal* 31, no. 1 (January 2021): 62–93, doi: 10.1111/isj.12293.

Ilan Oshri, Julia Kotlarsky, and Leslie P. Willcocks, "Global Software Development: Exploring Socialization and Face-to-Face Meetings in Distributed Strategic Projects," *Journal of Strategic Information Systems* 16, no. 1 (January 1, 2007): 25–49, doi: 10.1016/j.jsis.2007.01.001.

Mary Beth Watson-Manheim, Katherine M. Chudoba, and Kevin Crowston, "Perceived Discontinuities and Constructed Continuities in Virtual Work," *Information Systems Journal* 22, no. 1 (January 2012): 29–52, doi: 10.1111/j.1365-2575.2011.00371.x.

54 Amy Abel, Amanda Popiela, and Rebecca Ray, *Trends and Directions in Organizational Human Capital Development: Building an Engaging Culture That Supports Learning and Talent Development*. Sage UK, 2022.

55 Rachit Dubey, Tom Griffiths, and Tania Lombrozo, "If It's Important, Then I Am Curious: A Value Intervention to Induce Curiosity" (Proceedings of the 41st Annual Conference of the Cognitive Science Society, 2019: 282–288).

56 John R. Childress, *Leverage: The CEO's Guide to Corporate Culture* (New York: Principia Associates, 2013).

Dave Eaton, and Gabriella Kilby, "Does Your Organizational Culture Support Your Business Strategy?" *Journal for Quality and Participation* 37, no. 4 (2015): 4–7.

Sarantuya Jigjiddorj, Altanchimeg Zanabazar, Tsolmon Jambal, and Buyankhishig Semjid, "Relationship Between Organizational Culture, Employee Satisfaction and Organizational Commitment," *SHS Web of Conf.*, 90 (2021): 02004, doi: 10.1051/shsconf/20219002004.

Tiago Melo, "Determinants of Corporate Social Performance: The Influence of Organizational Culture, Management Tenure, and Financial Performance," *Social Responsibility Journal* 8, (2012): 33–47.

Yasas L. Pathiranage, "Organizational Culture and Business Performance: An Empirical Study," *SSRG International Journal of Economics and Management Studies* 6, no. 6 (2019): 1–12, doi: 10.14445/23939125/IJEMS-V6I6P101.

José C. Pinho, Ana P. Rodrigues, Sally Dibb, "The Role of Corporate Culture, Market Orientation, and Organizational Commitment in Organizational Performance," *Journal of Management Development* 33 (2014): 374–398.

57 *Seinfeld*, season 8, episode 15, "The Susie," directed by Andy Ackerman, written by David Mandel, featuring Jerry Seinfeld, Jason Alexander, Julia Louis-Dreyfus, and Michael Richards, aired February 13, 1997, on NBC.

58 *Arrested Development*, season 1, episode 4, "Key Decisions," directed by Anthony Russo, written by Mitchell Hurwitz, Brad Copeland, and Abraham Higginbotham, featuring Will Arnett, aired November 23, 2003, on Fox.

59 *Martin*, season 1, episode 6, "Really, Gina's Not My Lover," directed by Gerren Keith, written by Topper Carew, featuring Martin Lawrence and Tisha Campbell-Martin, aired on October 15, 1992, on Fox.

60 *How I Met Your Mother*, season 2, episode 9, "Slap Bet," directed by Pamela Fryman, written by Carter Bays, Craig Thomas, and Kourtney Kang, aired November 20, 2006, on CBS.

61 Avraham N. Kluger and Guy Itzchakov. "The Power of Listening at Work." *Annual Review of Organizational Psychology and Organizational Behavior* 9 (2022): 121–146.

62 Pam A. Mueller, and Daniel M. Oppenheimer, "The pen is mightier than the keyboard: Advantages of longhand over laptop note taking," *Psychological Science* 25 (2014): 1159–1168.

63 Reem Rachel Abraham, Surekha Kamath, and K. Ramnarayan, "Impact of Note-Taking on Cognition During Lectures," *South-East Asian Journal of Medical Education* 4, no. 2 (2010): 44–45.

64 Ferris Jabr, "Why Walking Helps Us Think," *The New Yorker* (September 3, 2014). www.newyorker.com/tech/annals-of-technology/walking-helps-us-think.

May Wong, "Stanford Study Finds Walking Improves Creativity," *Stanford News* (April 24, 2014). news.stanford.edu/2014/04/24/walking-vs-sitting-042414.

65 Kristin Froemming, "Listen Up! You're Tuning Out! Emotional Triggers That Serve As Listening Barriers in Senior Populations," *Master's Theses,* UW Whitewater (2009). minds.wisconsin.edu/handle/1793/47507.

66 Marc A Russo, Danielle M Santarelli, Dean O'Rourke, "The Physiological Effects of Slow Breathing in the Healthy Human," *Breathe* 13 (2017): 298–309, doi: 10.1183/20734735.009817.

67 Amy Cuddy, *Presence: Bringing Your Boldest Self to Your Biggest Challenges* (New York: Little, Brown and Company, 2015).

68 Aleksandra Siedlaczek-Szwed, Agata Jałowiecka-Frania, "Yoga—A Way to Achieve Emotional Balance," *European Journal of Sport Sciences* 1, no. 3 (2022): 7–10, doi: 10.24018/ejsport.2022.1.3.22.

69 "Dialectical Behavior Therapy." Cleveland Clinic, accessed August 14, 2023, my.clevelandclinic.org/health/treatments/22838-dialectical-behavior-therapy-dbt.

70 Weathers, M. Troy. (2022). "Dissertation: Mindful attention for reading and class (MARC): A DBT-Informed Group Intervention for College Students with Attention-Deficit/Hyperactivity Disorder." www.proquest.com/openview/5cc898a5cc06e10897fe1fc66ca4ec9b/1?pq-origsite=gscholar&cbl=18750&diss=y.

71 Pamela K. Adelmann, and R. B. Zajonc, "Facial Efference and the Experience of Emotion," *Annual Review of Psychology* 40 (1989): 249–280, doi: 10.1146/annurev.ps.40.020189.001341.

72 Meifen Wei, Kelly Yu-Hsin Liao, Tsun-Yao Ku, Phillip A. Shaffer, "Attachment, Self-Compassion, Empathy, and Subjective Well-Being among College Students and Community Adults," *Journal of Personality* 79, no. 1 (2011), doi: 10.1111/j.1467-6494.2010.00677.x.

Guasp Coll Marian, Navarro-Mateu Diego, Giménez-Espert María Del Carmen, Prado-Gascó Vicente Javier, "Emotional Intelligence, Empathy, Self-Esteem, and Life Satisfaction in Spanish Adolescents: Regression vs. QCA Models," *Frontiers in Psychology* 11, (2020), doi: 10.3389/fpsyg.2020.0162.

73 George A. Bonanno, and Charles L. Burton, "Regulatory Flexibility: An Individual Differences Perspective on Coping and Emotion Regulation," *Perspectives on Psychological Science* 8, no. 6 (2013): 591–612, doi: 10.1177/1745691613504116.

74 Manuel London, *Job Feedback: Giving, Seeking, and Using Feedback for Performance Improvement,* 2nd ed. (Mahwah, NJ: Psychology Press, 2003).

75 Tim Hopf, and Joe Ayres, "Coping with Public Speaking Anxiety: An Examination of Various Combinations of Systematic Desensitization, Skills Training, and Visualization," *Journal of Applied Communication Research* 20, no. 2 (May 1, 1992): 183–198–198, doi: 10.1080/00909889209365328.

76 Pamela K. Adelmann and R. B. Zajonc, "Facial Efference and the Experience of Emotion," *Annual Review of Psychology* 40 (1989): 249–280, doi: 10.1146/annurev.ps.40.020189.001341.

77 Maarten Van Someren, Yvonne F. Barnard, and Jacobijn Sandberg, *The Think Aloud Method: A Practical Approach to Modelling Cognitive* (London: Academic Press, 1994), 29–41.

78 Lisa Feldman Barrett, Nathan Williams, and Geoffrey Fong, "Defensive Behavior Assessment," *Personality and Social Psychology* 28, no. 6 (2002), doi: 10.1177/0146167202289007.

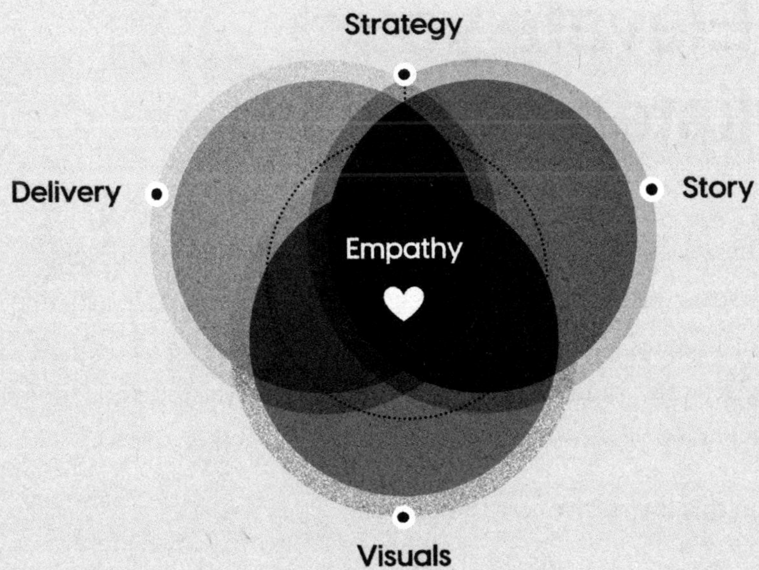


contact@duarte.com | 650.625.8200 | www.duarte.com

# Elevate your listening skills.

Improved listening strengthens workplace relationships and boosts the bottom line, but memorable and actionable listening techniques have been scarce—until now. Adaptive Listening™ gives you, your team, and your organization the tools and common language to cultivate trust and traction at work.

In this interactive workshop, you'll:

- Discover the characteristics and cautions of your S.A.I.D. Listening Style™
- Identify the influences that shape your ability to focus on the speaker
- Determine the speaker's S.A.I.D. Listening Goals™ for the interaction
- Adapt the way you process and respond to meet the speaker's goals across situations

Led by expert facilitator
Real-time practice and discussion
Adaptive Listening
How to Cultivate Trust and Traction at Work
Nicole Lowenbraun & Maegan Stephens
Foreword by Nancy Duarte
Adaptive Listening™ Canvas
Focus your Listening LENS™
DUARTE
Adaptive Listening™
Build Trust and Grow Your Professional Influence
Your Workbook
Engaging multi-media
Small group exercises

Mango Publishing, established in 2014, publishes an eclectic list of books by diverse authors—both new and established voices—on topics ranging from business, personal growth, women's empowerment, LGBTQ studies, health, and spirituality to history, popular culture, time management, decluttering, lifestyle, mental wellness, aging, and sustainable living. We were named 2019 *and* 2020's #1 fastest growing independent publisher by *Publishers Weekly*. Our success is driven by our main goal, which is to publish high-quality books that will entertain readers as well as make a positive difference in their lives.

Our readers are our most important resource; we value your input, suggestions, and ideas. We'd love to hear from you—after all, we are publishing books for you!

Please stay in touch with us and follow us at:

Facebook: Mango Publishing
Twitter: @MangoPublishing
Instagram: @MangoPublishing
LinkedIn: Mango Publishing
Pinterest: Mango Publishing
Newsletter: mangopublishinggroup.com/newsletter

Join us on Mango's journey to reinvent publishing, one book at a time.